The History of Sweets

About the author
Paul Chrystal has Classics degrees from the Universities of Hull and Southampton; he is the author of a hundred or so published books, a number of which are about confectionery and beverages. He has written features on aspects of the history of food and drink for the *Daily Express* and has appeared on the BBC World Service, Radio 4's PM programme and various BBC local radio stations talking on a wide range of subjects, but notably confectionery. Paul has also contributed to a six-part series for BBC2, celebrating the history of some of Britain's most iconic craft industries' – in this case chocolate in York, which aired in 2019. He has been history advisor for a number of York tourist attractions relating to chocolate. He is also History Editor of *the Yorkshire Archaeological Journal*. In 2019 he was guest speaker for the Vassar College (New York) London Programme with Goldsmith University speaking about the history of chocolate.

paul.chrystal@btinternet.com

By the same author
Chocolate: The British Chocolate Industry
A History of Chocolate in York
Cadbury & Fry through Time
The Rowntree Family of York
Old Bournville
Confectionery in Yorkshire
Tea: A Very British Beverage
Coffee: A Drink for the Devil
Rowntrees: The Early History

The History of Sweets

Paul Chrystal

PEN & SWORD
HISTORY

First published in Great Britain in 2021 by
Pen & Sword History
An imprint of
Pen & Sword Books Ltd
Yorkshire – Philadelphia

Copyright © Paul Chrystal 2021

ISBN 978 1 52677 885 7

Typeset by Mac Style
Printed and bound in India by Replika Press Pvt. Ltd.

Pen & Sword Books Limited incorporates the imprints of Atlas, Archaeology, Aviation, Discovery, Family History, Fiction, History, Maritime, Military, Military Classics, Politics, Select, Transport, True Crime, Air World, Frontline Publishing, Leo Cooper, Remember When, Seaforth Publishing, The Praetorian Press, Wharncliffe Local History, Wharncliffe Transport, Wharncliffe True Crime and White Owl.

For a complete list of Pen & Sword titles please contact

PEN & SWORD BOOKS LIMITED
47 Church Street, Barnsley, South Yorkshire, S70 2AS, England
E-mail: enquiries@pen-and-sword.co.uk
Website: www.pen-and-sword.co.uk

Or

PEN AND SWORD BOOKS
1950 Lawrence Rd, Havertown, PA 19083, USA
E-mail: Uspen-and-sword@casematepublishers.com
Website: www.penandswordbooks.com

Contents

Acknowledgements

This book has benefited from the kindness and generosity of a number of people; without their help it would be considerably inferior in many ways. I must especially thank John Lazenby, grandson of Percy Lazenby, founder of Lazenby and Son (York) Ltd for the information about his grandfather's company, and the Tordoff family for the images of the Oldest Sweet Shop in Pateley Bridge. Thanks too to Mark Simmons, Curator (Museum Development) Hartlepool Borough Council for permission to use the photo showing the end of sweet rationing in West Hartlepool. Charlotte Borger, Communications Consultant at Divine Chocolate Ltd, was extremely helpful with information and photos, as was Rachael Gartland, Communications Assistant at Beamish Museum in the provision of images for Jubilee Confectioners. Susan Major, John Stevens and Mavis Morris of Clements Hall Local History Group kindly provided the information on York's Clementhorpe chocolate companies. Thanks also to Sophie Jewett, Managing Director of York Cocoa House, for providing the image on page 238 showing one of their school demonstrations on chocolate making. Finally, thanks to Elisabeth Maselli, Assistant to the Director and Assistant Editor, Rights and Permissions Manager and eBook Coordinator at Rutgers University Press in New Brunswick for permission to quote from their Children and Drug Safety: Balancing Risk and Prevention in Twentieth-Century America (New Brunswick: Rutgers University Press, 2018) by Cynthia A. Connolly.

Party girl promoting Caley's of Norwich chocolates in this poster from the late 1920s.

Introduction

The defining characteristics of a sweet (or candy in the US) is that it is just that – sweet – and that what makes it sweet is sugar or sugar substitutes, the main constituent of a sweet. What we can also call sugar confectionery encompasses any sweet confection, and that takes in chocolate, chewing and bubble gum, fudge, sugar candy, as well as other sweets. Vegetables, fruit, or nuts which have been glazed and coated with sugar are said to be candied sweets.

Sweets are usually made in small, individual, bite-size pieces. Although a packet or box of sweets may well be shared, the individual sweets in a packet or chocolates in a box are often just for you and for you only. Give some away or swap them for someone else's sweets at your own discretion. Unlike a sweet dessert – often itself called 'sweet' – sweets are usually

Sweets at a souk in Damascus, Syria. (*Candies; photographer Elisa Azzali. This file is licensed under the Creative Commons Attribution 2.0 Generic license*)

eaten casually, with the fingers, and as a snack between meals. There is a grey line between sweets and dessert which fluctuates from culture to culture and from country to country. What is regarded as a dessert in one country may be considered a sweet in the neighbouring country. For example, in western countries including Greece and Cyprus, baklava is served on a plate and eaten with a fork as a dessert, but in the Middle East, Northern Africa, and Eastern Europe it may be treated as a sweet.

The overlap, confusion even, is best seen in parts of India with the hundreds of varieties of confectionery desserts which are called *mithai* or sweets. Sugar and desserts have a long history in India where by about 500 BC, people there had developed the technology to produce sugar crystals. In the local language, these crystals were called khanda (खण्ड), which is where our word candy comes from.

Food chemistry obviously pays a part in the definition and classification of sweets, which are categorised into non-crystalline and crystalline types. Non- crystalline candies are homogeneous and may be chewy or hard, so include caramels, toffees, seaside rock and nougats. Crystalline candies have small crystals in their structure, so are creamy, melt in the mouth or

A selection of Indian sweets. Mishri Ki Roti With Edible Flowers. A delicate cookie garnished with edible flowers and strands of saffron. (*Published by Nidhi Bothra. https://naturallynidhi. com/category/desserts/indian-sweets/*)

are chewy; they include fondant and fudge. Fudge is made by mixing and heating sugar, butter and milk.

A sweet has never just been a sweet: sweets have acted as a medicine, they perform the role of a pacifier, they are breath fresheners, they are tokens of love and vehicles of seduction with their amorous and risqué messages, they satisfy primeval urges for cannibalism and mutilation, they are to meditate with, mediate with, bribe, comfort and distract with, they soothe and they satisfy. Some of the quirky names adopted to brand sweets bear all of this out with such wonderful creations as Opoponax, Heliotrope, Pink Aromatics, Tsfani-Ihang, Phul-Nana and Shem el Nessim, Sweet Lips and Kiss Call.

Fairtrade chocolate making in action.

(a)

(b)

(c)

(d)

A selection of sweet marketing: (a) Murraymints; (b) Cioccolato Venchi – founded in 1878 in Piedmont; (c) Fry's famous 1920s milk churn poster; (d) and a delightful GB Chocolate, Red Lion Square, London postcard from 1910 posted and franked at 10.30 am, asking the recipient (Alice) to meet for tea at 3.30pm that very afternoon.

Chapter 1

A Sweet Timeline

Much of what is covered in the following pages features in this timeline which delineates the development of sweets over 8,000 years.

8000 BC – Prehistoric honeycomb depicted in wall art
The first record we have of the 'sweet' is the honeycomb depicted in a Stone Age cave painting discovered near Valencia. The image shows a caveman dangling on a vine while he raids a bees' nest for honeycomb; this he throws down to a friend waiting below, as the bees buzz around him.

800 BC – Liquorice
Like a lot of sweets, liquorice was first valued for its medicinal qualities, and the thirst-quenching nature of liquorice root meant it was issued to Roman legionaries on long route marches.

AD 1000 – Arabic almond lozenges
These are mentioned in one of the earliest of all cookbooks, written in Persia, which describes *lawzinaj* – aromatic almond sweets laced with musk and amber.

1350 – Sucket – candied fruit
One of the most popular (and accidentally onomatopoeic) sweets imported from the east – oranges, lemons and pineapples preserved in sugar; they are the forerunners of boiled sweets and are still obtainable today. While suckets remind us of a sweet to be sucked, comfits tell us that comfits are comforting comfort food.

1450 – Comfits – aniseed balls and similar
Hard sugary sweets which started life as medicines in which the herbs and spices encased in the sugar were valued for their medicinal qualities.

1550 – Lollipops
Our first references to sweets on sticks, made by means of a special box into which syrup would be dropped onto upright sticks.

1650 – Gums and pastilles
The French perfected these: it was a French master confectioner who turned up at Rowntree's – M. Gaget – with the idea for fruit pastilles, in the mid-nineteenth century.

1820s – Boiled sweets
Originally conceived as cheap versions of crystallised fruits, the 'sweetie wives' of the Scottish Lowlands perfected the art, creating sweets such as 'soor plooms', Hawick balls and Berwick cockles.

1840s – Rock
Morecombe is famous for more than its bay and pier: seaside rock, decorated with letters, was first produced in Morecambe in the 1830s. Early rock sticks rolled off the production lines to be given as courting gifts, with the letters spelling out risqué messages, not place names. In York, to cement Anglo-Greek relations, sticks of rock were produced with 'Athens Police' lettered all the way through during an exchange visit.

1871 – Chewing gum
Or 'chuddy' – invented by a New York entrepreneur who had first tried to market tyres, toys, masks and boots using chicle sourced in Mexico: chicle is a natural gum traditionally used in making chewing gum. The tyre connection is a bit worrying.

1870s – Penny chews
Chewy sweets began to be made with intense fruit, liquorice and chocolate flavours.

1890s – Toffee
First commercially marketed by a Scotsman, while the French developed their caramels. One of the more interestingly named brands was Rocket Rinking Toffee, popular around 1910.

1899 – Liquorice Allsorts

Liquorice Allsorts were inadvertently invented by a salesman who clumsily spilled the samples he was carrying all over the floor. Before this he routinely sold the sweets individually; the 'allsorts' selection proved an enduring success.

The irrepressible Bertie Bassett from the 1920s.

1900 – Marshmallow

The medieval medicine based on the sticky root of the marsh mallow plant was imitated by French confectioners using egg whites and sugar, and later took the world by storm.

1926 – Bubble gum

This was invented after-hours by Walter Diemer, an accountant who enjoyed 'messing around in the lab' at the sweets firm where he worked in Philadelphia. The pink colour was a spur-of-the-moment choice.

1940 – Sherbet

Sherbet became the fizzy powder we know today only in the mid to late nineteenth century, as a kind of imitation of the exotic original.

1953 –Sweet rationing ends in the UK

1960s – Packaging

The traditional selling of sweets in the sweetshop as loose sweets sold from jars in quarter-pound paper bags began to be challenged by brightly packaged and wrapped sweets or multi packs.

1960s – Penny chew

The 'penny chew' – small chunky and chewy sweets (more often halfpenny or four-for-a-penny chews, such as Fruit Salads, Blackjacks and Mojos). Pick-and-mix continued as a High-Street sweets staple, with Woolworths the 'go to' place.

Sweet Timeline by brand to 1977

1866	Fry's Chocolate Cream Bar
1902	Fry's Milk Chocolate (5 Boys)
1905	Cadbury's Dairy Milk
1910	Cadbury's Bournville Plain Chocolate
1911	Wrigley's Juicy Fruit and Spearmint Gum
1915	Cadbury's Milk Tray
1921	Cadbury's Fruit & Nut
1929	Fry's Crunchie
1932	Terry's All Gold
1932	Mars Bar
1933	Rowntree's Black Magic
1935	Milky Way
1935	Rowntree's Aero
1935	Rowntree's KitKat
1936	Quality Street; Rowntree's Dairy Box
1936	Maltesers
1937	Rolos; Smarties
1948	Polo Mints
1950	Spangles
1951	Bounty
1958	Galaxy; Picnic
1962	After Eight Mints
1967	Twix
1967	Marathon (now Snickers)
1976	Rowntree's Yorkie
1977	Double Decker

Chapter 2

How it all Started:
Honey, Fruit and Nuts in Downtown Cairo?

As we have just seen, it was probably the Indians who gave us our first sweets. The Persians and Greeks, between the sixth and fourth centuries BC, came across the people of India and their 'reeds that produce honey without bees': sugar cane is indigenous to tropical South and Southeast Asia. As with all good things, this sugar was taken home and taken on by the traders in their respective countries to become widespread through sugar cane agriculture; by the seventh century, the Persians were operating sugar refineries. In ancient India, pieces of sugar were produced by boiling sugar cane juice and consumed as *khanda*; this was the original candy and explains the origin of that word. Sweets started to emerge in different shapes and sizes – from Sanskrit

92 EGYPTIAN TYPES AND SCENES.- Sweet Seller "Good weight.- LL.

Postcard depicting an Egyptian sweet seller, happy with the weight. From around 1930.

texts describing 'milk-based sweets laced with sugar' in India, to Arabic almond lozenges featured in Persian cookbooks.

But before sugar was widely available, all sweets were based on honey. About 8,000 years ago, caveman drawings found near Valencia, Spain depict honey from a honeycomb being dried out to form a sweet confection. Honey was used in ancient China, the Middle East, Egypt, Greece and throughout the Roman Empire to coat fruits and flowers, either to preserve them or to make them into sweets. Egyptian hieroglyphics from at least 3,000 years ago suggest that the art of sugar confectionery was already well established: in ancient Egypt, sweets were being spiced up with figs, dates and spices. Sweets also took on a powerful role in votive offerings and religious ceremonies. Later, the Romans and Chinese were heating up their sweets in ovens. The Romans considered the confectioner a skilled artisan while a confectioner's kitchen excavated at Herculaneum (so pre-AD 79) was fitted out with pots, pans, and other implements not dissimilar to those used today. In India, Sanskrit texts reveal milk laced with sugar.

We have noted how, before sugar imports into Europe made it widely available and much cheaper, honey was the main constituent of the sweet. During the Middle Ages, the Persians had a huge role to play by spreading sugar cane cultivation, developing refining methods, and making sugar-based sweets. The mysterious sweets called 'Manus Christi' – or 'hands of Christ' – refer also to a stage in the medieval candy-making process, but mainly to a medicinal hard candy that first appears in medieval recipe and medical books and keeps cropping up until its disappearance in the early nineteenth century. It was thought to be a life saver and usually took the form of a stick of hard sugar candy flavoured with violets, cinnamon and rose water. Its miraculous properties led it to be embellished with gold leaf in many recipes as many (very rich) people considered gold to be a panacea. Henry VIII was one such believer and always had a ready supply to hand.

Sweets, comfits and sweetmeats were an essential part of the medieval feast, served up as a finale to the meal. Initially this was known as the voidee, but by the sixteenth century it was known as the banquet or banket course. This had been going on, though, for centuries and is first recorded in the first detailed menu we have as given in the late thirteenth-century Anglo-Norman *Treatise of Walter of Bibbesworth*:

> 'And when the table was cleared
> There was white powder with large dragées:
> Mace cubeb, clove gillyflower
> And other spices to try
> And not forgetting the wafers

The 1468 wedding of Charles the Bold of Burgundy to Margaret of York at Bruges gives us an instance of the custom in the houses of the great and good of giving guests a *drageoir* groaning with sweets to take home with them.

The Venetians later took on the mantle of spreading the sweet revolution during the fourteenth century, when they began to import sugar from Arabia. Around 1450, aniseed balls were one of many comfit sweets available and sought after for the medicinal content of the herbs and spices inside the sugar casing. Sugar cane cultivation had spread to Sicily, Spain, Madeira, southern USA and the West Indies; in time it also reached most tropical and subtropical areas of the world. The fifteenth century, though, was a time of crisis in the confectionery world. The Ottoman Turks had taken the city of Constantinople in pursuit of their rampant expansionism and promptly closed down the trade routes from the east to Europe. Sugar was badly affected, only adding to the parlous state of the Mediterranean-Arabian industry and harvests in general. The upshot was that the Portuguese, through the endeavours of Vasco da Gama in 1497, found part of the solution when the passage to India and beyond by way of the Cape of Good Hope was opened up. However, the notion of growing your own sugar cane was becoming all the more popular and to this end the island of Madeira was colonised, yielding its first harvest to the Lisbon market in the 1450s and Bristol in 1456. The Portuguese made good use of their success and planted sugar on São Tomé, the Azores and in Brazil. The Spanish followed on the Canary Isles, Mexico, Jamaica, Cuba and Puerto Rico.

Slavery was already established in the medieval Middle East and Mediterranean sugar markets; Pope Nicolas I sanctioned the use of pagans as slaves and the Italians were using black slave labour on Crete and Cyprus, while the Genoese had similar arrangements in Spain. Slaves were soon active in São Tomé and Brazil under the Portuguese. Brazil was important because it dominated the sugar market for a hundred years

Children on a Louisiana sugar cane plantation around 1885. (*Schomburg Center for Research in Black Culture, New York Public Library*)

or so from the mid-sixteenth century and Brazilian sugar cane yielded a high amount of sugar with no irrigation required (on account of the climate). The English, French and Dutch naturally were not going to stand by as this Iberian monopoly flourished, and so it was from 1630 to 1660 they each invaded the islands of the Caribbean: England took Barbados and Jamaica, the French Guadeloupe, Martinique and St Kitts, while the Dutch colonised northern Brazil. The workforces were, of course, made up of African slaves. During the seventeenth century the British shipped over 250,000 slaves; in the eighteenth century they transported 45,000 every year.

There was opposition, not least from Coleridge, and William Cowper who penned his vivid *Sweet Meat has Sour Sauce, or, the Slave Trader in the Dumps* from 1788:

> Here's padlocks and bolts, and screws for the thumbs
> That squeeze them so lovingly till the blood comes.
> They sweeten the temper like comfits or plums,
> Which nobody can deny.

By the sixteenth century, confectionery manufacture was a hand-made commercial business with confectioners making sweets by moulding boiled sugar with fruits and nuts into various interesting forms. The

The Mill Yard: Grinding sugar cane in a windmill. 1823. (*Image taken from 'Ten Views in the Island of Antigua, in which are represented the process of sugar making, and the employment of the negroes … From drawings made by W. Clark', etc. Originally published/produced in London: Thomas Clay, 1823. Held and digitised by the British Library, and uploaded to Flickr Commons*)

Cannes à sucre – Réunion, 1879 Centre des archives d'outre-mer. Henri Georgi (Vers 1853–1891) (*Cane Cutters, Jamaica* (*13227614553*))

development of sweet-manufacturing machinery began in the late eighteenth century with the Industrial Revolution. Beet was another source of sugar: this process was accelerated by the Napoleonic Wars and the two world wars.

The Industrial Revolution

As with many other aspects of social and industrial history, the Industrial Revolution and the technological advances which came with it changed everything in the world of sweets. In 1847, the invention of the candy press machine enabled manufacturers to become creative and produce multiple shaped and sized sweets at the same time. In 1851, confectioners began using a revolving steam pan for boiling sugar. This meant that the confectioner no longer had to endlessly stir the boiling sugar. The heat from the surface of the pan was also much more evenly distributed and made it less likely to burn the sugar. From now on you only needed only one or two people to run a confectionery business.

Needlers of Hull could boast at the end of the nineteenth century a Cyclone Pulveriser for reducing sugar to dust and nuts to paste. Dog-paddling mixers did the mixing while guillotines did the cutting. The first caramel wrapping machine came in 1894 when a converted shag packing machine did the trick, the forerunner of automated packing, one of which was named the Oliver Twister while another was the Lightning Twister which turned out fifty-eight wrapped sweets per minute. A steam sugar boiling machine was named The Eureka – Archimedes would have been impressed. The Blackcurrant Strigging Device did the work of thirty girls; as could a Patent Gooseberry Snuffer.

Confectionery was, by the eighteenth century, considered a valuable and honourable skill in the comfortable households of the comfortably off. Samuel Richardson's eponymous hero, Pamela (1740), lists sweetmaking among her domestic credentials: 'I will assist your housekeeper...in the making of jellies, comfits, sweetmeats...and candy.' In 1760, Hannah Glasse in her *Complete Confectioner* name-checked Lady Leicester and her Hollow Gumballs made of a lemony fondant.

Out on the streets amongst the people, the confectioner was also held in high regard as probably the most accomplished and admired of all food tradesmen. Sweets were very much in demand as were the confectioners' skills. An example is Italian Domenico Negro, who traded from the sign of the Pot and Pineapple in London's Berkeley Square in the 1670s. He listed amongst his confections: marshmallow, sugar plums, Ghimauve or Lozenges for Colds & Cough. The provinces too shared in the confectionery treasure trove as evidenced by the advertisement placed by French confectioner Nicolas Seguin in the *York Courant* of 11 December 1764:

SEGUIN, Confectioner from Paris in the Minister Yard, YORK Makes and sells all Sorts of dry and wet Sweetmeats, Apricots, Green Gages, Pears, Apples &c...Comfits of all Kinds, perfumed Ginger, Carrimum, (Cardamum), Raspberries, Carraway, Images, and Sugar-Boxes.... All sorts of Biscuits and Macroons, as made in Paris... The true Paste and cakes of Mallows for Coughs; Syrup and Paste of Orgeat: Syrups of Mallows, and Capilair of Orange Flower... He makes Deserts of all Kinds, either to sell or lend; besides he makes Sealing wax fine and common... The whole in Wholesale or Retale, at the most reasonable Prices.

York at that time had its share of poverty, but for the well off it was a cosmopolitan, fashionable and relatively affluent place patronised by the landed and professional classes. In 1871, it could boast eight confectioners in a city of 17,000 inhabitants and the market to keep them busy, demanding impressive desserts and sweets with which to round off the many frequent dinners in the Yorkshire Club and the Assembly Rooms – to name but two high-end establishments. The shops also sold or hired out the latest in tableware and silver and the very best in sugarwork ornaments.

Vending machines were springing up everywhere, even on buses at the foot of the stairs, on railway stations and in theatres. A machine at Euston or Paddington could comfortably take £200 a day in 1896. The more sophisticated the machines became, the more ingenious did the methods of robbing them become; with hair and hat pins, nails and tin discs all deployed to get that free chocolate bar or chewing gum.

Manufacturers soon latched onto their customers' love of a gamble: chewing gum machines cleverly delivered a free packet every fourth transaction while The Automatic Cackling Hen Company filled its machines with cackling hens which chorused as the paper eggs were delivered along

Typical scene inside a sweetshop in the 1950s.

with a cheap boiled sweet and a voucher entitling the customer to a free box of chocolates or a jar of jam. Lucky Potatoes and Sensation Balls came with a coupon giving entitlement to a prize. Clinker's Lucky Bags meanwhile gave you a monkey on a stick or a tiny spinning top.

In the nineteenth century, mass production and a fall in the price of sugar made sweets cheaper, so the new market was no longer just for the rich, but it also consumed the working classes, and working-class children in particular. By the end of the nineteenth century, the ubiquitous sweet shop was the 'go to' place on the way to and from school and at weekends.

Tuck shops sprang up in schools. Pear Drops, Sherbet Lemons, Cough Candy, Rhubarb and Custard, Aniseed Twists, Marshmallows,

Typical scenes outside the school tuck shop in the 1950s.

Candy Floss, Fruit Pastilles and Fruit Gums all originate from the mid-nineteenth century to the turn of the twentieth century. Marshmallows came about after French confectioners imitated a medieval medicine using egg whites and sugar.

Meanwhile, the first chocolate bar was made in 1847 and milk chocolate was produced in 1875. Fudge was invented in the USA in the 1880s. Peanut brittle and jelly beans were also created in the nineteenth century. Kendal mint cake came onto the market in 1869, while Turkish delight, invented in 1777, became popular in Europe in the same century.

Henry Mayhew's 1851 *London Labour and the London Poor* gives us some idea of the relative size of the confectionery market in mid-nineteenth-century London: it stood at £10,000 per annum compared with £31,200 for tea and coffee, £19,448 for hot eels, £14,000 for baked potatoes, £11,400 for fried fish, £6,000 for muffins and crumpets and £3,000 for pies. There were 230 sweet sellers in the capital. In Manchester there were two confectioner's shops in 1772, increasing to 308 in 1872 (by comparison there were 804 butchers and 374 bakers).

One of the most famous sweets launched during the early twentieth century was the wine gum – aimed unusually at adults, hence the grown up name. Peace Babies were very popular when they were launched in 1918 to celebrate the end of the Great War; these are still made today although they now go by the name Jelly Babies.

Choc-ices went on sale in the USA in 1921. The ice-lolly was patented in 1923. Meanwhile, bubble gum was invented in 1906 and the first lollipops were sold in 1908. In 1922, ice cream was sold in the street in Britain for the first time.

After the Second World War, the privations suffered by the chocolate companies were to continue until 1953 when rationing was finally ended. To make matters worse, cocoa disease wiped out 16 per cent of the world's cocoa supply in 1948, thus pushing up the price to £237 per tonne – six times the pre-war price. It was a period of consolidation for all the confectionery companies.

Sweet definitions: sweets, candy and confectionery

In Britain, Ireland, and some Commonwealth countries, sweets (from which the Scottish Gaelic word *suiteis* is a derivative) is the word for sugar confections. Candy is used specifically for rock candy and occasionally for (brittle) boiled sweets. Lollies are boiled sweets fixed on sticks.

In Australia and New Zealand, lollies is generally the word for sweets, whereas in North America, candy is the word – although this usually refers to a specific range of confectionery and does not include such items of sugar confectionery as ice cream. Ice cream and sorbet are classified with dairy products. Sweet is occasionally used, as well as describing a treat.

The United Nations' International Standard Industrial Classification of All Economic Activities (ISIC) scheme (revision 4) classifies both chocolate and sugar confectionery as ISIC 1073, which includes the manufacture of chocolate and chocolate confectionery; sugar confectionery proper (caramels, cachous, nougats, fondant, white chocolate), chewing gum, preserving fruit, nuts, fruit peels, and making confectionery lozenges and pastilles. In the European Union, the Statistical Classification of Economic Activities in the European Community (NACE) scheme (revision 2) matches the UN classification, under code number 10.82.

Etymologically speaking, the word sugar is derived from the Sanskrit word *Sharkara*. In English, it was about c. 1300 when the noun sweet was first recorded, meaning 'something sweet to the taste'. It also means 'beloved one' from sweet (adj.); 'candy drop' is 1851 (earlier sweetie, 1721) designating a sweetmeat such as a lozenge or drop type sweet. The meaning 'one who is dear to another' is from 14c. Old English *swete* (n.) which meant 'sweetness'.

The Middle English word candy began to be used in the late thirteenth century. To candy (as a verb) means to 'preserve or encrust with sugar' (1530s) from candy (noun) which means 'crystallised sugar' from Old French *sucre candi* 'sugar candy' – crystallised sugar made by boiling and slow evaporation, to preserve by boiling with sugar; to encrust with sugar from the Old French *candir*. And before that from Arabic *sukkar kandi*, from Persian *kand*, cane sugar, probably from Sanskrit *khanda* 'piece (of sugar)' perhaps even from Dravidian (compare the Tamil kantu 'candy,' kattu 'to harden, condense').

In Britain, candy is usually sweets made only from boiled sugar and striped in bright colours. In the United States, by 1962, a 'candy-striper' was a young female volunteer nurse named thus from the pink-striped design of her uniform, similar to patterns on peppermint candy. Candy-striped (adj.) is from 1886. 'Eye candy' was not without a whiff of sexism, an attractive woman on a TV show, etc. by 1978; based on the same anatomical metaphor, we have 'nose candy' – cocaine – from 1930. A candy man was an itinerant seller of candy, especially in the north of England and Scotland, and an alternative name for a 'bum bailiff' – a bailiff empowered to collect debts or arrest debtors for non-payment.

As for confectionery, Mrs Beeton, in 1861, gives us a definition which excludes sweets as we know them today, but instead describes the type of confection to be seen weighing down the tables of the rich:

In speaking of confectionery, it should be remarked that all the various preparations above named come, strictly speaking, under that head; for the various fruits, flowers, herbs, roots, and juices, which, when boiled with sugar, were formerly employed in pharmacy as well as for sweetmeats, were called confections, from the Latin word conficere, 'to make up;' but the term confectionery embraces a very large class indeed of sweet food, many kinds of which should not be attempted in the ordinary cuisine. The thousand and one ornamental dishes that adorn the tables of the wealthy should be purchased from the confectioner: they cannot profitably be made at home. Apart from these, cakes, biscuits, and tarts, &c., the class of sweetmeats called confections may be thus classified:-1. Liquid confects, or fruits either whole or in pieces, preserved by being immersed in a fluid transparent syrup; as the liquid confects of apricots, green citrons, and many foreign fruits. 2. Dry confects are those which, after having been boiled in the syrup, are taken out and put to dry in an oven, as citron and orange-peel, &c. 3. Marmalade, jams, and pastes, a kind of soft compounds made of the pulp of fruits or other vegetable substances, beat up with sugar or honey; such as oranges, apricots, pears, &c. 4. Jellies are the juices of fruits boiled with sugar to a pretty thick consistency, so as, upon cooling, to form a trembling jelly; as currant, gooseberry, apple jelly, &c. 5. Conserves are a kind of dry confects, made by beating up flowers, fruits, &c., with sugar, not dissolved. 6. Candies are fruits candied over with sugar after having been boiled in the syrup.

Mrs. Beeton's Book of Household Management,
by Isabella Beeton, 1861 – Chapter 30 –
Preserves, Confectionery, Ices and Dessert Dishes

Modern definitions are much closer to what you would expect: confectionery is sweets or chocolate; confectionery is also the art of making confections, foodstuffs that are rich in sugar and carbohydrates. Confectionery is divided into two broad and overlapping categories: bakers' confections and sugar confections. Bakers' confectionery, also known as flour confections, are mainly sweet pastries and cakes and do not concern us here.

Sugar confectionery, however, includes sweets: candied nuts, chocolates, chewing gum, bubble gum, pastillage, and other confections that are mainly made of sugar. Chocolate confections are sometimes categorised separately, as are sugar-free versions of sugar confections. As noted, the words candy (US and Canada), sweets (UK and Ireland), and lollies (Australia and New Zealand) are the usual nouns for the most common varieties of sugar confectionery.

We shall see in the next chapter the strong links between confectionery and its derivative words and medicine. In terms of language, the earliest use of confect as a verb comes in 1545, where it means 'to make in to a confection or to prepare food' (1605). In 1580, we had the sentence 'The Phisitions prescription confected by the Apothecary.' By 1477, confection not only meant making by ingredients or mixture, but also, more specifically, a preparation of drugs, a conserve, an electuary – a medicinal substance mixed with honey or another sweet substance; also a preparation of fruits, spices, sugar. The year 1651 saw a confectioner defined as 'a compounder of medicines, poisons etc.'

Some iconic sweets

Most things are considered iconic or an icon these days so there are very few real icons left to wow us or make us exclaim (the equally bankrupt) 'awesome!' However, here are a few generic types of sweets which do deserve to be called exceptional:

Neapolitans

Terry's of York first produced Neapolitans (which never had anything to do with Naples) in 1899. Once a Christmas staple for millions, these sadly missed mini-choc bars were wiped off the face of the earth in 2005, twelve years after Terry's was bought out by multinational food monolith, Kraft. The distinctive foil-paper wrappers and flavours were Milk Chocolate (Blue); Plain Chocolate (Red); Mocha – coffee flavoured plain chocolate – (Brown); Café Au Lait – coffee flavoured milk chocolate – (Turquoise); Orange Milk Chocolate (Orange); Orange Plain Chocolate (Pink). Terry's also produced a selection of mint-flavoured Neapolitans and cream-filled Neapolitans.

Luckily, other companies now make and sell Neapolitans, for example Marks & Spencer's Neapolitans and Lindt Napolitans.

Polos

We have the Nazis to blame for delaying the launch by Rowntree's in 1939 of Polo Mints when they invaded Poland in 1939. The 'mint with a hole' was scheduled for launch in that same year, but the outbreak of war scuppered the manufacturer's plans. The 1940s were equally sparse sweet-wise and even the production of Peace Babies was suspended.

Polo Mints are a breath mint whose defining feature is something that does not exist: that hole in the middle. The peppermint-flavoured Polo was eventually first manufactured in the UK in 1948, invented by employee John Bargewell at the Rowntree Factory in York – a range of flavours (Polo Fruits) followed. The name is a play on 'polar', conjuring up the cool, fresh taste of the mint.

These are the Polo's vital statistics: all Polos are 1.9 centimetres (0.75 in) in diameter and 0.4 centimetres (0.16 in) thick, with a 0.8-centimetre (0.31 in)-wide hole. The word 'POLO' is embossed twice on the upper flat side of the ring, hence the popular slogan 'The Mint with the Hole'. Polos are usually sold in individual packs of twenty-three mints,

Two years before the Polo Mint's arrival, Parma Violets appeared on the shelves. Parma Violets are manufactured by the Derbyshire company Swizzels Matlow and named after the Parma violet variety of the flower.

Polos, of course, were predated by the US Lifesavers by some twenty years and owed much of their success by clever marketing which exploited the confectionery equivalent to a black hole – the selling of nothingness – the hole.

Spangles

Mars used Spangles to help lift post-war austerity while sweets were still on ration. When Spangles were introduced in 1950, as with cough sweets you only needed one ration point instead of the two required for other sweets and chocolate. This was a valuable bonus; marketing slogans included Hoppy's favourite sweet' – a reference to Hopalong Cassidy (William Boyd) who featured in the adverts, and 'The sweet way to go gay!'

Love Hearts

In the 1950s, Love Hearts came into our (love) lives – hard tablets stamped with daft messages such as: 'I'm Shy', 'Kiss Me', 'It's love' and 'I Love You'. These, of course, were a variant of Terry's earlier Conversation Lozenges. Love Hearts manufacturers Swizzels Matlow also launched the world's first chewable lolly in 1957 with the 'Drumstick'. Apparently, the son of one the company's owners was experimenting with a new machine and discovered that he could make a sweet with two different flavours. Raspberry and milk were chosen and the Drumstick had arrived.

Chapter 3

The Rise and Rise of Sugar

As we have already said, despite the good job honey had done, without sugar there would be no such thing as sweets as we know them today. Sugar is everywhere in food and drink, often a clandestine, sinister ingredient in the myriad foodstuffs and beverages into which it is shovelled on a biblical scale. According to *dw.com* the average German, for example, ingests more than 30kg (66lbs) of sugar every year, Germans being reasonably typical of western Europeans and North Americans and so on. We all know that such levels of consumption has deleterious effects on our health – both medical and dental. Before sugar was refined on an industrial scale, we derived our sweeteners from fruits: the Romans cultivated fruit trees and bushes throughout their empire and so set in train centuries of fruit cultivation. The extracted and preserved fruit juice was processed into a mush or jelly. Sugar to the Romans came from trade with Arabia and India; it was called *saccharon* (Pliny the Elder, *Natural History* 12, 32), but they only used it for medicinal purposes. Dioscorides recommended it for stomach and bowel disorders (*Materia Medica* 2, 82, 4). When in the early Middle Ages, cane sugar arrived in Europe from the Middle East it was far too expensive for most people to afford – even the aristocracies reserved it for special occasions.

During the eighteenth century, the British and other empire builders began to cultivate sugar cane in their colonies, producing massive quantities of sugar. Napoleon tried to put Britain out of business with his Continental Blockade, which attempted to interrupt sugar imports. From the middle of the nineteenth century, sugar beet, and therefore, sugar, was available to everyone and – above all – it was affordable.

We discuss the health implications of sugar consumption in a later chapter, but suffice to say here, the 'white poison' is a contributory factor in numerous diseases. It will come as no surprise to learn that, like the sweets they gave rise to, sugar was, for many years, believed to have therapeutic properties and was a constituent in medicines available at pharmacies.

In the twelfth century, *sine confectiones* drugs (without wrappers) consisted of 90 per cent sugar. In the seventeenth century, pharmacists were still using sugar in medicines for preserving and masking the bitter taste of some drugs; on a more positive note it was also being dispensed as a source of energy. Indeed, it did not take long for apothecaries to realise that sugar spelled money, so in order to boost profits they simply did away with any active medical ingredients and just sold the sweet element – and so was confectionery, and the sweet shop, born.

Typically, sugar was delivered to the apothecaries, and later to the confectionery companies, in conical sticks weighing up to 14lbs. It came in various exotically named varieties including Dutch Crushed – best for boiled sweets; Russian Crystal, Madras Cane Jaggery, Pale Porto Rico, Yellow Crystallised Trinidad, St Kitt's Syrup Crystallised Demerara and the decidedly less exotic, mundane Tate's # 1 and #2. Tate apart, a veritable geography lesson on a conical stick.

When is sugar not sugar?

Glucose syrups

W.W. Cargill, for example, manufactures glucose syrups for liquid formulations under the name C* PharmSweet™; its website tells us that:

> Glucose syrups are aqueous solutions of α-D-glucose based natural sugars obtained by starch hydrolysis. They are widely used in the manufacture of sucrose-based medical syrups. These syrups often contain high amounts of sucrose and have the tendency to crystallize over time. The shelf-life of medicated syrups can be improved dramatically by adding glucose syrup, as the polysaccharide portion of the glucose syrup acts as an anti-crystallizing agent. They also provide extra viscosity for liquid preparations.

Sugar-free bulk sweetening agents

Liquid sorbitol and liquid maltitol are syrups obtained by the hydrogenation of glucose or glucose syrups with high maltose content. Cargill makes these agents under the names C* PharmMaltidex™ and C* PharmSorbidex™; they are used in the formulation of sugar-free medical syrups.

The website continues:

> Sorbitol liquid is useful as a bulking agent with stabilizing properties, while maltitol syrups are well suited for the production of cough syrups and linctuses where their clean sweet taste and non-cariogenicity are particularly useful. Maltitol syrups are extremely stable against crystallization – so the caps on bottles containing syrups and oral solutions do not get stuck because of crystal formation.
>
> Most polyols are non-cariogenic, meaning that they do not promote tooth decay. This is because polyols cannot be metabolized by the Streptococci bacteria in the mouth. This makes them an ideal substitute for sugar and glucose syrup and the sweetener of choice in modern medical syrup formulations, especially in childcare.
>
> (www.cargill.com/pharmaceutical/pharma-applications/
> medicated-confectionery)

If cutting out sugar is not a plausible option, there are healthy alternatives: not least honey and coconut sugar. (*Image from* India Times, *December 3 2020*)

Chapter 4

'A Spoonful of Sugar...':
Sweets as Spurious Medicine

In the Middle Ages, sweets doubled up as medicine to deal with a wide range of complaints ranging from settling the digestive system (combined with spices) or soothing a sore throat. Obviously these therapies were, at first, very much the preserve of the wealthier classes. Stomach problems were common because food was often less than fresh, so anything that could help to ease the discomfort was welcomed. One of the prophylactics was appropriately called chamber spice; it was made from cloves, ginger, aniseed, juniper berries, almonds and pine kernels, all dipped in melted sugar and guaranteed to get you running for the chamber pot.

Every healthcare professional and parent knows how difficult it can be to persuade a child to take medicine. Bitter tastes are anathema to young patients who respond by point blank refusal or who just spit out their medicines. Julie Mennella, from the Monell Chemical Senses Center in Pennsylvania, warns that children's non-compliance is a 'public health priority', and in some instances may impede recovery from illness, or even be life-threatening. In response, scientists at the 241st National Meeting of the American Chemical Society in 2011 launched a new compound that inhibits the tongue's perception of bitter tastes, nicknamed the 'bitter blocker GIV3616' – a potential replacement therapy to Mary Poppins's doling out a spoonful of sugar to disguise those nasty flavours. Nevertheless, research in 2012 on children's medicine in the seventeenth century, by Dr Hannah Newton, a science historian at the Department of History and Philosophy of Science, University of Cambridge, reveals that doctors and parents had a varied armamentarium of imaginative strategies to fall back on to make medicines 'grateful & pleasing to the Sick Child, & such as...trouble not its Pallate'.

She reveals that it is a common misconception that children's preference for sweet over bitter flavours is a modern phenomenon and that recently scientists are saying that children's predilections are 'a reflection of their basic biology', evolved as a mechanism for survival. The taste buds are formed in the foetus at seven weeks gestation and within hours of birth, infants reject bitter tastes in preference to sweet ones: acerbity, like pain, is nature's warning, a sign of the potential harm that might ensue if the bitter substance is ingested.

Nothing much, then, has changed in 300 years: the Sussex doctor John Pechey wrote in 1697, 'sweet things which Children eat, and are delighted with…[they] eat greedily', while a physician from Kent, Robert Pemell, noted in 1653 that children 'will hardly take' anything that is 'so bitter'. These doctors attributed children's penchants to the heightened sensitivity of the 'teats' of their tongues – the taste buds.

As today, substitution was one popular seventeenth-century method for making medicines palatable, swapping unpleasant ingredients with substances of a more agreeable flavour.

When treating children for threadworms, Dr Pemell advised giving children 'juyce of Lemons or Citrons' in place of the bitter herb wormwood. Where the use of disagreeable ingredients was unavoidable, practitioners tried to disguise the taste by putting the medicine into the child's normal food or drink. The Dutch physician Franciscus Sylvius declared, 'Knowing that children are nice [fussy], and can scarce be prevailed with to take even the smallest doses' of bitter medicines, he suggested that 'these may be given in their milk or drink, they may be [the] better beguiled; scarce discerning them'. Medicines could be mixed with mashed apple, or in the case of babies, breast milk. In addition to disguising the noxious taste, practitioners suggested giving pleasant drinks after the child had taken the medicine, to counter any lingering bad taste. In the 1680s, Thomas Davies fed his child 'a little beere posset drink…to take away the ill taste' of a remedy containing castor oil and piony. This adaptation might raise eyebrows today, but weak beer was a standard drink for children in the seventeenth century.

Sugar soon makes an appearance in this seemingly intractable battle of wills: the historian Joan Thirsk has shown that although honey was the 'traditional sweetener', by the 1650s, sugar was becoming more fashionable generally, because it was regarded as a healthier food. In 1651, the physician Francis Glisson advised adding 'some pleasant and agreable Liquor, or candid Cherries' to his medicine on the grounds that the child 'delights in such things'. It is a short step from this generalised behaviour to sweetening children's medicines. In 1660, Abigail Harley gave her young niece 'a drink of maidenhaire & violet leaves & hyslop' which she had 'swetened with syrop of violets & sugar candy'. And it wasn't just taste that was proving a problem; some parents attempted to better the smell. Sarah Hughes' recipe for 'A purge for Children', dated 1637, had to be tempered with 'soe much of cinnamon water as will mend the smell'.

Distraction was another much applied strategy, for example the French midwifery expert François Mauriceau suggested that infants suffering from painful teething should be given 'a Silver Coral, furnish'd with small Bells, to divert the Child'. As was emotional blackmail: the well-named father of 6-year-old Joseph Scholding from Suffolk told his son, 'If you love me, take it', to which, the boy responded, 'to satisfy you, I will take it'. Bribery sometimes worked as when in 1726, John Yorke from London complained that his nephew James 'is so refractory [about] taking what is proper for him', that '[it is] a hard taske to govern him'. Yorke had to 'use all my perwasion' to get the child 'to take what the Dr order'd'; in particular, he 'wou[l]d by no means submit to a glister [enema] to cool his body'. Eventually, by promising James a copy of *Robinson Crusoe*, the uncle managed to coax his nephew into taking the medicine.

Dr Newton concludes that adding sugar may be harmful to children's teeth, but it certainly seems to 'please and comfort' the sick child, as one seventeenth-century doctor put it. There may be some extra benefits to sweetening children's medicines: recent investigations show that sugar acts as a form of pain relief in infants, and may even improve the efficacy of antibiotics.

(Adapted from www.cam.ac.uk/research/discussion/
a-spoonful-of-sugar-or-a-bitter-blocker; © Hannah Newton)

Candy aspirin

In 2018, Cynthia Connolly published her *Children and Drug Safety*, a disturbing, but important book which, according to the blurb:

[T]races the development, use, and marketing of drugs for children in the twentieth century, a history that sits at the interface of the state, business, health care providers, parents, and children. This book illuminates the historical dimension of a clinical and policy issue with great contemporary significance-many of the drugs administered to children today have never been tested for safety and efficacy in the pediatric population. Each chapter of Children and Drug Safety engages with major turning points in pediatric drug development; themes of children's risk, rights, protection and the evolving context of childhood; child-rearing; and family life in ways freighted with nuances of race, class, and gender. Cynthia A. Connolly charts the numerous attempts by Congress, the Food and Drug Administration, the American Academy of Pediatrics, and leading pediatric pharmacologists, scientists, clinicians, and parents to address a situation that all found untenable.

Indeed, the intentional blurring of safety considerations with the pursuit of profit in over the counter (OTC) children's medicine where drugs are developed and made to masquerade as more palatable sweets is probably the most sinister manifestation of the (deliberate) confusing of pharmaceuticals with sweets.

The essence of the story is that in 1947, the Plough Company, founded by entrepreneur Abe Plough, successfully reformulated an old, off-patent medication – aspirin – into a flavoured, small-dose chewable tablet designed to appeal to the finicky palates of medicine-averse children. Aspirin – acetylsalicylic acid (ASA) – is a medication which used to be used to reduce pain, fever, or inflammation. It had originally been manufactured and patented by Bayer of Leverkusen in 1853. Plough had made his money buying ailing proprietary drug companies and remarketing their products aggressively. Although Plough purchased one of these companies, St. Joseph in 1921, by the 1940s things were not going too well.

But the boom in births after the Second World War gave him an opportunity. Plough set St. Joseph chemists to work developing a paediatric aspirin formulation that would be attractive to children through colour and taste. In September 1947, the company released the bright orange St. Joseph Aspirin for children amid a frenzy of aggressive creative marketing in all media. Particularly insidious though was his use of newspaper and magazine adverts, particularly those in *Parents* magazine,

St Joseph's child unsafe pharmaceutical masquerading as sweets.

in which he depicted homely and idealised scenarios and a stereotyped, class and racially exclusive vision of the comfortable American family in well-appointed living rooms.

Mothers appeared relaxed, but no. The copy implied that parenting was stressful and difficult. According to Cynthia Connolly, 'the ads were designed to tap into mothers' anxieties by persuading them that post-war parenting was much more complex. As a result, the ads implied, children could face danger if a mother purchased a product that had not been scientifically formulated to accommodate her children's physiological and psychological needs.' The persuasive message was that Plough's attractively coloured formulation met all the scientific safety criteria, unlike other medicines.

Plough's new product achieved blockbuster status almost immediately. By the early 1950s, low-dose, flavoured aspirin was the number one drug ingested by children, far outstripping its chief competitor, penicillin. Plough's profits increased by double digits, in some years by as much as 50 per cent. All of this spurred Bayer and other generic manufacturers to bring competing versions to market.

Connolly goes on to tell us that 'within a few years the American Academy of Pediatrics (AAP) recorded an alarming dramatic increase in aspirin poisoning in young children. The statistics seemed irrefutable: by 1951, three years after St. Joseph Aspirin for Children became available, pre-school-age children represented 80 per cent of aspirin deaths. Children loved the taste of St. Joseph Aspirin for Children.'

There was nothing anywhere in Plough's advertisements which mentioned the importance, the necessity indeed, of keeping these pills away from toddlers and pre-school children; many parents remained blithely unaware of the threat from an overdose. They were, no doubt, 'horrified to learn that a toxic dose of aspirin could cause ringing in the ears, sleepiness, rapid and deep breathing, vomiting, and vision problems. An especially high dose could result in seizures, coma, even death.' Stomach bleeds too must have been an issue.

In the event, some parents did inadvertently overdose their children. There was no requirement or regulation for a standardised children's aspirin preparation. Each generic company decided themselves how much acetylsalicylic acid to put in a tablet. The AAP reported that 50 per cent of accidents in children were now poison-related: paediatricians, nurses, and public-health officials began tracking all accidental swallowings in children. In most cases, aspirin topped the list.

[Cynthia Connolly holds the Rosemarie B. Greco Term Endowed Associate Professorship in Advocacy and is an associate professor of nursing in the School of Nursing. She is also associate director of the Barbara Bates Center for the Study of the History of Nursing and the co-faculty director of the Field Center for Children's Policy, Practice & Research in the School of Social Policy & Practice. The text above is adapted and extracted from 'Children and Drug Safety: Balancing Risk and Prevention in Twentieth-Century America' (New Brunswick: Rutgers University Press, 2018.) © Cynthia A. Connolly].

Indeed, sweets and medicine were inextricably associated with each other; so much so that in the early days of sweets in Europe, it was the apothecary who was the key player in the production of sugar-based preparations. Medieval European physicians were well-versed in the medicinal uses of sugar, having learnt them from the Arabs and Byzantine Greeks. For example, one Middle Eastern remedy for rheums (a thin mucus naturally discharged from the eyes, nose, or mouth during sleep) and fevers was little twisted sticks of pulled sugar which the Arabs called *al fānād* or *al pānād*. These became known in Britain as alphenics, or more commonly, as penidia, penids, pennet or pan sugar. They were the precursors of barley sugar and modern cough drops. In 1390, we know that the Earl of Derby paid 'two shillings for two pounds of penydes'.

Nevertheless, the non-medicinal applications of sugar burgeoned and the comfitmaker, or confectioner, gradually took centre stage in what became a separate trade. In the late medieval period the words confyt, comfect or cumfitt were generic terms for all kinds of sweetmeats made from fruits, roots, or flowers preserved with sugar. By the sixteenth century, a cumfit was usually a seed, nut or small piece of spice enclosed in a round or ovoid mass of sugar. The production of comfits was a basic and core skill of the early confectioner, who in the sixteenth and seventeenth centuries was known in England as a comfitmaker. But the apothecaries refused to let go and comfits were also produced by apothecaries – with directions on how to make them published in dispensatories as well as cookery books. An early medieval Latin name for an apothecary was *confectionarius*, overlapping into the sweet trade and giving us the word confectionery.

The relationship between apothecary and the confectionery industry is clearly illustrated by the origins of Joseph Terry in eighteenth-century York. Confectionery was beginning to emerge as a major force helped in part by the freighting opportunities the railways offered. By 1851,

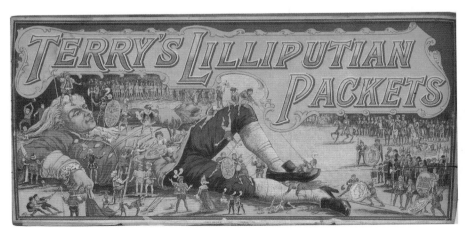

Terry's of York Lilliputian Packets – a marvellous piece of art from 1885.

Joseph Terry employed 127 workers in St Helen's Square, and Thomas Craven was working with 63 men and 60 boys; both companies were manufacturing sugar confectionery.

Joseph Terry had been making cocoa and chocolate since 1886; by the end of the 1920s the firm had become the market leader in chocolate assortments and was building a sound reputation for producing the best in dark and bitter chocolate. The origins of the company go right back to 1767 when:

> [T]here was founded near Bootham Bar, York, a confectionery business which was destined to develop, at first into a centre where the elite of the County enjoyed their sweetmeats, and, at last after phases of success with various specialties and operation at different centres in the City, into a Chocolate Factory the name of which is recognised throughout the World as synonymous with excellence of quality.

This confectionery business was run by Messrs William Bayldon and Robert Berry. Joseph Terry came to York from nearby Pocklington to serve an apprenticeship in an apothecary in Stonegate. In 1823, Joseph married Harriet Atkinson, a sister-in-law of Robert Berry; he then gave up being a chemist and druggist and joined Berry who had moved from Bootham to St Helen's Square in 1824 – the site of the first Old Factory. George Berry succeeded his father to form the pleasantly rhyming Terry & Berry, but George left in 1828 leaving Joseph to develop what then was essentially an expanding confectionery business. Chocolate production began in earnest around 1867, with thirteen chocolate products – although the company would for some thirty more years or so remain primarily a confectionery company. The new chocolate lines complemented the other 380 or so confectionery lines.

Jordan Almonds

If anything typifies the elision of medicines into sweets, then it is the dragée, or more specifically, the Jordan Almond – a bite-sized confection with a hard outer shell, often used for decorative, symbolic or medicinal purposes.

Jordan Almonds originated in ancient Rome, where honey-covered almonds, *dragati*, were introduced by a Roman baker and confectioner named Julius Dragatus. His confections were, of course, the exclusive preserve of the upper echelons of Roman society and were served by the nobility at weddings and births. When sugar became more readily available in the fifteenth century, the nuts were coated in sugar, as perfected in Sulmona, Italy, by the Pelino family.

The term Jordan is a corruption of the French word *jardin*, for garden, indicating the use of a cultivated rather than wild almond. Others would have it that the term refers to a variety of almonds originally grown along the Jordan River while others still believe that Jordan is a corruption of the name of the town of Verdun in France. In the thirteenth century, when the medieval crusaders brought sugar back to Europe, it was extremely valuable and considered medicinal. Accordingly, an apothecary in Verdun began coating his other medicines with sugar (calling them dragées) to make them easier to swallow. Verdun became famous for its Dragées de Verdun.

The Verdun apothecary knew that his dragées increased the tolerability of bitter medication and improved compliance.

Jordan Almonds, also known as mlabas (ملبس, 'coated' or 'covered') in Arabic, are often used as wedding favours – like the Italian Bomboniere – with the 'bitter' almonds and the 'sweet' sugar symbolising the bitter-sweet nature of life and love. The treats are often dispensed in fives to represent happiness, health, longevity, wealth, and fertility. The odd number is also significant because it is indivisible and thus symbolises the unity of husband and wife. In the Middle East, Jordan Almonds are considered an aphrodisiac.

Today M&M's are probably the most popular example of dragées. They were initially designed to facilitate transportation and the consumption of chocolate for the US military and are sold as decorative dragées in twenty-five different colours.

Ayds

Ayds Reducing Plan Candy was an appetite-suppressant sweet that was popular in the 1970s and early 1980s, originally manufactured by Carlay Company from 1937. In 1944, the US Federal Trade Commission objected to the claim that the product could help to 'lose up to 10 pounds in 5 days, without dieting or exercising'. Chicago firm Campana's takeover of Carlay Company brought the 'Ayds Reducing Plan vitamins and mineral candy' into the Campana portfolio. It was available in chocolate, chocolate mint, butterscotch, and caramel flavours, and later peanut butter. The original packaging used the slogan 'Ayds Reducing Plan vitamin and mineral Candy'; a later version was more pithy: 'appetite suppressant candy'. The active ingredient was originally benzocaine, presumably to reduce the sense of taste and so reduce eating, later changed to phenylpropanolamine.

The emergence and spread of AIDS and HIV in the mid-1980s effectively torpedoed this hybrid sweet-medicine: public awareness of AIDS was increasingly problematic due to the phonetic similarity of names and the fact that, ironically, the disease caused dramatic weight loss in patients. By 1988, the company announced that it was seeking a new name because sales had crashed by 50 per cent due to awareness of the disease. A number of ownership changes followed and the name was changed to Diet Ayds (Aydslim in Britain), but was eventually withdrawn from market.

Cold and throat lozenges – sweets or medicine or medicated sweets?

Many early sweets, then, claimed some medicinal benefit; indeed early pharmaceuticals sweetened with sugar or honey coatings were called electuaries, or confections. Confectionery soon became another word for sweets as the medicinal element receded. Medicated confectionery is widely used in the formulation of drugs for many conditions such as minor throat irritations, coughs, colds, respiratory tract congestion and allergies. Other medicines containing active ingredients such as antacids, vitamins and herbal extracts can also be formulated as confectionery products. The no man's land between the numerous over the counter cold and throat lozenges is decidedly grey and murky – are they sweets or pharmaceuticals? Here are some definitions designed to plot a way through the minefield that is medicated sweets:

Pastille

A pastille is a type of sweet or medicinal pill full of thick liquid that has been solidified and is designed to be consumed by light chewing and allowing it to dissolve in the mouth. A pastille is also known as a troche, which is a medicated lozenge that dissolves like a sweet. Pastilles were originally a pill-shaped lump of compressed herbs, which was burnt to release its medicinal properties. Literary references to the burning of medicinal pastilles include the short story *The Birth-Mark* by Nathaniel Hawthorne, the poem *The Laboratory* by Robert Browning, and *Jane Eyre* by Charlotte Brontë.

Vocalzone Throat Pastilles is a brand of throat pastille, or throat lozenge, used to help with colds as well as public performance and singing. The company was founded in 1912 by William Lloyd, who adapted a medicine he had created for the tenor Enrico Caruso into a pastille form. After Lloyd's death in 1948, Vocalzone was sold to Ernest Jackson in 1955 before later being acquired by Kestrel HealthCare Limited (now Kestrel Medical Limited) in 1993.

A number of singers, actors and public speakers swear by Vocalzone: they include Theresa May, Sir Tom Jones, Derek Jacobi, Hilary Duff, The Swingle Singers, Katherine Jenkins, Dionne Warwick, Wendi Peters and Jack Savoretti.

J. Dobson & Son of Elland still produces Voice Tablets to this day – efficacious in sore throats. CT&W Holloway, Birmingham confectioners, made Voice Confectionery. In 1895, Holloway somehow obtained the endorsement of the famous Spanish soprano Adelina Patti; they eponymously rebranded their lozenges Pattines, put her likeness on the tin and added the pithy Patti endorsement: 'much pleased' – brief, but to the point – she was obviously saving her voice.

Rowntree's Fruit Pastilles on the other hand (rebranded in Australia as Wonka Fruit Pastilles, Fruit Joy in Italy, Frutips in Canada, China, Hong Kong, Singapore and Taiwan after the 1988 acquisition of Rowntree by Nestlé) make no pretence to being medicinal in any way – quite the opposite: they are small round sugar coated sweets with a jelly-like consistency, due to the gelatin they are made from.

Throat lozenge

Also known as a cough drop, troche, cachou, pastille or cough sweet, a throat lozenge is a small, usually medicated tablet intended to be dissolved slowly in the mouth to temporarily suppress coughs, lubricate, and soothe irritated tissues of the throat made sore possibly from the common cold or flu. Cough tablets get the name lozenge due to their original shape, a diamond. Lozenges can contain benzocaine, an anaesthetic, or eucalyptus oil. Non-menthol throat lozenges generally use either zinc gluconate glycine or pectin as an oral demulcent. Several brands of throat lozenges contain dextromethorphan. Other varieties, such as Halls, contain menthol, peppermint oil and/or spearmint as their active ingredient(s). Honey lozenges are also available.

We can trace sweets used to soothe the throat back to 1000 BC in Egypt's Twentieth Dynasty, when they were made from honey flavoured with citrus, herbs, and spices. More recently, in the nineteenth century, physicians discovered methamphetamine and heroin, which suppress coughing at its source – the brain. Popular formulations of that era included Smith Brothers Cough Drops, first advertised in 1852, and Luden's, created in 1879. Concern over the risk of opioid dependence led to their withdrawal and the development of alternative medications.

The Smith Brothers story tells us much about early branding and trademarks. The brothers (William Wallace and Andrew) were makers of the first cough drops produced in the United States and became one of the most famous brands in the country. They were the sons of James Smith (c1800–1866) of Poughkeepsie, New York. In New York, James had opened an ice cream shop; he bought a cough drop recipe from a peddler named Sly Hawkins and in 1852 made his first batch of 'Smith Brothers Cough Drops'. William and Andrew inherited the business after their father died in 1866.

Originally the drops were sold from glass jars on countertops. To prevent competing drug stores from selling generic versions, the company began packaging drops in branded boxes in 1872. To distinguish their drops from imitators, the brothers created a logo featuring their portraits and stamped it on their boxes. When trademarked in 1877, the word 'Trade' appeared under the picture of William and the word 'Mark' under Andrew's. The brothers became known as Trade and Mark, nicknames that stick to this day. Recent flavours include Honey Lemon, Wild Cherry and Warm Apple Pie.

William H. Luden created the Luden's brand in 1879. He was the son of a jeweller who died just a few years after emigrating from the Netherlands; Luden left school at 15 and became an apprentice confectioner. In 1879, aged 20, he was selling sweets made in his widowed mother's kitchen, behind the jewellery shop.

Luden did things differently: most sweets at that time were sold door to door, but Luden persuaded shopkeepers to display and sell his wares.

He developed the menthol cough drop, effectively doing away with the cumbersome vials of menthol that cold sufferers carried to relieve their symptoms. He cleverly handed out samples of his cough drops to railroad workers, giving the product massive national exposure in an early example of disruptive guerrilla marketing – one of the aims of which is to effect an emotional reaction in clients, and to get people to remember products or brands in a different way than they are used to.

Luden's was acquired in 1928 by Food Industries of Philadelphia and went on to produce over 500 varieties of sweets in addition to its better-known cough drops; they employed more than 1,200 people. By the 1930s, Luden's products were selling in twenty-six countries and the firm was turning out tens of millions of pounds of sweets. In 1967, animator Ed Seeman and musician Frank Zappa worked together on a television commercial for Luden's Cough Drops. The commercial won a Clio award for Zappa's soundtrack.

Luden's Inc. was sold to Hershey Foods Corp in 1986; Luden's Throat Drops brand was sold by Hershey's to Pharmacia in 2001. In 2003, Pharmacia was acquired by Pfizer. In 2006, Pfizer sold its consumer products division, including the Luden's line, to Johnson & Johnson.

Luden's brand throat drops are demulcents (a swelling or irritation reliever) and mild oral anesthetics. The active ingredient in fruit flavours is pectin, a soluble gelatinous polysaccharide found in ripe fruits. Pectin places a coating on the throat to reduce irritation and swelling. Original Menthol and the various honey flavours contain menthol, an oral anesthetic and irritant reliever.

An example of their modern products is *Melatonin Soothers* described as Deliciously Soothing for Restful Sleep[†][*]

The website boasts:

Use to aid in occasional sleeplessness, helping you to fall asleep faster and wake up feeling refreshed. Luden's® Melatonin Soothers are great tasting, 100% drug free, and won't cause next day grogginess.[*]

† Aids in occasional sleeplessness[*]
* These statements have not been evaluated by the Food and Drug Administration. This product is not intended to diagnose, treat, cure or prevent any disease.

The market for medicated sweets is huge, with a wide choice, including Barnips Lozenges, Coltsfoot Rock, and Teddy Gray's Herbal Tablets. Here are the stories behind more of these products:

Teddy Gray's Herbal Tablets

Established in 1826, the Edward Gray of Dudley company is still a family-run business – now in its fifth generation – and has four retail outlets across the West Midlands. The tablets, like many in this category, are supposedly made according to a secret family recipe.

When John Gray set up the company it was to buy and sell other people's sweets as he criss-crossed and traversed the region in his horse and cart. Soon he decided to make his own sweets, and, with his son Teddy, took the business from strength to strength. Once rationing had ended in 1953, Gray junior was able to concentrate on wholesale, thus making the herbal tablet the success it remains today.

Fisherman's Friend

Fisherman's Friend was developed in 1865 by Fleetwood pharmacist James Lofthouse for the benefit of local fishermen on stormy and freezing trips into the North Atlantic. The main market has expanded somewhat since then and you don't have to be a fisherman to enjoy them. Holidaymakers to Fleetwood were early non-fisherman customers when the Lofthouse family started selling to shops in the surrounding area from their van. The shape of the lozenge is based on the design of the buttons on one of the dresses Doreen Lofthouse wore to the office.

Early branding told us that the Friend was suitable for 'internal and external use'; the answer to how the sweet can be administered externally is revealed when we know that Fisherman's Friend was originally a liquid, dispensed in a glass bottle. Now no one has to rub a lozenge on his chest any more.

The combination of choppy seas and breaking glass led to the 'lozenging' of the liquid mixture into the form we know today. A Fisherman's Friend 'delivers instant relief from problems caused by the prolonged exposure to hostile conditions' – a kind of 'special forces' of the sweet world.

Original Extra Strong lozenges ingredients are: Sugar, Liquorice extract, Menthol, Eucalyptus oil, Dextrin, Tragacanth (a natural gum extracted from dried sap), Capsicum tincture.

In 1972, the new packaging in black and red reflected the very early typewritten labels of the brand, which were produced directly from the red and black colours on the typewriter. In 1979, Fisherman's Friend became the first confectionery company to produce a sugar free mint. A 1980s' advert proudly, yet absurdly, announced that 'These Fisherman's Friend super strong mints really make you blow!'

The company is still family-owned and dispenses more than 5 billion lozenges a year. In 2013, chocolatier Adam Chandler created a Fisherman's Friend Truffle at the International Chocolate Awards, filling a dark chocolate shell with a ganache made from Original Extra Strong lozenges melted into whole cream and a dark chocolate base.

Victory V

Originally manufactured in Nelson, Lancashire, the Victory V liquorice-flavoured lozenge was invented by Thomas Fryer and Edward Smith MD in the mid-nineteenth century and was initially made by hand to ensure that each sweet contained the correct amount of therapeutic ingredients: ether, liquorice and chloroform. In the 1960s the company acquired the Alverthorpe, Wakefield firm of A. Talbot and Son.

Unsurprisingly, Victory V lozenges no longer contain chloroform or ether. However, their scent and flavour is still vividly reminiscent of diethyl ether – recreated by artificial means to preserve the original flavour. Today they are manufactured by Crediton, Devon company Ernest Jackson & Co. Ltd.

Legend has it that Victory V was named after the famous 'V' sign used by English archers in the Battle of Agincourt to show the French that their bow fingers were still intact.

Nigroids or Vigroids

Nigroids were invented by Ferris & Co. Ltd., manufacturing chemists of Bristol in 1900. Nigroids was the brand name of this liquorice sweet – small black pellets marketed as an expectorant lozenge for singers, using the slogan 'for clarity of voice'. The company promoted them 'For Hoarseness, Tickling of the Throat, etc. They afford protection to the Voice, Throat, and Chest, against ill-effects of fog, cold and damp. Invaluable to singers and speakers.'

Ernest Jackson acquired the brand in 1974 and in November 2010 changed the brand name from Nigroids to Vigroids.

The main ingredient of Vigroids is liquorice block juice. The company warns that liquorice can raise blood pressure, and that those with a history of hypertension should take them with care. They suggest limiting consumption to ten per day. No sugar is used. Small quantities of other flavourings such as menthol, eucalyptus and peppermint are added to help the pellets act as a breath mint.

Barnett's Winter Nips

Now called Barnips to signify their manufacture by Barnett's, they have been produced by Barnett's Confectionery in Radford, Nottingham since 1896 and are still hand made in traditional copper pans by this family firm. The nips – menthol lozenges – were particularly popular with workers in heavy industries like the iron foundries and mining, to allay dry throats caused by the heat and dust.

As with any pharmaceutical, contraindications are possible when more than one drug is administered to a patient. The same may be true, albeit in extremely rare cases, of medicated lozenges if a paper in *Endocrine Abstracts* (2002) 3 P54 by K.C. Lewandowski & W.A. Burr (Pinderfields General Hospital, Wakefield) entitled *Apparent mineralocorticoid excess caused by Barnips cough tablets*, is anything to go by.

A 66-year-old woman, was admitted as an emergency with one-week history of profound weakness ('had to crawl to the fridge to get milk for tea'), lethargy, productive cough and hypokalaemia. Her medication: Amlodipine 5mg od, Bendrofluazide 2.5mg od, Aspirin 75mg. The cause of her profound hypokalaemia at presentation became more clear when she admitted consuming at least a packet of 'Barnips' throat sweets a day (probably more during episodes of chest infections). We eventually obtained a sample of these and established that they contained 3.8 per cent oil of liquorice (~250 mg of deglycyrrhizinised liquorice extract/pack of 'Barnips' sweets). Conclusions: Though liquorice preparations are no longer used in the treatment of peptic ulcer disease, there are reports that in susceptible individuals, hypokalaemia can develop after chronic ingestion of about 500 mg of liquorice/day. We therefore concluded that in our patient such profound and life-threatening hypokalaemia was caused by chronic liquorice ingestion in the form of 'Barnips' cough sweets, in the setting of concomitant treatment with a thiazide diuretic [Bendroflumethiazide].

Lun Jeelers

One of Barnett's most popular sweets are 'Lun Jeelers'; these were originally called 'Lung Healers', but trading standards prohibited the company from using the name in the 1950s as it suggested the sweets may cure lung problems. The firm exports to various countries, including Iceland, where the menthol and eucalyptus treats are very popular. Sugar-free versions are available.

Coltsfoot

Coltsfoot rock has been made by Stockleys Sweets in Lancashire for over ninety years. It is a paste dried hardened stick infused with coltsfoot extract, an ingredient from the plant *Tussilago farfara*.

Originally the leaves of the plant were dried, then smoked. Despite serious safety concerns, people take coltsfoot for respiratory problems such as bronchitis, asthma, and whooping cough (pertussis). They also take it for sore mouth and throat, cough, and hoarseness. Some people inhale coltsfoot for coughs and wheezing.

It also goes by the name of Coughwort and numerous others including Ass's Foot, Brandlattich, British Tobacco, Bullsfoot, Chasse-Toux; in Paris, the flowers were often painted as a sign on the doorpost of an apothecary's shop.

Stockley's was set up after the First World War by Malcolm Stockley who had been a toffee-maker in earlier days. His products were exhibited at the World Exhibition in San Francisco in 1939. Visitors to Stockley's Sweet Shop at Oswaldtwistle Mills will see the world's largest pear drop, which is on display there.

Proctor's Pinelyptus Pastilles

These medicinal sweets date back to 1817 and were endorsed by such celebrities as Shakespearean actress Ellen Terry and opera star Charles Santley. Medicated followers of fashion?

The pastilles contain eucalyptus oil and menthol and are made today by pharmaceutical company Ernest Jackson, manufacturers of medicated confectionery and vitamin products, in Crediton, Devon.

It all started in 1817 when a Crediton pharmacist, William Searle, was asked to prescribe 'something effective but soothing' for a troublesome sore throat. As a result, he developed a range of medicated lozenges which he manufactured and sold from his pharmacy on Crediton High Street. In 1891, William Searle sold the company to Edward Ernest Jackson.

A 1908 advert proclaimed the pastilles 'are unequalled for clearing the throat and giving tone and strength to the voice…They are of immense service to Speakers, Singers, Teachers, Travellers, and all who have much talking to do.'

This Ernest Jackson timeline illustrates the complex path such·a product takes in the market place with its product development often confounded by serial mergers and acquisitions in the industry:

1817 – William Searle starts making medicinal lozenges in Crediton
1891 – Edward Ernest Jackson buys the business from Searle
1896 – Ernest Jackson diversifies into Pastilles & Pellets
1923 – Imps liquorice and menthol pellets launched
1925 – Throaties medicated pastilles launched
1964 – Proctor's brand acquired
1974 – Vigroids brand acquired
1977 – Vitamin C pastilles launched
1984 – Ernest Jackson merges with Bassett Foods PLC
1989 – Cadbury Schweppes take over Trebor Bassett
1991 – Potters Catarrh Pastilles and Zubes brands acquired
1992 – Victory V and Hacks acquired by Trebor Bassett
1995 – Bassett's Soft & Chewy Vitamins launched; Kia Ora Fruit
        Pastilles launched
2000 – Confectionery unites in the UK as Cadbury Trebor Bassett
2003 – Adams acquisition brought Halls into Ernest Jackson
2005 – Bassett's Soft & Chewy Omega 3 products launched
2008 – Bassett's Soft & Chewy brand relaunched
2011 – Kraft Foods acquires Cadbury PLC
2017 – MAC relaunches and introduces two brand new offerings for sore
        throats

Paregoric

Paregoric, or camphorated tincture of opium, also known as *tinctura opii camphorata,* is a traditional patent medicine known for its anti-diarrheal, anti-tussive, and analgesic properties.

According to Goodman and Gilman, *Pharmacological basis of therapeutics* 'Paregoric is a 4 per cent opium tincture in which there is also benzoic acid, camphor, and anise oil. … Paregoric by tradition is used especially for children.'

Confusingly the name paregoric has also been used for a kind of boiled sweet, originally (and by some reports still currently) containing paregoric – in particular the Army & Navy brand sweet produced by British confectioner Paynes.

In the early eighteenth century, Jakob Le Mort (1650–1718), a professor of chemistry at Leiden University, prepared an elixir for asthma and named it paregoric. Le Mort's elixir, comprising 'honey, licorice, flowers of Benjamin, and opium, camphor, oil of aniseed, salt of tartar

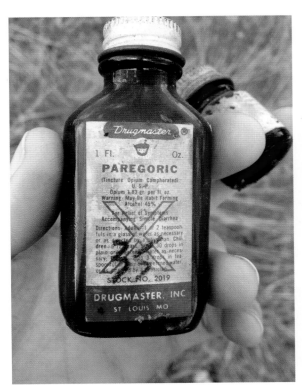

A bottle of Paregoric, circa 1940s. The large red X on the label indicates that it was classified as an 'exempt narcotic', sold without prescription even though it contains morphine. The name paregoric has also been used for a kind of boiled sweet, originally (and by some reports still currently) containing paregoric – in particular the Army & Navy brand sweet produced by British confectioner Paynes. (*Photographer: User: Jwilli74; This file is licensed under the Creative Commons Attribution- Share Alike 3.0 Unported license*)

and spirit of wine', became official as 'Elixir Asthmaticum' in the *London Pharmacopoeia* of 1721. Its ingredients were assembled out of the obsolete humoral philosophy and quasi-scientific reasoning of the Renaissance. Paregoric was used in various formulations for hundreds of years.

Paregoric was a household remedy in the eighteenth and nineteenth centuries when it was widely used to control diarrhoea in adults and children; as an expectorant and cough medicine; to calm fretful children, and to rub on the gums to counteract the pain from teething.

Army & Navy Sweets

Army & Navy sweets are a type of traditional boiled sweet. They are black, lozenge-shaped and flavoured with liquorice and herbs. They were issued to servicemen during the First World War, hence the name. They used to contain tincture of opium.

Not for the Camp Fire Girls though.

The branding departments, if they were not busy fooling the market with spurious medicinal benefits, did their best to promote non-existent health- giving qualities with some doubtful ingredients: there were, for example, Grapejuice Caramels and All Fruit Nutlets, while Keillor's Lactor Chocolate boasted highly active bacillus in its contents derived, no less, from Bulgarian sour milk as recommended by a Professor Metchnikoff, a key opinion leader of the day no doubt, who vouched for its efficacy in rheumatism, neuritis, indigestion and the somewhat mysterious and worrying auto-intoxication.

Ingesting Teasdale's 1911 New Season Kali, marketed more like a fine wine, could have fatal consequences, as sadly discovered by the parents of a Huddersfield girl who swallowed a bagful of kali, a constituent of fizzy drinks; kali, when taken dry, fizzes madly and has a detrimental effect on anyone with a weak heart.

On a more positive note it seems as though the bad health messages about sweets were getting through to some people. Members of the Camp Fire Girls Movement could earn a Healthcare Badge by desisting from sweets and ice cream for two weeks. Such abstemiousness cut little ice with their Boy Scout counterparts who kept on scoffing regardless, badge or no badge: indeed, they could indulge themselves with chocolate scouts courtesy of Pascall who sold them in boxes (sixes ?) of eight complete with a paper tent.

Chapter 5

Cultural Issues: Rationing, Racism, Smoking Sweets, Women's Rights

Rationing

During the First World War, imported ingredients were dangerously scarce. Gum Arabic supplies dried up when Sudan fell to the Germans and remained unobtainable until 1918. Sugar too was in short supply. Not only that, it was also a very dangerous substance when pocketed by munitions workers. This was evidenced by the case of the munitions worker who was found with two barley sugars on his person and fined £2 – a week's wages; sugar can react explosively with chemicals used in munitions. Because of the shortages of sugar, by 1916 confectionery was *verboten* in cinemas, theatres and music halls while all milk products – fresh, condensed and powdered – were banned from use in chocolate.

In the Second World War general rationing started on 8 January 1940 with bacon, butter and sugar the first items to be restricted. Sweet and chocolate rationing started on 26 July 1942, giving an allowance of 2oz per person per week to everyone over 5 years old, a penny choc and toffee bars counting as 1oz. The allowed amount of sugar, and therefore sweets, fluctuated during the war, ranging from 16oz a month down to 8oz (227g) a month. Before the war, weekly confectionery consumption was 6¼ oz per person; rationing slashed that by two-thirds. Valiant attempts were made to find suitable sugar substitutes as the Japanese overran more and more of the sugar producing countries in the Far East: pulped apple and treacle, and plum syrup all failed. Milk chocolate was deemed unnecessary as plain chocolate would suffice according to the Food Ministry. It passed the Use of Milk (Restriction) Order in 1941, banning milk use in chocolate, sweets and ice cream.

Rationing ended on 5 February 1953 – a very big day in Britain. Now children all over the country raided their piggybanks and headed for the nearest sweet shop to take their fill of all those sweets the war had denied them. If you had the coupons you could get your hands on and lips around lemon sherbets, flying saucers, barley sugar twists, liquorice, jelly babies, Fry's chocolate creams, pear drops and cola cubes.

Toffee apples were the bestsellers, closely followed by nougat and liquorice strips. Many firms simply gave their sweets away, handing out sweets to anyone who wanted them – guerrilla marketing at its best. Not, though, as generous or as imprudent as it seems – what better way to seed the market? Free samples often meant that the recipients came back for more, many times thereafter. One firm in Clapham Common gave 800 children 150lbs of lollipops to share during their midday break from school; a London factory opened its doors to hand out free sweets to all comers. Amongst adults, the 2lb boxes of chocolates were always a favourite. The end of rationing resulted in spending on sweets growing by £1,000 million in the first year. Consumers nowadays spend more than £5.5 billion.

Because 1953 was the second attempt to de-ration sweets, the government and manufacturers were quick to reassure the public that there would be no repeat of the first attempt, when in April 1949 demand far outstripped supply and they were put back on ration after just four months. Bizarrely, sugar itself remained rationed so that manufacturers had to make enough sweets to meet the demand of a de-rationed market, but with only 54 per cent of the sugar supplies they had before the war.

In spite of the heavy sales, there were no signs of panic buying, even though there were already shortages of the most popular brands. One reason may be that the price of confectionery nearly doubled during the course of the war, and many people had not been taking up their full ration. Sweet coupons, though, were around still for some time as it takes a long time to print 50 million ration books and the 1954 version had been designed and printed already, sweet ration and all.

As if the bombing and rationing were not bad enough, the wartime nanny state in the guise of London County Council listed sweet eating in their six deadly sins, along with going to 'picture palaces', riding in trams and omnibuses unnecessarily, throwing away jam pots and bottles, wasting bread and not making do and mending.

Patriotism loomed large with brands such as John Bull Caramels, Duchess Chocolates, Tally-ho Mixture and Colonial Assortment. Sales of Hindenburg Toffee did not do so well in Edinburgh.

Racism

British companies were not immune from the nostalgic and, by today's standards, racist advertising harking back to the days of slavery and recently evaporating colonialism. A Fry advert from the turn of the century has a crowd of Negroes marvelling at a cargo of Fry's cocoa washed up on their island: *a new discovery*. Somewhat insensitive and patronising if one recalls the tens of thousands of slaves employed in the cocoa industry not so many years before.

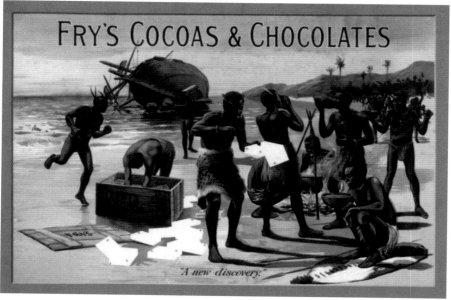

Even by the *mores* of the time, the shipwreck poster is somewhat ironic and hypocritical, given that it was black slaves who were responsible for much of the world's cocoa-chocolate production during the nineteenth century.

In 1920, one of the UK's favourite sweets, the Black Jack, was born. However, the wrapper of this iconic aniseed-flavoured chew was originally emblazoned with the image of a grinning golliwog, leaving a bad taste in the mouth, culturally speaking at least. Florence Kate Upton, author of numerous golliwog books, designed the label which was withdrawn in the more enlightened 1900s and replaced by a pirate. Wonder what the pirates thought of that?

Other racist brands down the years included Black Boys and Nigger Babies.

In 2014 *DW Com* reported:

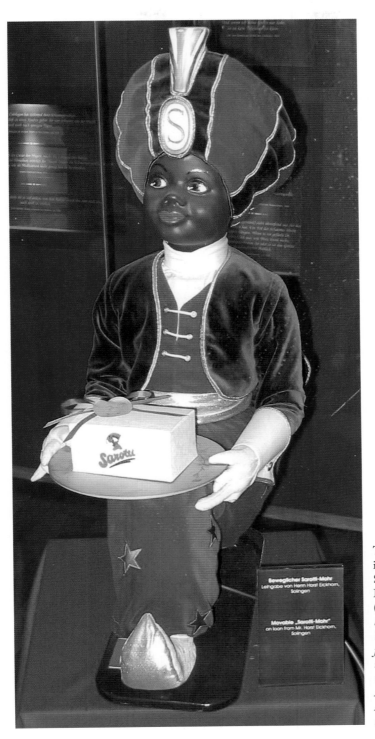

The Sarotti Moor in the Imhoff-Stollwerck-Museum, Berlin. (*Photographer Stephan Windmüller. This file is licensed under the Creative Commons Attribution–Share Alike 3.0 Unported license*)

German candy producer Haribo to take liquorice sweets that are shaped like ethnic masks and faces off the Swedish and Danish market.

Haribo has decided to stop selling some of its black licorice sweets in Denmark and Sweden in response to increasing customer complaints on the Internet dubbing the candies 'racist'. The black licorice sweets are part of Haribo's 'Skipper Mix' salty blend and are shaped like ethnic masks or faces resembling those found in African, Asian, or Native American art. ...Ola Dagliden, Head of Haribo Sweden added that Haribo never intended to offend anyone and that the Skipper Mix was designed to remind people of the things sailors might have collected on their travels around the world. 'It wasn't something we saw as having negative connotations,' he said.
(www.dw.com/en/haribo-takes-racist-sweets-off-the-market/a-17376231)

Haribo is not alone. In Germany and Austria chocolate-coated marshmallows are still referred to as Negerküss or Mohrenkopf, meaning 'Negro kiss' and 'Moor heads'. On the packaging, however, producers now generally print Schokokuss, 'chocolate kiss'. Sarotti's corporate symbol of the Sarotti Moor was depicted with racially exaggerated features similar to the banished golliwog. Sarotti is a Berlin chocolate brand owned by Stollwerck GmbH since 1998.

Bristol firm Packer's had no qualms about racial stereotyping when they launched their Pickaninny Assorted with ads featuring a brown person with curly hair exclaiming 'Ooh dey's nice!'

Smoking sweets

Almost as insidious as the Candy aspirin scandal discussed in Chapter 4 is the production, sales and marketing of sweet cigarettes, or candy cigarettes and chocolate cigars – unashamedly designed to provide children with replicas of real world tobacco products and deliver significant profits to the makers at the expense of children's health in later life as adults.

Sweet cigarettes started rolling off the production lines in the late nineteenth century, usually made from chalky sugar and red tipped, but also of bubblegum or chocolate, wrapped in paper and packaged and

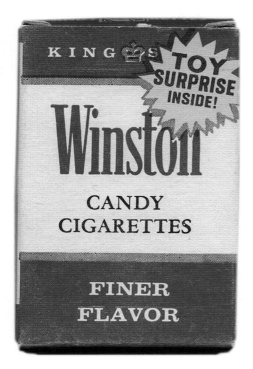

Sinister marketing of sweet cigarettes designed to hook the child – on cigarettes.

branded so as to closely resemble cigarettes. Some products even contained powdered sugar concealed in the wrapper, allowing the 'smoker' to blow into the cigarette and produce a cloud of sugar that imitated smoke, which was emitted from the other end.

An indication of how intent devious sweet manufacturers were to facilitate the fantasy that children enjoyed emulating the grown-ups in their lives is the Jack Tar Smoker's Outfit marketed with the unedifying slogan: 'the famous brands that father smokes, specially blended to suit the juvenile palate'. Even given changes of attitude and *mores* over the years, this is particularly despicable and puts the manufacturer on a par with cigarette companies who dish out free cigarettes to children in developing countries to hook them into the habit.

Medical research in cutting edge medical journals like *The British Medical Journal* and *Paediatrics* clearly shows that there is a direct link to eating sweet cigarettes and smoking in later in life. At the same time, sweet cigarettes represent a cynical way of marketing real cigarettes to children, as many sweet cigarettes are sold in branding clearly reminiscent of cigarette branding and offer a sly way

to market for real cigarettes. For these reasons sales of sweet cigarettes are banned in many countries even though they continue to be manufactured and consumed in many parts of the world with the flaccid mitigation that manufacturers now describe their products as candy sticks, bubble gum, or just candy.

To make matters worse, there is a history of tobacco companies colluding with sweet cigarette manufacturers where tobacco companies have allowed candy cigarette companies to use their branding; Brown and Williamson went so far as to send copies of its labels to candy cigarette companies.

A 1990 study found that UK sixth-form students who used candy cigarettes were twice as likely to smoke cigarettes than those who did not 'smoke' candy cigarettes.[Klein, J. D. et al. (January 1992). 'Candy cigarettes: do they encourage children's smoking?' Pediatrics 89 (1): 27–31.]

A 2007 study surveyed 25,887 adults and found that: 'candy cigarette use was reported by 88 per cent of both current and former smokers and 78 per cent of never smokers'; a statistically significant difference that the authors suggested indicates a connection between candy cigarette use as a child and smoking as an adult. [Klein, J. D. et al. (July 2007). 'History of childhood candy cigarette use is associated with tobacco smoking by adults' Preventive Medicine 45 (1): 26–30].

Rosie Mestel, (*Los Angeles Times* 15 September 2012) 'Candy cigarettes and 'Toddlers & Tiaras', California Life & Style quotes:

The Stanford School of Medicine says that 'although these products clearly desensitize children to smoking by normalizing cigarette usage amongst younger generations, efforts to outlaw candy cigarettes in the United States (both in 1970 and again in 1991) have been unsuccessful. Other countries, such as Canada, the United Kingdom, Saudi Arabia, and Finland, have been proactive in banning candy cigarettes.

But it was not just children and adolescents who were being turned into smokers; the chocolate companies in particular were busy preaching that certain of their brands were just the thing for that snack in between smokes. Nestlé's Smoker's Semi-Sweet Milk Chocolate from the 1930s are 'Specially blended to suit smokers. It is just sweet enough, very sustaining, and does not create thirst. You will find it particularly pleasant between smokes.' Chocolate cigars and cigarettes were popular and packaged to look like the real thing with Dunn's, Fry's and Rowntree's all involved.

Most candy cigarettes continue to be manufactured in the United States, with the largest maker of candy cigarettes, World Confections Inc. based in New Jersey.

Joke Sweets

Joke sweets are exactly that. The history of confectionery is peppered with joke sweets containing a wide range of non-sweet sweets such as garlic, olives, gherkins, chilli, mustard or cayenne pepper. Freak Chocolates were 'all the rage in the US'. In the UK, though, Marylebone Borough Council failed to see the funny side: they took a shop to court for selling joke sweets amid concern that a child could choke to death.

Women's rights

Women workers at R.S. Murray's Clerkenwell, London confectionery factory went on strike complaining of the sweltering conditions there. The women had earned themselves the support of women's rights campaigners including Mary Macarthur (1880–1921) and the name Murray's White Mice because they clocked off coated in white starch dust. The management at Murray's were intent on crushing the strike and were contemptuous of the 'agitating ladies'; but eventually they relented and gave a pay rise and proper tea breaks. One assumes that they also did something about the ventilation. The women's anthem and rallying call was a dirge set to the tune of Three Blind Mice: 'Murray's White Mice, see how they fight…'

The Ladies Confiserie Company was established in London's Buckingham Palace Road by the fascinatingly named Miss Spenderel Moody; the aim was to train, educate and enable women to infiltrate the higher echelons of the confectionery companies instead of having to make do with packing and filling chocolate boxes.

The Piping and Ornamentation School opened on London's Tottenham Court Road – one lesson cost 7s 6d, ten were five guineas while a six-month course was £50. Predictably the men were scornful and patronising, if not sexist, referring to the students as 'a pretty sight, to watch them arrive for their lessons with their dainty embroidered satchels…'

Chapter 6

Sugar and Slavery

In the seventeenth century, sugar cane was imported into what was then the British West Indies from Brazil when most local Caribbean farmers were busy growing cotton and tobacco. However, strong competition from the North American colonies meant that prices of these crops were crashing, which led to the owners of the large Caribbean plantations turning to growing sugar cane instead.

Sugar cane became the principal crop on the numerous plantations throughout the Caribbean during the eighteenth and nineteenth centuries. These plantations produced 80–90 per cent of the sugar consumed in Western Europe. The main source of labour was African slaves.

Between 1700 and 1709, the trade in sugar increased dramatically due to the increasing popularity of sugar to sweeten what were then luxury drinks such as tea and coffee. In 1700, Britain's sugar consumption was 4lbs per person, in 1800 that had risen to 18lbs per person. By 1750, sugar overtook grain as the most valuable commodity in European trade – it made up 25 per cent of all European imports. In Barbados, for example, sugar amounted to 93 per cent of the island's exports.

In around 1903, Rowntree's had found itself implicated by association in what sections of the press called the 'Cocoa Scandal'. Quaker opposition to slavery had always been fervent, and is well recorded. In 1657, George Fox was vocal in denunciation, travelling in 1671 to the West Indies and America to see the situation for himself. In 1736, Benjamin Lay summed up the Quaker position when he dubbed slavery 'hellish practice … a filthy sin … the greatest sin in the world … [slavery is] of the very nature of Hell itself and is the belly of Hell'. Quakers made up the majority of the 1787 Abolition Society and were responsible in part for The British Slave Trade Act of 1807 and The Slavery Abolition Act of 1833; they formed the Anti-Slavery Society in 1823. The Cadburys were particularly active, especially William, a Cadbury buyer and George, Cadbury's nephew.

At the time Cadbury sourced 45 per cent of their high quality cocoa beans from Príncipe and São Thomé – Portuguese colonies off the West African coast in the Gulf of Guinea. Rumour had it that the workers there were slaves; this was confirmed in a sale notice for a São Thomé plantation which included '200 black labourers worth £3,555'. William Cadbury's investigations confirmed the worst: outlawed slavery was rife in São Thomé, under the aegis of the Portuguese government. A fact-finding mission under Joseph Burtt was despatched to Príncipe and São Tomé, commissioned by Cadbury's, Fry's, Rowntree's and Stollwerk.

Some years previously, though, *Harper's Monthly Magazine* had hired an English journalist, Henry Nevinson, to investigate the story from Angola where he eventually found indisputable evidence of a slave trade – shackles and skeletons and allegations of witchcraft. The hub of 'this deed of pitiless hypocrisy' was Benguala where the captured natives were press-ganged into becoming 'voluntary workers' (*serviçais* in Portuguese) over on São Thomé for five years. This contracted labour was slavery by a different name. Nevinson visited the islands and saw 30,000 slaves on São Thomé and 3,000 more on Príncipe. Twenty per cent of the *serviçais* died each year in 'okalunga' – hell on earth, 'their dead bodies lashed to poles and carried out to be flung away in the forest' (D. Cadbury, *Chocolate Wars* pp. 196–7). Nevinson's findings were serialised in *Harper's* and published in a book, *A Modern Slavery*, which exposed the sordid and shameful working conditions there for contracted workers as just that – modern slavery; the Cadbury-Rowntree-Fry-Stollwerk research in 1907 confirmed the situation. Burtt convinced the Rowntree board on 2 May 1907 'beyond all doubt'. Attempts to enlist the Foreign Office to take action against the Portuguese resulted in little more than a Foreign Office cover up to protect Portuguese labour contracts in South African mines.

All the while, though, the chocolate companies were facing increasing criticism and accusations of hypocrisy, led by the *London Standard* of 26 September 1908 exposing 'that monstrous trade in human flesh ... the very islands which feed the mills and presses of Bournville.' The outcome was a boycott of cocoa from São Tomé and Príncipe in March 1909 by the Quaker companies and a protracted libel case: Cad*bury Brothers Ltd vs the Standard Newspaper Ltd.*, which began in November that year.

Sweet and chocolate manufacturers were always guilty of embracing slavery, if only by association. Sweets and chocolate require sugar and sugar was one of the main drivers of slavery for many decades.

Sven Beckert's review of James Walvin's *Sugar: The World Corrupted: From Slavery to Obesity* published in *The New York Times*, 23 July 2018 under the headline 'How Sweet It Is. And How Malignant' pulls no punches and says it all:

> Sweets have invaded the English language the way they have invaded our diet, with almost universally positive connotations. Sweet love, sweet people and sweet deals all suggest pleasant experiences, as do the sugary confections that grace our tables and fill our stores. James Walvin's new book, 'Sugar: The World Corrupted: From Slavery to Obesity', will thoroughly disabuse you of such agreeable associations and may make you reluctant to reach for something sweet. Sugar, he shows, is a blood-soaked product that has brought havoc to millions and environmental devastation to large parts of the planet, premature death to the poorest populations in many parts of the world and huge health costs for societies from the United States to India. After reading this book the mere mention of sugar should make you think of slavery and cavities, imperialism and obesity – and remind you to check the label on the products you consume… 'Sugar' is an entertaining, informative and utterly depressing global history of an important commodity… 'Sugar' raises fundamental questions about our world. It does not resolve all those questions, but it provides enough information for its readers to begin to see some answers and to see how troubling and disconcerting they are.

Walvin reveals that 'In 1770, rum – made from sugar cane – provided possibly one-quarter of the caloric needs of British North America. By the mid-twentieth century, the average annual consumption of sugar in Britain was an astonishing 110lbs per person.' And if we thought that slavery, sugar slavery, came to a nice tidy end with William Wilberforce and the victory of the Abolitionists then prepare to be sorely disappointed. Walvin reminds us that the only thing that really changed was the geography of sugar as brutalised indentured workers from India and China took up sugar production in Guyana and Fiji, Mauritius and Trinidad. Beet sugar producers in Germany and the American Midwest gained market share. And by the late twentieth century, American corn growers were feeding huge quantities of high fructose corn syrup into global markets, enabling an ever-increasing quantity of sweeteners to be poured into soft drinks and cereals.

And into sweets and chocolate.

However, now there is much good work being done by Nestlé and others, into increasing action against child labour and expanding a cocoa sustainability program. In December 2019, Nestlé released its latest 'Tackling Child Labor' report in its efforts to tackle the issue of child labour in the cocoa communities of West Africa through its 2012 Child Labor Monitoring and Remediation System which allows Nestlé to identify, track and address child labour in its supply chains. Remedial action is provided through community-wide solutions as well as those tailored to individual needs.

Why do we still tolerate slavery in the confectionery industry? This from http://www. slavefreechocolate.org/: 2.3 million children work in the cocoa fields of Ghana and Côte d'Ivoire. These children are vulnerable to brutal labour practices, including trafficking and slavery. Candy companies – including, but not limited to, Nestlé, Hershey, Cargill, ADM, and Barry Callebout – have admitted accountability and promised to remedy this situation. Sadly, seventeen years have passed since this agreement and little has changed. Additionally, the abject poverty these farmers are forced to endure in has also resulted in deforestation of sensitive and important national forests. The candy industry is a $70 billion dollar industry. It should have changed.

Help us make this happen.

The website relates how

> Over the past two years, Nestlé has almost doubled its outreach to include 78,580 children across 1,750 communities. In the development phase of the system from 2012 to 2017, Nestlé monitored over 40,000 children in Côte d'Ivoire and identified 7,002 as child laborers.
>
> The system continues to be successful in identifying children involved in child labor, with over 18,000 children found. Through awareness raising and assistance, 55% of these children have been able to stop child labor activities… Since 2012, over 87,000 children within and outside Nestlé's supply chain have benefited from remediation, including the following educational activities: Building and renovating schools and funding bridging classes; Providing school kits / uniforms; Financing the issuance of birth certificates that give access to the education system; Raising awareness on the importance of preventing child labor with half a million farmers and community members; Improving women's literacy as well as providing support on other income-generating activities to support livelihoods.
>
> (www.nestle.com/media/news/nestle-action-against-
> child-labor-cocoa-sustainability-program)

Nestlé adds that in the last ten years, the company has invested 220 million Swiss francs (CHF) or £71 m in the Nestlé Cocoa Plan in the pursuit of making cocoa farming more sustainable and improve the lives of those living in farming communities. Alexander von Maillot, Global Head of Confectionery at Nestlé, said: 'While we have made progress, we will not stop here. Our goal is to source 100 per cent of our cocoa for confectionery from the Nestlé Cocoa Plan by 2025.'

Long may it continue.

Chapter 7

Poisoning Sweets: Adulteration

An adulterant is a hostile matter found in substances such as food, cosmetics, pharmaceuticals, fuel or other chemicals that compromises the safety or effectiveness of that product.

There are few, if any, foodstuffs or beverages which have escaped the blight of adulteration; short-changing on ingredients and supplementing them with additives and rubbish – some of it toxic – has always been an easy way to increase profits. Some manufacturers introduced bright colours in sweets by illegally adding toxins: green (chromium oxide and copper acetate), red (lead oxide and mercury sulphide), yellow (lead chromate) and white (chalk, arsenic trioxide). All have found their way into your sweet packet or chocolate bar, and into your and your children's stomachs.

In an 1885 cover cartoon for *Puck*, Joseph Keppler famously satirised the dangers of additives in sweets by depicting the 'mutual friendship' between striped candy, doctors, and gravediggers. Research into the dangers of additives, exposés of the food industry, and public pressure led to the passage of the 1860 Adulteration of Food and Drink Bill to regulate food and drugs, including sweets.

Sweet colourants, particularly yellow colourants such as E102 Tartrazine, E104 Quinoline Yellow WS and E110 Sunset Yellow FCF, have many restrictions around the world. Tartrazine, for example, can cause allergic and asthmatic reactions and was once banned in Austria, Germany, and Norway. Some countries such as the UK have asked the food industry to phase out the use of these colourants, especially for products marketed to children. They clearly need to do more than just ask.

The adulteration of food and drink, though, has been around forever; the recent case in 2013 of horses masquerading as cows was nothing new when we thought we were eating beef although it was horse meat on our plates and in our burgers.

"OUR MUTUAL FRIEND."

Joseph Ferdinand Keppler's (1838–94) 'Our Mutual Friend', 7 January 1885, cover, warning of the dangers of colour additives in sweets. It shows a doctor and a sexton, happily greeting a striped candy cane, whose coloured lines are marked with the names of dangerous additives that have been used to create the colours: green (chrome green, chromium oxide); white (chalk); red (red lead, lead oxide); white (arsenic, arsenic trioxide); yellow (chrome yellow, lead chromate); red (vermilion, mercury sulfide); green (verdigris, copper acetate); white (glucose, an adulterant for sugar).

Before that, the famous scandal of 1948 saw thousands of unsuspecting Britons eating horse when they thought they were eating beef. Over 750,000 horses – not just old nags but young foals too which were served up as veal – ended up on 3 million plates up and down the country, although half the diners would have put their money on it being beef.

In ancient Rome, water and wine drinkers adulterated without knowing they were doing it: lead poisoning was a chronic problem caused by lead water pipes and utensils; it was made even worse by the use of lead in some medicinal potions. Interestingly, our word for a plumber is derived from the Latin word for lead, *plumbum*. Wine drinkers often preserved wine with a syrup called *sapa* which was stored in lead containers; this would give a regular *Falernian* drinker 20mg of lead per litre of wine consumed – forty times the chronic toxicity level; it went down like the proverbial balloon.

The first legislation to regulate the production and sale of food was in 1266, when the *Assisa Panis et Cervisiæ*, or Assize of Bread and Ale was enacted in late Medieval English Law to regulate the price, weight and quality of manufactured bread and beer. At this time, we were able to formulate objective measurements relating to the size or weight of foods, but not to the quality. Food quality was judged subjectively based on appearance, smell and taste.

As society advanced, food began to be prepared, produced and marketed – which was when it became essential for consumers to be protected from hazards instigated by others either accidentally or deliberately.

We have the medieval guilds to thank for early attempts to regulate quality standards, but these were intended to protect the market rather than the customer or consumer. Moreover, the guilds only operated in towns and cities, so adulteration in the countryside remained unregulated.

As soon as the distinction between consumer and manufacturer became more distinct, the opportunities for systematic food fraud were seized upon by the less scrupulous. By the eighteenth century, there was adulteration on an industrial scale. Bakers were at it: they used chalk and alum, more commonly found today in deodorants and medications used in the treatment of piles, to whiten bread. Potatoes, plaster of Paris, clay and sawdust helped to bulk up their buns and loaves. Brewers were at it, apart from the time-honoured use of water as a dilutant, poisons such as strychnine – rat poison – were introduced to give that lovely hoppy bitter taste, and to reduce the hop bill. Cocoa manufacturers mixed in arrowroot, potato starch, sago flour and powdered seashells to reduce the required cocoa content; iron rust, red lead or brick dust were used to give that rich brown colour and to ensure a good night's sleep. Grocers coloured their cheeses with lead. The list goes on and includes, spirits, olive oil, cheese, pickles, anchovies, mustard, confectionery – all found to be adulterated and often in ways which had a serious and adverse impact on health. The use, for example, of copper was widespread and anchovies were dyed red with lead oxide. A twelve-year study published in 1848 concerning the adulteration of food found not a single loaf of bread subjected to analysis that was unadulterated. Anthony Wohl gives us an interesting list of the adulterants:

The list of poisonous additives reads like the stock list of some mad and malevolent chemist: strychnine, *cocculus inculus* (both are hallucinogens) and copperas in rum and beer; sulphate of copper in pickles, bottled fruit, wine, and preserves; lead chromate in mustard and snuff; sulphate of iron in tea and beer; ferric ferrocynanide, lime sulphate, and turmeric in chinese tea; copper carbonate, lead sulphate, bisulphate of mercury, and Venetian lead in sugar confectionery and chocolate; lead in wine and cider; all were extensively used and were accumulative in effect, resulting, over a long period, in chronic gastritis, and, indeed, often fatal food poisoning. Red lead gave Gloucester cheese its 'healthy' red hue, flour and arrowroot a rich thickness to cream, and tea leaves were 'dried, dyed, and recycled again'.

As late as 1877, the Local Government Board found that approximately a quarter of the milk it examined contained excessive water, or chalk, and 10 per cent of all the butter, over 8 per cent of the bread, and 50 per cent of the gin had copper in them to heighten the colour.

Anthony S. Wohl,
Endangered Lives: Public Health in Victorian Britain,
Harvard UP, 1983

Not everyone minded, it seems: in 1771 Tobias Smollett reported in his *The Expedition of Humphrey Clinker* that while London bread was

[a] deleterious paste, mixed up with …bone ashes, insipid to the taste and destructive to the constitution. The good people are not ignorant of this adulteration; but they prefer it to wholesome bread, because it is whiter than the meal of corn. Thus they sacrifice their taste and their health.

Nevertheless, scientific investigation was developing apace as were scientific analysis and the detection of adulteration.

Frederick Accum

In 1820, it took a visiting German chemist and laboratory assistant to Humphry Davy, Frederick Accum, to do anything about it: he identified numerous toxic additives in many foods and drinks. The title page of his best-selling book, *The Treatise on Adulterations of Food and Culinary Poisons* featured a skull and an ominous quotation from the Old Testament: 'there is death in the pot.' Accum's argument, quite reasonably, was that 'The man who robs a fellow subject of a few shillings on the highway is sentenced to death, but he who distributes a slow poison to the whole community escapes unpunished.'

Accum's verbose, but descriptive, subtitle is: *Exhibiting the Fraudulent Sophistications of Bread, Beer, Wine, Spiritous Liquors, Tea, Coffee, Cream, Confectionery, Vinegar, Mustard, Pepper, Cheese, Olive Oil, Pickles, and Other Articles Employed in Domestic Economy.*

The book describes in detail methods for detecting adulterants within foods and drink. It was so popular that within one month of publication it had sold 1,000 copies. Shortly after, it was reprinted with the addition of milk, cinnamon, isinglass and Spanish liquorice juice. Accum followed this up by publishing the names and addresses of each of the convicted food traders that had knowingly sold adulterated food and drink.

Accum may have liked a pint because he noticed the adulteration of English beer. Taste notwithstanding, his analyses uncovered evidence of ferrous sulphate; extracts of *cocculus indicus*, a poisonous plant used to stun fish and which is sometimes used in the treatment of vertigo (so that's why we feel dizzy, sick and fall over after a pint or three); quassia, liquorice juice; ground coriander and *nux vomica*, a source of strychnine. Jellies and sweets – and therefore children – did not escape: the bright colourants were found to contain lead, copper or mercury.

All this, of course, irked the food manufacturers no end. They, in turn, discredited Accum by alleging that he had wilfully damaged books in the Royal Institution of Great Britain library. His home was searched and the damaged books were discovered. No one knows for sure whether he had damaged the books himself or whether they had been planted to incriminate him; probably the latter, but either way he was arrested and charged. When he appeared before Court he was granted bail; however, by this stage his reputation was in ruins and his work invalidated so he returned to Germany – all his good and valuable work wasted while the foul trade went on for the next thirty years.

Dr Arthur Hill Hassall

Things started to happen again in the 1840s when the public, scientists and health professionals were becoming more and more aware of the realities of adulteration – on the pocket and on health. In 1848, Mitchell's *Falsification of Food* set new standards using chemical analysis of food, but his work had limited circulation. A key turning point in the public's recognition of the adulteration of food was in 1850, when it was widely believed it to be quite impossible to obtain basic foods in a pure state. Dr Arthur Hill Hassall (1817–1894), a physician, presented a paper to the Botanical Society on the Adulteration of Coffee and refuted government statements that no foolproof methods existed to detect certain kinds of adulteration. Between 1851 and 1854 *The Lancet* published weekly articles – the Hassall Reports – under the title *Analytical Sanitary Commission* which demonstrated not only financial fraud, but foods seriously hazardous to health, giving full details of hundreds of transgressors. Hassall's work, naming and shaming, was hugely popular and, for the first time, engaged the medical profession in public health in a significant way.

In 1857, Hassall published a second volume and, happily, identified improvements by some manufacturers. The phrase 'pure and unadulterated' became a popular advertising slogan in the late 1850s, highlighting purity as a unique selling point. This improvement, however, was largely felt by the middle class. Legislation was needed to deal with a continuing large number of fraudsters who were swindling the poor working classes who formed the majority of the population; as today, governments' flaccid response to the problem was to tolerate vested interests who, naturally, still favoured voluntary reform.

All the while, in the background, factory and mill owners the length and breadth of the country were growing more and more annoyed by a surge in absenteeism blamed largely on the consumption of adulterated foods and drink.

The first bill to control the adulteration of food and drink was introduced in the House of Commons, but following strong opposition, was withdrawn. In 1857–58, Hassall revealed that adulteration was rife in Manchester, Birmingham, Leeds and Liverpool, but it was not as bad as it was in London in 1851. Two further bills were brought forward in 1858, but these were abandoned when the change in government prevented them from becoming law. In October, the 'Bradford lozenge scandal' erupted when about 200 were poisoned and 20 died, bringing the issue of adulteration into the public glare.

It is hard to say how far the stark realisation that most foods were being systematically polluted and poisoned, the conclusive findings of Dr Hassall, or even the fatalities in the Bradford humbug scandal provided the impetus for legislation. What we can say with greater confidence is that Britain's reputation with regard to exports was suffering and that is a more likely reason why adulteration legislation was finally passed. Once again money spoke loudest.

The Adulteration of Food and Drugs Act 1860

Adulteration was eventually made illegal under The Adulteration of Food and Drugs Act 1860 and The Adulteration of Food Act 1872 and 1875. One of the issues which gave impetus to this was publication in 1851 of one of the Hassall Reports mentioned above in which Hassall found over half of all chocolate he sampled was found to contain brick dust. He and his editor, Thomas Wakley, surgeon and MP, had also identified gamboge, a violent purgative and irritant, lead, copper and mercury in various sweets; even the brightly coloured wrappers were polluted with the same toxins. Hassall sampled 2,500 products making use of the microscope for food analysis for the first time, publishing his findings in the *Lancet* reports and later in a book, naming and shaming, like Accum, the 'adulterers'. Hassall and Wakley catalogued each of the vendors, locations, dates and products purchased. Each food and drink item was analysed and the results were published with the conclusion that food adulteration was a lot more common than was believed and that many of the adulterated foods were actually poisonous. Chocolate products which were exposed by this research included oatmeal chocolate, acorn chocolate, Icelandic moss, barley chocolate. In France 'ferruginous chocolate' was considered 'so beneficial to women who are out of order, or have the green sickness' and was made from dissolving good chocolate in rusty water.

Hassall's meticulous, but frustrating, work was even mentioned by Charles Kingsley in the *Water Babies* of 1863: those who 'invent poisons for little children and sell them at wakes, fairs and tuck shops...Dr Hassall cannot catch them ...'; this highlighted the ubiquity of food adulteration. Karl Marx described 'the incredible adulteration of bread' in *Das Kapital*.

The first general Act of 1860 permitted the appointment of public analysts, but only seven were appointed. It was a compromise, permissive in nature and not generally acted upon, it 'passed on to the statute book and into oblivion'. While the Act was a failure, it did set a precedent in which the State had shown a willingness to intervene.

In 1861, Dr Edward Lankester delivered a lecture to the Royal Society of Arts claiming that 87 per cent of bread and 74 per cent of milk sold in London was adulterated.

The Adulteration of Food and Drink and Drugs Act 1872 made the appointment of public analysts mandatory and made it an offence to sell mixtures (chicory and coffee, for example) unless this was declared. Despite the difficulty of securing convictions due to continuing requirement for *mens rea*, more than 1,500 convictions were secured within three years. In 1873, the case Fitzpatrick v Kelly partially negated the need to prove *mens rea* to secure a conviction for offences under the 1860 Act.

In 1874, the Society of Public Analysts was founded. The landmark Sale of Food and Drugs Act 1875 was enacted in August; it defined food and had a profound impact in improving the quality of basic foods, the suppression of adulteration and in establishing food purity. It confirmed offences of strict liability and introduced heavy penalties for adulteration of food including three months' hard labour for a second offence. The Public Health Act 1875 provided powers to inspect and seize unsound food. The Act became the basis for modern food legislation: the offences it created have stood the test of time. It paved the way for an approach to food law which can be traced to the present day Food Safety Act 1990.

While the 1875 Act sought to address the chemical contamination of food, the Public Health Act 1875 introduced basic controls concerned with the biological contamination of food, including the inspection, seizure and destruction of unfit food.

Coffee and tea were now all the rage in Britain – but they were expensive. No problem: tea could be cheapened for the manufacturers by using tea leaves that had already been used (the exact equivalent of a second-hand teabag today). They were boiled up with ferrous sulphate and sheeps' droppings, coloured with a veritable palette of Prussian blue, verdigris, tannin, or black carbon before resale. Some teas sold contained no tea at all, made instead from the dried leaves of other plants. So much for a nice cup of tea.

A similar fraud was visited on the prestigious cup of coffee with the use of old coffee grounds: these were mixed with sand, gravel, chicory and dandelions. Chicory itself was often polluted by roasted carrots and turnips – for the aroma – with a sprinkling of 'black jack', burnt sugar, to give it a rich coffee colour.

In the United States, adulteration was so prevalent in the early twentieth century that a journalist on New York's *Evening Post* was inspired to compose these lines which have an eerie resonance today:

> *Mary had a little lamb,*
> *And when she saw it sicken,*
> *She shipped it off to Packingtown,*
> *And now it's labeled chicken.*

Perhaps the most famous, and lethal, case of adulteration (although in this instance it was accidental) was the Bradford humbug poisonings.

The Bradford Humbug Poisoning 1858

This was the accidental arsenic poisoning of more than 200 people. Twenty people died and over 200 became seriously ill when sweets inadvertently made with arsenic were sold from a market stall in Bradford. For centuries before, sugar was extremely expensive and was called 'white gold'. The

THE GREAT LOZENGE-MAKER.
A Hint to Paterfamilias.

Adulteration was a major problem especially in the nineteenth century. This was published in Punch on 20 November 1858; it references a famous case of poisoning in Bradford in 1858 when dozens fell ill and over twenty people died, including many children, after eating adulterated humbugs. 'A Hint to Paterfamilias' – indicates that it is a warning to parents about the potential dangers of treating their children to sweets.

government recognised the opportunities here and taxed it severely: in 1815 the tax raised from sugar in Britain was £3 million. To defray the costs of raw materials, sweet and chocolate manufacturers resorted to adulteration and their products were often mixed with cheaper, substances or 'daff'. Daff (also known as 'multum', 'flash' and 'stuff') was a concoction of harmless substances such as powdered limestone and plaster of Paris.

William Hardaker, known locally as 'Humbug Billy', routinely sold his sweets from a stall in the Green Market in Bradford; his supplier, James Appleton, the manufacturer of the sweets – including peppermint humbugs – used daff in his sweet production, daff that was supplied by a druggist in Shipley. Tragically, 12lbs of arsenic trioxide were sold instead of the harmless daff. Both daff and arsenic trioxide are white powders and look alike; the arsenic trioxide was not properly labelled and negligently stored next to the daff.

The mistake went undiscovered during the manufacture of the sweets: Appleton combined 40lbs of sugar, 12lbs of arsenic trioxide, 4lbs of gum, and peppermint oil, to make 56lbs of peppermint humbugs. The sweets contained enough arsenic to kill two people per humbug.

As usual, Hardaker sold the poisoned sweets from his stall. Of those who bought and ate the sweets, twenty people died, with a further 200 or so becoming severely ill with arsenic poisoning within a day or so. All involved in the production and sale were charged with manslaughter, but no one was convicted.

Good did, however, come from this tragedy: there was new legislation to protect the public in the form of the 1860 Adulteration of Food and Drink Bill which changed the way in which ingredients could be used, mixed and combined. The UK Pharmacy Act of 1868 introduced more stringent regulations regarding the handling and selling of named poisons and medicines by pharmacists. The abolition of the sugar tax in 1874 meant sugar became affordable to all, thus making daff redundant.

Terry's and the Edinburgh Poison Case 1941

In 1941, Terry's of York was embroiled in the Edinburgh Poison Case when a disaffected Brigadier General Tredegar (actually John Millar) attempted to poison Georgina Ferguson with a box of Terry's Devon Milk, which he laced with toxic permanganate of potash and sent through the post to her. He was duly convicted of attempted murder and sentenced to three years' penal servitude.

The case of Jessie Blake, a 12-year-old Birmingham girl, is altogether more tragic. She died from peritonitis two days after eating some chocolate chumps bought at her corner sweet shop. Chocolate chumps are the size of a small rolling pin smeared with brown paraffin wax – poor man's chocolate. Some say that added ingredients included the shop sweepings, soap, sawdust and candle wax.

Manufacturers and traders, of course, stood by their paraffin wax, with one even going so far as to retort that he was happy to eat it for breakfast in a sandwich. The medical profession pointed out, though, that it dissolved at a temperature far in excess of that sustained by the human body and that digestive acids had no impact on the stuff.

There were also cases of pearl drops sprinkled with powdered glass to achieve that all-important sparkly sugar finish, and of brown sugar cut with sand.

Adulteration is not the only hazard sweets has to offer. In 1962, a consignment of chocolate bunnies exploded on arrival in Denver, Colorado. Why? Because Denver is a mile above sea level (hence Mile-High City) and the change in pressure turned the bunnies into potential weapons of mass destruction.

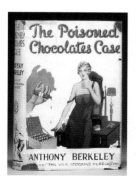 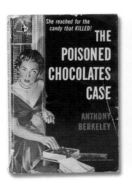 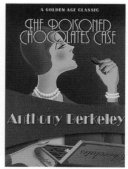 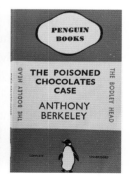

Four of the many editions of Terry's of York 'Edinburgh Chocolates Case'.

Chapter 8

Special Sweets: Liquorice, Chewing Gum, Rock, Candy Floss, Gobstoppers, Jelly Babies, Dolly Mixtures ...

Rock

Rock is unique as it often known and distinguished by its place of origin, for instance Blackpool rock, Redcar rock or Brighton rock; it is a hard stick-shaped, cylindrical boiled sugar confectionery usually flavoured with peppermint or spearmint. Its principal market place is usually seaside resorts in the United Kingdom (such as those mentioned above as well as, for example, Southend-on-Sea, Scarborough or Margate) and in Ireland (Bray and Strandhill); in Gibraltar; in Denmark in towns such as Løkken and Ebeltoft; and in Sydney and Tasmania, Australia.

What defines rock? It usually takes the form of a cylindrical stick (hence 'a stick of rock'), normally 1–2.5cm (0.39–0.98in) in diameter and 20–25cm (7.9–9.8in) long. These cylinders often have a pattern embedded throughout the length, usually the name of the resort where the rock is sold, so that, magically, the name can be read on both ends of the stick and remains legible even after pieces are bitten off. Rock is sometimes sold in the form of individual sweets, with writing or a pattern in the centre; these are, in effect, slices of rock.

Those magical letters are formed by combining thin strips of multi-coloured and white toffee. When they are made, the face of each letter is approximately the size of a thumbprint, not the minuscule size seen in the final, stretched product.

The letters are not made, as you would think, in order of appearance in the name (B, L, A, C, K, P, O, O, L), but by their shape 'square' letters, (B, E, F, H, J, K, L, M, N, P, R, T, W, X, Y and Z), are made first, as they keep their shape, while 'triangular' (A and V) and 'round' (C, D, G, O, Q, S, U) letters are made last to prevent them from losing their shape, as the toffee is still reasonably soft at this point. For example, the letters that make up 'BLACKPOOL ROCK' would be made in this order: B, P, R, K (×2), L (×2), A, C (×2) and O (×3). The individual letters are now placed between blocks or sticks to prevent them from losing shape and going flat. The letters are then placed in their correct spelling order with a 'strip' of white, aerated toffee between each letter to make it legible.

The 1830s saw Morecambe in Lancashire being credited with creating the first seaside rock.

Coltsfoot Rock

But it's not just at the seaside where you can enjoy your rock. As noted, coltsfoot rock is a confectionery product created from coltsfoot extract by Stockley's Sweets, based in Oswaldtwistle, Lancashire. Essentially, it is a hardened stick of brittle rock candy flavoured with coltsfoot.

It now enjoys the status of a recognised product of importance with regional heritage, like Dundee Cake and Kendal Mint Cake. The recipe is secret to Stockley's Sweets and, as they are the only manufacturer, all products that are labelled as such have originated from Stockley's factory.

Edinburgh Rock

Edinburgh Rock or Edinburgh Castle Rock is a traditional Scottish confection, and is very different from conventional rock. It consists of sugar, water, cream of tartar, colourings and flavourings. It is formed into sticks, and has a soft and crumbly texture.

Edinburgh rock was first made in the nineteenth century by Alexander Ferguson, who had the nickname 'Sweetie Sandy'. Alexander was born in Doune, Perthshire in 1798 and learned his confectionery in Glasgow before moving to Edinburgh to set up his own business. The success of Edinburgh Rock was such that he was able to retire back to Doune a very rich man. In the early twentieth century the rock was produced and sold at 1 Melbourne Place, now demolished, but previously on the corner of George IV Bridge with the Royal Mile.

Candy floss

Candy floss contains only one ingredient: sugar, although it may contain small amounts of flavouring and/or food colouring. Surprisingly, an average 1oz serving gives you about 100 calories. We call it candy floss, but in the US it was originally 'fairy floss and then 'cotton candy' from the

Russian girl eating candy floss. Originally posted to Flickr as 'candy girl'; photographer: Alex Yosifov. This file is licensed under the Creative Commons Attribution-Share Alike 3.0 Unported license.

1920s. It is still fairy floss in Australia and candy floss in Ireland, New Zealand, South Africa, Egypt, India and Sri Lanka. The Indian *sohan papdi* and the Iranian *pashmak* are similar.

It is made by heating and liquefying sugar, spinning it centrifugally through minute holes – and finally allowing the sugar to rapidly cool and resolidify into fine strands. It is often sold at fairs, circuses, or at the seaside; it usually comes on a stick.

Its origins are obscure. Some ascribe it to a form of spun sugar found in Italy in the fifteenth century. Machine-spun cotton candy was invented in 1897 by dentist (!) William Morrison and confectioner John C. Wharton; they invented the world's first electric candy floss machine and first successfully introduced cotton candy at the 1904 St Louis World's Fair as 'Fairy Floss' with great success, selling 68,655 boxes at 25¢ (= $6.97 in 2018) per box. That same fair also saw the introduction of the world's first ice-cream cone. Joseph Lascaux, another dentist (!) from New Orleans invented a similar cotton candy machine in 1921. Tootsie Roll Industries, the world's largest candy floss manufacturer, makes a bagged, fruit-flavoured version called Fluffy Stuff. Modern commercial machines can hold up to 3lbs (1.4 kg) of sugar and have compartments for extra flavours. The rotating bowl at the top spins at 3,450 revolutions per minute.

Humbugs

The humble humbug is a traditional hard boiled sweet usually flavoured with peppermint and striped in two different colours – often black and white. Humbugs may be cylinders with rounded ends wrapped in a twist of cellophane, or more traditionally tetrahedral formed from pinched cylinders with a 90-degree turn between one end and the other (shaped like a pyramid with rounded edges) loose in a bag. Records of humbugs exist from as early as the 1820s, and they are mentioned in Elizabeth Gaskell's 1863 *Sylvia's Lovers* set around Whitby, as being a food from the North.

Variations on a humbug:

The bull's eye

The typical bull's eye has black and white stripes like a humbug, but is spherical, more like an aniseed ball. These are peppermint flavoured and are also known as bullets in the UK as they resemble smooth bore musket balls.

In the US, the bull's eye is a very different animal. Goetze's Candy Company, Inc. based in Baltimore, Maryland specialises in caramel-based candies. Goetze's was established in 1895, as the Baltimore Chewing Gum Company by August Goetze and his son, William. In 1917, the family developed a soft, caramel candy known as 'Chu-ees' which ultimately evolved into their signature candy, Caramel Creams, (also known as Bull's Eyes) a soft chewy caramel with a cream-filled centre.

Maintaining the bovine theme, Goetze also makes Cow Tales, originally launched in 1984. Cow Tales are produced in vanilla, chocolate, strawberry, and caramel apple flavours. Over the years, the company has experimented with peanut butter and banana flavours.

Everton mints

Another popular mint in the humbug family is the Everton mint, which is also striped black and white, but with a toffee centre. There are a number of contenders for the origin of the sweet. The mints were first produced in a Liverpool sweet shop close to Goodison Park, home of Everton FC

– hence the name. The owner of the sweet shop, one Mother Noblett, created the mints to appeal to Everton fans, making them black and white reflecting (confusingly) the team's black and white kit at the time.

You could be forgiven for thinking that that was that, and for believing as well that the Everton FC nickname, the Toffees, come from Ma Noblett's toffee centre. Not so. Ma Noblett's wasn't the only toffee shop in town: there was also (confusingly) Ye Anciente Everton Toffee House in head-on competition.

Situated close to the Queen's Head Hotel in Village Street, where St Domingo's Football Club was renamed Everton Football Club in November 1879, Ye Ancient Everton Toffee House was run by Old Ma Bushell, a woman famous for her Everton Toffees and another go-to place for fans making their way to watch the Everton matches firstly at Stanley Park, then Priory Road and then (very confusingly) to Anfield which was Everton's ground before it was Liverpool FC's.

Despite the similarities in origin, the two sweets sold by the rival toffee shops were remarkably different. Mother Noblett's Everton Mints, as we have seen, had a toffee centre, with a hard sugar shell striped, humbug-like, black and white. By contrast, Old Ma Bushell's Everton Toffees were traditional English toffees. Sadly Old Ma Bushell doesn't get the credit for inventing Everton Toffees – that honour goes (confusingly) to a Molly Bushell who invented the sweet back in the 1760s from a house on Everton Brow.

Whatever, competition between the two shops was intense and guerrilla marketing skills had to be razor sharp. And so it was that Old Ma Bushell had to raise her game if she was to reverse the decline in sales she was suffering at the hands of Mother Noblett. Ma Bushell saw that her customer base was stuck inside Goodison Park for the best part of the match days so she obtained permission from the owners to distribute her toffees to the crowds from inside the ground. Glamour and wardrobe played a part: enlisting the help of her beautiful granddaughter Jemima Bushell, Old Ma Bushell had the girl dress in her best frock and a large bonnet, ensuring that the fans flocked to her for the sweets.

The Everton Toffee Lady is still there at home games today, with a lucky teenage girl chosen from the Everton Supporter's Club to perform that star role.

Bêtises de Cambrai are a French boiled sweet made in Cambrai. 'Bêtise' means 'stupid mistake' in French and the sweets are said to have been invented by accident by the son of a confectioner named Afchain. The original flavour is mint, but many others are now produced. Stripes of caramel add sweetness.

Gobstoppers

Gobstoppers or jawbreakers are a type of hard candy, usually round, and range from 1 to 3cm (0.4 to 1.2in) across though they can be up to 8cm (3.1in) in diameter.

The name gobstopper comes from 'gob', slang for mouth, as in 'shut your gob!' In his 1964 *Charlie and the Chocolate Factory*, Roald Dahl described 'Everlasting Gobstoppers', a fictional type of gobstopper that would never get smaller or be finished.

Gobstoppers usually consist of a number of layers, each layer dissolving to reveal a differently coloured (and sometimes differently flavoured) layer, before dissolving completely. Gobstoppers are too hard to bite without risking dental or maxillofacial trauma – or both, hence the name 'jawbreaker'. As gobstoppers dissolve very slowly, they last a very long time in the mouth, larger ones can take days or even weeks to finally disappear.

In 2003, Taquandra Diggs, a 9-year-old girl in Starke, Florida, suffered severe pain and burns on her face, neck and arm after being assaulted in an unprovoked attack by a gobstopper; it exploded in her face after she went to bite into it after it had been left out in the sun. Diggs and several other alleged victims' families filed lawsuits against Nestlé for medical bills resulting from plastic surgery as well as pain and suffering; the matters were later settled out of court for an undisclosed amount.

Dolly Mixtures

Dolly mixtures consist of a variety of small soft sweets and sugar-coated jellies in multi-coloured fondant shapes, such as cubes and cylinders, with various flavourings.

Where did that name come from? Some say that it derives from the daughter of one of the confectioners that created the product, Mr Clayton – Dolly being the pet name for his eldest daughter Dorothy. Others say that it originated around the time of the British Raj in India, where dahl is a dried mixture of beans, peas, or legumes of different sizes and colours.

In the UK, Dolly Mix is produced under the Barratt brand, now owned by Tangerine Confectionery. The Goon Show's Bluebottle was often rewarded, or bribed, with a quantity of dolly mixtures, jelly babies, or similar sweets.

Liquorice

Liquorice is an extract from the Glycyrrhiza glabra plant which contains glycyrrhizic acid, or GZA. GZA is made of one molecule of glycyrrhetinic acid and two molecules of glucuronic acid. The extracts from the root of the plant can also be referred to as liquorice, sweet root, and glycyrrhiza extract.

The name liquorice is derived (via Old French licoresse) from the Greek γλυκύρριζα (glukurrhiza), meaning 'sweet root', from γλυκύς (glukus), 'sweet' and ρίζα (rhiza), 'root', this being the name given by Dioscorides. Pedanius Dioscorides (c. 40–90 AD) was a Greek physician, pharmacologist, botanist, and author of De Materia Medica – a 5-volume Greek encyclopedia about herbal medicine and related medicinal substances, a pharmacopeia.

Liquorice, as we know it, is made by macerating liquorice roots and supplementing the juice with dried liquorice juice from Spain; this is the derivation of the Yorkshire, County Durham, and Lancashire colloquialism 'Spanish'; others contend that the name comes from Spanish monks who grew liquorice root at Rievaulx Abbey near Thirsk in North Yorkshire. The area around Pontefract, Yorkshire, is famous for its cultivation of liquorice with a number of companies exploiting its popularity.

It was Sir George Saville who invented the Pontefract cake, or pomfret, in 1614 when he stamped the small, round liquorice cakes with an image of the local castle. Over the years, a sweet empire mushroomed in the surrounding towns, and by the nineteenth century, around twenty sweet companies had set up. At the height of production, there were ten enormous factories in Yorkshire, and inside each, teams of around forty-five female workers processed a daily ration of 25,000 'cakes' individually stamping the candy medallions with that design to look like Pontefract Castle.

Dunhills

By 1720, maybe earlier, the Dunhill family was renting the land around Pontefract Castle for the cultivation of liquorice; storing harvested liquorice roots in the castle cellars, which had previously been an arsenal and prison.

Dunhills' packaging claims that they had been making liquorice confectionery since 1760, all thanks to the precocious George Dunhill, who became a chemist; he is reputed simply to have added sugar to his medicinal recipes, thus transforming a medicinal confection into a sweet to make the first liquorice sweet. He was apparently only 7 years old at the time.

Dunhill worked at his liquorice business until his death in 1824, when it was taken over by his son Francis. Ann Dunhill, Francis' widow, ran the company after her husband died.

In 1872, the company played a vital part in national politics. Parliament passed the Secret Ballot Act and Pontefract had the first by-election held under the new system. Wax seals on surviving ballot boxes show that instead of the stamp of the borough, Dunhills' famous Pontefract cake stamp was used instead.

Craven's of York bought the business in 1883; the Dunhill name was kept and proceeded to trade in liquorice root distributed amongst wholesale and retail chemists across the UK.

Dunhills Ltd bought out competitors Sampson and Gundill in the 1920s and expanded its export trade, shipping liquorice worldwide including to the United States, Canada, British Guiana, various African countries, the Gulf States and Asia. In 1964 Dunhills Ltd acquired Robinson and Wordsworth Ltd.

Dunhills still operates from Pontefract under the ownership of Haribo. Haribo was founded in 1920 by Hans Riegel Sr in Bonn, the name is an acronym for Hans Riegel + Bonn. Until the 1960s, Pontefract cakes were handmade and hand stamped; an experienced stamper could turn out 30,000 cakes a day.

Robinson and Wordsworth Ltd

In 1877, Robinson and Wordsworth established a factory in Pontefract – Victoria Works – refining their own juice. They continued until 1886 when the death of Robinson left J. N. Wordsworth sole proprietor.

The company expanded with a new wing in 1890, which doubled the size of the works. By 1893, the works operated on three floors. That same year, the curator of Kew Museum visited the firm to research the cultivation of liquorice and published its findings in *The Leisure Hour*. The firm also had a display in Kew Gardens.

When Wordsworth died, the business was sold to a W. H. Lorriman who built a new factory off Ferrybridge Road. During the Second World War, the factory was diverted to aero-engine renovation. As noted, rivals Dunhills Ltd acquired the company in 1964.

Sampson and Gundill

The company set up the Tower Liquorice Refinery on Northgate, Pontefract in 1889 as a wholesale-only business. By 1893, the refinery employed sixty workers with a successful network selling to wholesale grocers, confectioners, and export merchants.

In the 1900s, one of the Gundill brothers travelled to Belgium to set up a liquorice refining company, but withdrew on account of the First World War.

The firm was part of a larger family business estate. The Gundill portfolio included firms of solicitors, builders, gasworks and Pontefract racecourse. Dunhills Ltd acquired the company in 1923.

Bellamy's, Castleford

Joseph Bellamy first started manufacturing confectionery in Leeds, but in 1900 moved to Castleford where sweets are 'spice' and liquorice is 'Spanish'. The factory in Queens Street was previously the Mountain Nail Works, but was converted to a liquorice refinery and a sweet factory.

W. R. Wilkinson

Wilkinson opened his first liquorice business in 1884 in a malt kiln in Pontefract's Southgate; soon after he moved to a new factory in Skinner Lane, the Britannia Works. In 1894 the company moved again, to a former brush factory in Monkhill, which was rebuilt in 1925 as a garden factory – with tennis courts, allotments, and housing for some of the workers, in the grounds.

Wilkinson employed fifty workers; its leading product was 'Perfected Pomfret Cake'. In 1894, Walter Marshall and William Haddock, who later became Pontefract's town clerk, bought out W. R. Wilkinson.

The company carried on sweet making at a reduced level throughout the Second World War; the factory was also used to machine tank parts.

The charismatic brand Willie Wilko ('Willie Wilko says try my mints!') was born in 1946: if you saved fifteen packet tops you qualified for a Willie Wilko bendy toy. In 1900, Wilkinson's and Dunhills were two of eleven firms manufacturing liquorice in Pontefract; Wilkinson's are now owned by Tangerine Confectionery of York, having been bought by Bassett in 1961. From 1901, under Walter Marshall's sole ownership the business continued to expand.

During the 1940s, the company created a trademark referred to as the 'company seal'. The five images represented Pontefract's rich liquorice heritage. The hooded figure signified the Cluniac monks who were despatched from France in the eleventh century to establish a new order in Pontefract. The image of a broken bridge is Pontefract's town symbol. The name of the town is said to derive from the Latin *pons fractus* meaning broken bridge. The round tower symbolises Pontefract Castle. The wise owl dates back to Charles I who visited Pontefract in 1623 and ennobled Lord Saville. He became the first Mayor of Leeds; the city adopted his owl symbol. On each side of the Pontefract seal are images of *Glycyrrhiza glabra*, the liquorice plant.

In 1961, the company merged with the Sheffield-based Bassett Group, their biggest rivals. Five years later their last commercial crop of liquorice was harvested. In 1985 it became Anglo Bellamy Wilkinson. In 1990, Trebor Bassett became the sugar confectionery division of Cadbury Schweppes. In 1999 the York and Pontefract factories combined to form Monkhill Confectionery. They employed 400 workers and produced about 13,000 tonnes of sweets each year, including dolly mixtures, coconut mushrooms and bubble gum as well as liquorice.

Ewbanks

Ewbanks was founded in 1810 by Thomas Firth as Pontefract's second liquorice factory, based in Elephant Yard. The founder was succeeded by David Longstaffe, who later sold to Robert Ewbank and W. R. Horsfall.

From 1810 to 1885 the company was known as Firth Confectioners. The Horsfall and Ewbank partnership prevailed until 1892 when Ewbank became the sole owner. Under his direction, the company grew and expanded into the larger Eagle Liquorice Works, Friarwood in 1887. The company employed sixty workers and boasted a handsome domestic and export trade.

On 8 August 1942, the factory was torched by German incendiaries. The pan, gum and liquorice rooms were all badly damaged, and the factory was put out of action. A new gum department was officially opened on 6 February 1948.

In January 1961, the business merged with the toffee manufacturers Arthur Holland of Southport (which later merged into the larger group J. A. and P. Holland Limited). The company closed in 1965.

Hillaby's

Entrepreneur John Hillaby established the Lion Liquorice Works, Pontefract in 1850. The company grew its own liquorice and by 1893 was the biggest producer in the world. It was taken over by Bellamy and Sons Ltd of Castleford in 1943. Its leading product was Hillaby's Improved Pontefract Cakes.

For the 1925 film *Goldrush*, Hillaby's provided a liquorice boot, which was eaten by Charlie Chaplin. In 1946, the factory on Back Street was destroyed by fire. The premises were rebuilt, but eventually closed as a liquorice factory in 1963 when Joseph Bellamy and Sons Ltd merged into the Mackintosh Group.

Other local manufacturers included R. Austerbery & Co founded in 1888 at the Castle Moat Liquorice Refinery; J.H. Addingley and Sons was founded in 1860 by Mr Charles Tinker and Co, and taken over by Addingley & Sons in 1872, operating from Baghill Refinery, Pontefract. The company closed in 1937. Then there was Longstaff's, Weve Monkman, and Voile & Wortley swallowed up first by Bassett in 1955 and then Wilkinson.

The world's leading manufacturer of liquorice products is M&F Worldwide, NYC which turns out more than 7 per cent of the worldwide liquorice flavours sold to end users.

Other liquorice facts

Originally liquorice was also used as a flavouring agent for tobacco in the manufacture of cigarettes, moist snuff, chewing tobacco, and pipe tobacco. Eating too much liquorice (more than 2 mg/kg/day of pure glycyrrhizinic acid, a liquorice component) is decidedly bad for you: it may result in adverse effects such as hypokalemia, increased blood pressure, and muscle weakness.

Liquorice was marketed squarely at a male market: it has no scent, no sugar coating, no nice colours – it was, in short, men's stuff. Indeed the no nonsense slogan confirmed this: 'men like them; they are the smoker's sweet. They have class appeal and mass appeal.'

Liquorice is amazingly versatile. The major use of liquorice is in the tobacco industry, at roughly 90 per cent of usage. The rest is split evenly between food and pharmaceuticals: 5 per cent of usage each. Liquorice extract is often found not just in sweets, but in some drugs, and beverages like root beer. It can also be used in chewing gum and toothpaste. The versatility and malleability of the sweet is reflected in some of the brand names: Pencil Cases, Twisty Telegraph Wires, Electric Drills and Rockets are just a few.

Liquorice lives on and not just through Haribo. The Pontefract Liquorice Festival takes place in July (www.experiencewakefield.co.uk/liquorice), and there is the art nouveau Pontefract Museum, which houses a special liquorice exhibit. Just outside Pontefract, at Farmer Copleys shop and dairy farm, Heather Copley and her husband Robert are the only present-day farmers to grow liquorice root successfully in the UK.

Marshmallow

The odd sounding word 'marshmallow' comes from the mallow plant species (*Althaea officinalis*), a herb which grows in marshes and other boggy areas. It goes back to around 2000 BC when high class ancient Egyptians ate them as a delicacy strictly reserved for gods and for royalty, who used the root of the plant to treat coughs and sore throats, and to heal wounds. These early marshmallows were made by boiling pieces of root pulp with honey until thick. Once thickened, the mixture was strained, cooled, and then used as required.

By the mid-1800s, French confectioners were supplementing the plant's traditional medicinal properties with honey, taking it half way to being a sweet in the form of a fluffy candy mould called Pâte de Guimauve – a spongy-soft dessert made from whipping dried marshmallow roots with sugar, water, and egg whites. It was also sold as a lozenge. In time, confectioners began to replace the mallow root with gelatin which created a stable form of marshmallow. This was developed around 1845 by Peter Cooper while he was trying to perfect his glue production.

In the late 1940s, the Greek-American confectioner Alex Doumak developed the extrusion process in which marshmallow mixture is pumped through extrusion heads with numerous ports aligned next to each other. These form continuous 'ropes' of marshmallow, giving us the familiar cylindrical shape. Today marshmallows comprise four ingredients: sugar, water, air, and a whipping agent/aerator (usually a protein). They are 50 per cent air; flavouring is usually vanilla.

Peppermint

Peppermint (*Mentha* × *piperita*, also known as *Mentha balsamea Wild*) is a cross between watermint and spearmint. Although the genus Mentha comprises more than twenty-five species, the most commonly used is peppermint. The ancient Egyptians and the Greeks used it. The peppermint featured in John Ray's *Methodus Plantarum Nova* in 1682 and was listed in the *London Pharmacopeia* in 1721, indicating its use as a medicine as well as being a sweet.

New Yorker Hiram G. Hotchkiss is the godfather of peppermint. According to an 1886 article in the *McCook Tribune*, Hotchkiss, then 75 years old, started out as a grocery man when he was 18, but soon saw the future of peppermint – with a handful of others he catapulted peppermint oil into a profitable industry, appreciated for its value as a medicine for stomach aches as well as being a popular sweet.

The peppermint has been used as a breath freshener, in such products as the turn-of-century Pep-O-Mint Lifesaver, especially useful in bars to mask the smell of smoke and drink; a holiday flavouring, especially at Christmas; and an addition to everything from cocktails to cakes.

In 2014, world production of peppermint was 92,296 tonnes, led by Morocco with 92 per cent of the world's total, and Argentina which accounted for 8 per cent. In the United States, the leaves of the peppermint plant are processed for the essential oil to produce flavourings which mainly go into chewing gum, sweets such as Polos, and toothpaste, shampoos, skin lotions and the like.

Lollipops

Lollipops or lollies are hard candies on a stick. The name lollipop was first coined by George Smith, owner of a sweet company called the Bradley Smith Company. George named his stick candy after Lolly Pop, his favourite racehorse and trademarked the name 'lollipop' in 1931.

The Jelly Bean

Jelly beans are those small bean-shaped sweets with soft candy shells and thick gel insides, sold in a wide variety of vivid colours and bold flavours. They are made mainly of sugar. In 1861, Boston confectioner William Shrafft urged Bostonians to send his jelly beans to Union soldiers during the American Civil War, indicating, if nothing else, just how popular they were. They still are.

The jelly bean obviously gets its name from its shape, but in the US a jelly bean was also used to describe someone who was useless: a shallow loser. It referred to a man who shows up for a date well turned out, nicely groomed, but has nothing else to commend him. Phil Harris wrote a song *Jelly Bean (He's a Curb-Side Cutie)* in 1940 – about a guy who was useless.

The jelly bean came into its own around 1930, as an Easter sweet due to its egg-like shape. Shortly after, the beans were being poured inside Easter eggs and soon no Easter was complete without a nest brimming with jelly beans. In the 1970s, an entrepreneur, David Klein, came up with the Jelly Belly, a jelly bean in which the whole sweet was infused with strong flavour, not just the shell. The name derives from when Klein was watching blues musician Lead Belly perform on the 1970s sitcom *Sanford & Son* and confused his name as 'Jelly Belly'.

Jelly beans have enjoyed considerable celebrity over the years: they made an appearance at the presidential inauguration in 1981 and were the first sweet to go on a space mission in 1983. People eat enough jelly beans in a year to circle the earth five times according to the Jelly Belly Company website. When Beatlemania shook the world in the 1960s, US Beatles' fans pelted the band with jelly beans, copying fans in the UK who threw Jelly Babies at George Harrison who reportedly liked them. The only problem was that Jelly Babies are soft and harmless while Jelly Beans casings are rock hard.

The soft part of a jelly bean is, of course, Turkish delight which brings us onto…

Turkish Delight

As you would expect, Turkish delight has an impressive and exotic history; started around AD 226 in the Persian Empire, where the ruling Sassanids enjoyed a sweet called *abhisa* made of honey, fruit syrups, and starch. By the ninth century, it was turning up in Arab apothecaries as a remedy for sore throats and called *rāḥat al-ḥulqūm* (راحَة الحُلْقُوم) which means 'throat comfort', later shortened to *lokum* which remains the name in Arabic. Its name in Greek is λουκούμι *(loukoumi)* where it is marketed as Greek delight. Things started to get interesting in the 1750s when Sultan Abdul Hamid I fell in love with the sweet and had his chefs prepare daily batches for his harem. Its reputation spread as far west as Britain where it was renamed the somewhat less exotic 'lumps-of-delight'.

Today Turkish delight can be made of chopped dates, pistachios, and hazelnuts or walnuts bound by gel; traditional varieties are often flavoured

Turkish delight on display at Koska Helvacısı; Koska Helvacısı, or just Koska, is the leading brand and trademark of helva (halva) and Turkish delight production in Turkey. Koska was a former quarter of Istanbul, near Laleli. The company takes its name from its old location at Koska. Helvacı means producer or seller of sweets in Turkish. 'Koska Helvacısı', then, 'Sweetshop of Koska'. (*Flickr: Turkish Delight – Variety; Author Quick fix. This file is licensed under the Creative Commons Attribution-Share Alike 2.0 Generic license*)

with rosewater, mastic, Bergamot orange, or lemon. The confection is often packaged and eaten as small cubes dusted with icing sugar, copra, or powdered cream of tartar, to prevent sticking.

Not all Turkish delight can boast an exotic provenance: Ling's Turkish delight originated not in Istanbul, but from a lock-up in south-east London.

Nougat

Nuts are literally at the centre of nougat; it is a confection made with sugar or honey, roasted nuts (almonds, walnuts, pistachios, hazelnuts, and macadamia nuts are most common), whipped egg whites, and sometimes chopped candied fruit. Nougat is chewy and it is used in lots of sweets and chocolates, including in Milky Way, Snickers and Double Decker. The word nougat ultimately comes from the Latin *panis nucatus* 'nut bread'.

There are three kinds of nougat. The first, and most common, is white nougat (mandorlato or torrone in Italy, turrón in Spain), made with beaten egg whites and honey; it first made an appearance in Cologna Veneta, Italy, in the early fifteenth century, subsequently in Alicante, Spain with the first published recipe in the sixteenth century, and in Montélimar, France, in the eighteenth century. The early recipes of white nougat were from Central Asia, found in a book in Baghdad in the tenth century. That nougat was called فطان *nāṭif*. One of these recipes indicates that the *nāṭif* comes from Harran, a city located between Urfa (now in south-east Turkey) and Aleppo, Syria. At the end of the tenth century, the traveller and geographer Ibn Hawqal wrote that he ate some *nāṭif* in Manbij in modern Syria and Bukhara in modern Uzbekistan.

The second type of nougat is brown nougat (nougat noir in French, literally 'black nougat'; in Italian croccante, meaning 'crunchy'), which is made without egg whites and has a firmer, often crunchy texture. The third is the Viennese or German nougat which is essentially a chocolate and nut (usually hazelnut) praline. It is nougat in southern France, or cupeta and cubbaita – from the Latin in Cremona, Taurianova and Sicily in Italy; in Greece, it is mandolato or mandola.

Fudge

You can make fudge by mixing sugar, butter and milk, heating it to the soft-ball stage at 240°F (116°C), and then beating the mixture while it cools so that it acquires a smooth, creamy consistency. Fruits, nuts, chocolate, caramel, candies, sweets and other flavours are sometimes added either inside or on top.

Fudge was first made in the US during the late nineteenth century when recipes were printed in many periodicals and advertisements during the 1880s. It was popular because the price of refined white sugar was coming down, and it could be made at home without the need for special equipment. Fudge-making was all the rage in US women's colleges: a student at Vassar College in Poughkeepsie, New York, claimed to have introduced it there in 1888 by selling her own 30lb (14kg) batch. The diary of another student mentions making fudges in 1892. An 1893 letter from another Vassar College student describes fudges as containing sugar, chocolate, milk and butter. A recipe for 'Fudges at Vassar' was printed in *The Sun* in 1895: the recipe comprises sugar, milk, butter and vanilla extract.

Fudge made from brown sugar is penuche. Pralines include nuts and Scottish tablet is a confection with similar ingredients. Other variants include Barfi – an Indian fudge made from cooking milk and sugar into fudge consistency with the addition of coconut, carrot, or nuts. Krówki is a Polish confection similar to fudge.

Toffee

As we have seen the word toffee makes an early appearance with Everton Toffee made by Molly Bushell in the 1750s and derives, probably, from taffy or tuffy, a northern dialect word for something chewy.

Toffee is made by caramelising sugar or molasses along with butter, and occasionally flour. The mixture is heated until it reaches the hard crack stage at 149 to 154°C (300 to 310°F). Toffee is sometimes mixed with nuts or raisins. The mixture is usually poured into a shallow tray and allowed to cool to form a slab.

One of the more popular brands in the 1920s was Harvino, a chewy toffee which owes its name to its creator, Harvey Vincent and was produced at the Lion Toffee Mills, founded in Hunnington, near Birmingham in 1898. Vincent went on to rename Harvino Blue Bird Toffee after attending a performance of Maeterlink's play *The Blue Bird of Happiness* (1908). Maurice Polydore Marie Bernard Maeterlinck (1862–1949) was also known as Count (or Comte) Maeterlinck.

In 1920, Vincent did not take too kindly to a rival branding his toffees Vyno and Vino (did they know no Italian?); Vincent took them to court on a charge of 'calculation to deceive'. Vincent won. Less successful was the Lancashire company Uncle Luke's Steam Confectionery Works, sellers of Uncle Luke's Balls, who tried to stop a rival selling their Uncle Jack's Balls. The judge ruled that everyone had a perfect right to sell their balls.

The previously litigious Harvey Vincent was obviously unconcerned that Boots had been using the Bluebird name since 1917 to brand their ginger beer and mineral waters.

Vincent emulated Cadbury's and Fry's with his insistence on making the workplace a pleasant environment in which to labour. He bought land in rural Worcestershire and spent £150,000 on a fine factory fit for workers. By 1927, Vincent was producing 1,700 tons of toffee every week.

Blue Bird became part of Needler's as Needler Bluebird. In 2002, Needler Blue Bird was purchased by Ashbury Confectionery who discontinued all lines previously made by Needler's and Blue Bird. Ashbury have donated the company's collection of historic Blue Bird packaging to the Black Country Living Museum.

A popular US variant is English toffee, a buttery toffee often made with almonds, sold in both chewy and hard versions. Despite its name it bears little resemblance to the toffee found in the United Kingdom.

Chewing gum

The primary benefit of chewing gum (as a verb and a noun), its raison d'être, is that it satisfies the primal urge to masticate. Other reasons to chew gum are to stimulate taste, teeth cleaning or breath-freshening; self-image too is a factor where idols or role models are characterised by their endless and repetitive gum chewing.

Chewing gum has taken many forms since its arrival in the Neolithic period. Excavations in Kierikki in Finland have revealed 6,000-year-old chewing gum made from birch bark tar, with tooth indentations. The tar from which the gums were made is believed to have antiseptic properties and other medicinal benefits. It is chemically similar to petroleum tar and is in this way different from most other early gum. The Mayans and Aztecs were the first to exploit the positive properties of gum: they used chicle, a natural tree gum, as a base for making a gum-like substance and to stick everyday objects together – early DIY. Forms of chewing gums were also found in Ancient Greece where the Greeks chewed mastic gum, made from the resin of the mastic tree and in so doing gave us our verb, to masticate. Mastic gum, like birch bark tar, has antiseptic properties and is believed to have been used to maintain oral health. Greek ladies used it as a fixative for their false eyelashes. Many other cultures have chewed gum-like substances made from plants, grasses, and resins. A Turkish sultan apparently got through 125 tons of the stuff in a year in his harem, which amounted to half the total harvest.

More recently, the American Indians chewed resin made from the sap of spruce trees; the New England settlers followed suit and in 1848, John Bacon Curtis from Maine developed and sold the first commercial chewing gum, calling it The State of Maine Pure Spruce Gum. He sold his goods nationwide before the railways or the luxury of motor car transport. In 1852, Curtis opened the Curtis & Son Company where about 150 employees produced 1,800 boxes of gum a day. Around 1850, a gum made from paraffin wax, which is a petroleum product, was developed and soon became more popular than spruce gum.

To sweeten their gum, the chewer would repeatedly dip the gum into a plate of powdered sugar. William Semple filed an early patent on chewing gum, patent number 98,304, on 28 December 1869. In seventeenth-century- England, chewing gum was made from isinglass from the guts of sturgeons: isinglass is a kind of gelatin obtained from fish, especially sturgeon, and used in making jellies and glue, and for fining real ale.

The first flavoured chewing gum came about in the 1860s when John Colgan, a Louisville, Kentucky pharmacist, mixed the aromatic flavouring tolu with powdered sugar; tolu is a powder obtained from an extract of the balsam tree (*Myroxylon*). He created small sticks of flavoured chewing gum he called 'Taffy Tolu'. Colgan also pioneered the manufacturing and packaging of chicle-based chewing gum, derived from Manilkara chicle, a tropical evergreen tree. He licensed a patent for the 'Chewing Gum Chip Forming Machine' on 2 August 1910, and one for automatically cutting wrappers for sticks of chewing gum.

What we might call modern chewing gum first appeared in the 1860s when chicle was brought from Mexico by the deposed former President, General Antonio Lopez de Santa Anna, to New York, where he gave it to Thomas Adams, worryingly, for use as a rubber substitute. Chicle did not work for rubber, but it did as a gum, which was cut into strips and marketed as 'Adams' New York Gum No. 1 – Snapping and Stretching…'

– a softer version of the spruce gum. De Santa Anna is better known as the man who led the charge against the US at the Alamo and killed Davy Crocket.

Adam's gum was good, but it was tasteless and sales were poor. So Adams simply added sugar and sales took off. Next, he added liquorice flavour, creating the first flavoured gum – Black Jack Gum, which he also marketed as a remedy for colds. That was followed by 'Tuttie Fruit Gum', the first fruit-flavoured gum; sour orange, and, around 1914, clove. In the 1880s, Frank and Henry Fleer added candy to the gum, importing the raw material from Merida in Venezuela by the ton.

In 1891, William Wrigley Jnr was sent out west by his father to grow the market for Wrigley's Scouring Soap; as a teaser he offered shopkeepers free baking powder and gum – the gum was more popular than the powder, and the rest is history.

Wrigley's Juicy Fruit, Lotta and Vassar were first out of the factory in 1883; Black Jack (1884), Chiclets (1899), and Wrigley's Spearmint Gum were other early gums that quickly dominated the market. By 1910, Spearmint Gum was the market leader followed by Doublemint in 1914, advertised as having the flavour of crème de menthe. Chewing gum gained worldwide popularity through Frank Sinatra's reference to the Wrigley Building in his *(Chicago) My Kind of Town* and by American GIs in the Second World War who were supplied chewing gum as a ration and traded it with locals.

Many of the ingredients used by manufacturers in their gum base have uses in inedible products, which naturally raises concern in some consumers. Polyethylene, one of the most popular components of gum base, is used in products ranging from plastic bags to hula hoops. Polyvinyl acetate is a sticky polymer found in white glue. Butyl rubber is typically used in caulking and the lining of car tyres. Paraffin wax is a by-product of refined petroleum.

Jelly Babies

Jelly Babies, for one reason or another, conjure up the macabre and sinister side of confectionery as much as they do the nurturing qualities of the human race. As one journalist has said, 'there's something of the night about them'; the pseudo-cannibalism implicit in their mutilation and consumption would have been very much at home in Book IX of

A dystopian-looking army of jelly babies. (*https://www.flickr.com/photos/father_jack/ 192744811/ Author https://www.flickr.com/photos/father_jack/ This file is licensed under the Creative Commons Attribution 2.0 Generic license*)

Homer's *Odyssey* with the man-eating Polyphemus in the Cyclops' cave. Remember the cold-jellied alacrity with which you bit off their heads as a child? This pseudo-cannibalism takes us back beyond nostalgia to our very earliest primal urges.

Companies will jump on any old bandwagon in pursuit of profits: hence the development of Rowntree's Body Parts and Barratt's Transplanters in the 1980s.

Jelly Babies are a soft sugar anthropomorphic jelly sweet, shaped as plump babies, reminiscent of cherubs and *putti*, in a range of colours. They were first born in Lancashire, when in 1864, an Austrian worker at the Fryer's sweet factory in Nelson, Lancashire made a mould for a new range of jelly bears. When he realised that the results looked more human than animal, he christened them Unclaimed Babies, after the foundlings frequently left on church steps at that time. Later the jelly variety were on the verge of extinction until reared back to survival by Bassett's of Sheffield who set up a programme for mass-producing Jelly Babies from

1918. Indeed every year they produce the population explosion to end all population explosions by delivering 1,000 million of the babies into a welcoming world.

Jelly Babies first featured on advertisements by Riches Confectionery Company of 22 Duke St, London Bridge in 1885, along with a variety of other baby-sweets, including 'Tiny Totties' and 'Sloper's Babies'. The pricing of these at a farthing each suggests that they were very much larger than the contemporary Jelly Baby, maybe 2–3in long and weighing 1oz. *The Burnley Express* reported on 16 December 1939 that, of all the comforts sent to troops abroad; 'The sweets which are in greatest demand are those which we all know as "unclaimed babies". Over 50lbs of these sweets have already been purchased.'

Bassett's have allocated individual name, shape, colour and flavour to different 'babies': they are Brilliant (red; strawberry), Bubbles (yellow; lemon), Baby Bonny (pink; raspberry), Boofuls (green; lime), Bigheart (purple; blackcurrant) and Bumper (orange).

A line of sweets called Jellyatrics was launched by Barnack Confectionery Ltd to commemorate the Jelly Baby's eightieth birthday in March 1999. In 2017, Bassett's released banana, pineapple and mango in their 'Jelly Babies Tropical' range – the first new flavours in almost a hundred years.

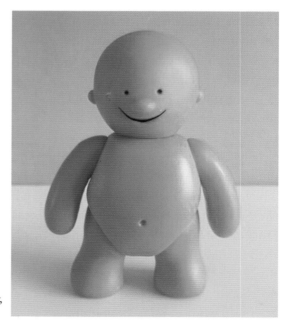

1988 Not just any old baby – this is a Bassett's Orange Jelly Baby: 'Poseable Figure' – spotted on eBay, December 2020.

Chapter 9

Chocolate's History

Early Days

Chocolate grows on trees; so, therefore, does money because chocolate means money. Montezuma and the Aztecs will show us this in due course. It grows on trees in the form of cocoa powder from the seeds or beans of the cacao tree, or, to give it its botanical name, *theobroma cacao* – literally, 'cocoa, food of the gods'. Cacao means 'bitter juice' in Mayan. The main growing areas are central and eastern South America and West Africa, all within 20° of the equator, below 1,000ft, in the shade and at a minimum temperature of 16°C. Between thirty and forty white pulp-covered seeds are to be found in the average, football-sized pod; it fruits all year round. In the very early days the beans were sun dried and the kernels or nibs (up to half their weight is made up of fat, or cacao butter) were roasted, shelled and crushed into a paste called cacao liquor – liquor in the liquid essence sense – and then made into cakes. These were then crumbled and immersed in water to form liquid chocolate. The drink was taken both hot and cold, thickened to make a soup or redried to make cakes. Four hundred beans make 1lb of chocolate.

There is some evidence that the pre-Mayan Olmecs from 1500 BC up to about 400 BC and, later, the Izapan knew cacao. But it is probably the Mayans who cultivated, manufactured, bartered and consumed chocolate on a large scale from around AD 600, in a bitter liquid form they called *xocloatl*. Cacao beans and roasting griddles have been found in excavated tombs bearing hieroglyphs which spell '*kakaw*'. These finds also tell us that the Mayans drank it unsweetened or sometimes spiced with vanilla, honey or chilli pepper. Cacao dissolved in 'virgin water' features in primitive Mayan baptism ceremonies as well as at sacrifices, betrothals and weddings. The Aztecs conquered the Mayans around AD 1200 and started chocolate's association with divinity by worshipping Quetzalcoatl as the bringer of chocolate. Cacao beans had been used as symbols for numbers by the Mayans; we know that the Mayans and others had traded with cacao, and Fray Bernadino de Sahagun tells us that forgeries were a problem in the first century BC with fake beans made from clay in circulation. Our phrases 'bean counters' and 'not worth a bean' are derived from these early transactions. To give some context, a porter's daily pay amounted to about one hundred beans, a fresh avocado cost three beans, a rabbit cost eight beans, a prostitute was negotiable around ten depending on the service required, a turkey or a slave one hundred, and a feather cape one thousand.

The dawn of the chocolate age: the Aztec Montezuma II briefing his envoys on a meeting with the conquistadores. Cortes had come looking for el Dorado but returned home around 1520 with cocoa, thus introducing cocoa, and ultimately chocolate, to Europe.

But it was Montezuma II (reigned AD 1502–AD 1520) who really exploited the fiscal power of chocolate: he adopted cacao as currency in place of gold, established a bean bank and allowed tribute to be paid in beans. The Dominican Bartolome de las Casas describes Columbus' landing in AD 1502 at Guanaja (off Honduras) and notes that the cargo on the natives' boats contained cocoa beans. Ferdinand Columbus (Christopher's son) adds 'those almonds which in New Spain are used for money…they seemed to hold these almonds at great price.'

Montezuma reputedly drank fifty cups of chocolate every day, partly because he believed it to be an aphrodisiac; he thereby helped to establish chocolate's pseudo-medical and sexual reputations. It was now being commonly used as a medicine for fevers and dysentery. We also know that cacao was an essential *vade mecum* on the journey to the next life. The Aztecs anticipated the temperance work of the English chocolate company Quakers in believing chocolate to be a socially more acceptable drink than their alcoholic *octli*.

To the Aztecs, chocolate was very much a beverage for the rich and regal, typically served at the end of a meal in much the same way as port or mint chocolates are today. Chocolate at the time was a very bitter drink and by no means universally popular. Like the Mayans the Aztecs adulterated it with the ground down bones of the dead, pimento and pepper. Giralamo Benzoni, in his 1575 *History of the New World*, considered it 'more a drink for pigs than humanity'*;* Jose de Acosta, Jesuit missionary and naturalist, in 1590 in his *Natural and Moral History,* tells us that 'the Spanish men – and even more the Spanish women – are addicted to the black chocolate', and thought that chocolate 'disgusts…it has a foam on top, or a scum-like bubbling'. Such antipathy gradually evaporated as Spanish ways and culture infiltrated local habits and diet. The Spanish drank it hot rather than cold and added more familiar spices such as black pepper and cinnamon.

The *conquistadores* went out west looking for *el dorado,* but they found chocolate too; Hernan Cortez was unimpressed when he tasted it as a post-prandial treat chez Montezuma, but unlike Columbus, he did recognise its commercial potential, for example as pay for porters. He promptly took the recipe and methods of cultivation and production back to Spain. It is, therefore, probable that chocolate was introduced to Europe around 1528 by way of the court of Charles V of Spain with some help from Jesuits and missionary Dominican monks who took a delegation of Kekchi Mayans home to meet Prince Philip (later Philip III of Spain) bearing chocolate amongst their gifts.

Charles' people added cane sugar to make it sweet and invented the *molinillo* to froth it up with; the king (no doubt with an eye on the military advantages) was impressed to hear from Cortez that chocolate was in fact an energy drink – allowing a man who had had a drink to march all day without need for food. Contemporary monks enhanced production and taste by shaping it into wafers or tablets for dissolving and by adding pepper, cinnamon and musk in place of the more usual chilli.

For most of the sixteenth century, chocolate was largely confined to Spain, but its spread to neighbouring countries was inevitable. Visitors to the Spanish court in the seventeenth century carried the recipe back to their various homes: the explorer Antonio Carletti detailed the process of cacao cultivation for the Italian court and Anne of Austria, daughter of Philip III, took it back to France when she married Louis XIII in 1615 – along with a maid dedicated to chocolate preparation and nicknamed *la Molina*. Louis XIV gave permission in 1659 for a Sieur David Chaliou of Paris 'to sell and deliver in all places of the kingdom a certain composition called chocolat, the use of which is very healthful'. Alphonse de Richelieu, Cardinal of Lyon, used chocolate to 'moderate the vapours of his spleen', having obtained the secret of its production from Spanish monks who had brought it to France. Dutch ships carrying chocolate were captured by the English, thus expediting its arrival in England.

The first known book on chocolate, *Libro en el Cual se Trata del Chocolat*, was published in 1609. Spanish colonists were busy planting cacao seeds throughout their colonies so that chocolate gradually became affordable to the less well off; it seems to have been routinely served up to dignitaries at bullfights and at *auto de fe*.

The Englishman Thomas Gage confirmed this in 1648 in his *A New Survey of the West Indies*: 'all, rich or poor, loved to drink plain chocolate without sugar or other ingredients.' He also tells the story of the Bishop of Vera Cruz, Don Bernadino de Salazar, who censured and prohibited the popular, but disruptive, habit white women had of consuming chocolate brought to them in mid-Mass or sermon by their Indian maidservants. The women insisted they had weak stomachs and needed a fortifying drink of chocolate to see them through the services. But the bishop was unsympathetic and served notice of excommunication on the persistent offenders. The women then threatened to withdraw their spiritual and financial support with threats on the bishop's life. Eight days later the bishop died, having been poisoned, ironically, by a chalice of laced chocolate allegedly served up by one of Gage's female friends assisted by a page with whom she was having an affair.

Chocolate's divine associations and its reputation as a healthy beverage steadily grew, as did its alleged medicinal and aphrodisiac qualities.

Pre-Columbian Nicaraguans had abstained from sex for thirteen days before beginning the cacao tree-planting season in the belief that their abstinence would cause the gods to look favourably upon their crop; the Aztecs gave sacrificial victims a cup of chocolate to drink just before ripping out their hearts – the heart-shaped cacoa bean symbolising the human heart.

Phillip II's physician, Francisco Hernandez, had in 1577 managed to combine the medical and the aphrodisiac when he confirmed that chocolate not only 'alleviated intestinal pains and colic' but also 'excited the veneral appetite'. In 1591, the Mexican Juan de Cardenas noted that 'green' chocolate caused fits, depression and tachycardia, but when roasted, cacao beans were 'nutritious and fortifying'. Giovanni Maria Lancisi, physician to Pope Clement XI, investigated a number of sudden deaths in Rome which had been attributed to bad snuff and too much chocolate; he absolved the chocolate, emphasising its life sustaining qualities. The Italian doctor Paolo Zacchia, in his 1644 *de mali Hipochondriaci,* was familiar with chocolate as a medicine that was good for the stomach. The French gastronomy writer Louis Lemery in the 1704 London edition of *Traite des Aliments* agreed: 'It helps Digestion, allays the sharp Humours that fall upon the Lungs. It keeps down the fumes of the Wine, promotes Venery.' To Dr Giovanni Batiste Felici, though, writing in 1728, chocolate was one of the 'many disorders which Mankind has introduced to shorten their lives', it changes normally quiet people into chatterboxes, making some angry, and turns children hyperactive. Geronimo Piperni's eulogy is more typical though, describing chocolate as a 'divine, celestial drink, the sweat of the stars, the vital seed…universal medicine'. For Dr Giovanni Bianchi of Rimini it was an effective cure for impotence.

A French thesis appeared *On the Healthful Uses of Chocolate* while a Dr Bachot declared it a 'noble confection…the true food of the gods'. Linnaeus gave it his endorsement when in 1737 he described it as 'a most healthy and nourishing drink', giving it its ambrosia-like label, *theobroma* – food of the gods. A native of Martinique died in 1720 at the age of 100 having subsisted for the last thirty years on a diet of chocolate and biscuits; in fact, he was so fit that he could mount his horse without the aid of stirrups until aged 85. The court of Cosimo III de' Medici (d. 1723) was famous for its jasmine-scented chocolate, thanks probably to the court physician Francesco Redi: with the addition of lemon peel, amber, musk, vanilla and cinnamon it had 'a prodigious effect' on drinkers. The French gastronome Jean Anthelme Brillat-Savarin is quite definite: 'persons who drink chocolate regularly are conspicuous for unfailing health and immunity from the host of minor ailments which mar the enjoyment of life.'

In 1664, chocolate received Papal approval when Cardinal Brancaccio pronounced *'liquidum non frangit jejunum'* – liquids do not break the (Lenten) fast. Even though chocolate was often very viscous and appeared in the form of cakes it passed the test for a liquid, and fasters were able to drink it with impunity. Associations with witchcraft and sorcery abounded, as did suggestions that chocolate led to unwifely conduct: during the Inquisition in seventeenth-century Guatemala, Juan de Fuenta testified that Cecilia, his wife, with 'spells and curses…treats him not as a husband, but as a servant…he mixes the chocolate and heats the food… and he gets up very early to do this while she stays in bed and sleeps until very late. And when his wife wakes, he brings her chocolate…in this way his wife has turned him into a coward, and all this cannot be a natural thing.'

If you were to believe the socialite and letter-writing gossip Marquise de Sevigne, chocolate had a defining role in embryology: one of her missives in 1671 tells us that 'The Marquise de Coetlogon took so much chocolate during her pregnancy last year that she produced a small boy as black as the devil, who died' – thus neatly if not outrageously merging sexual and diabolical associations. She probably epitomised French society generally, blowing hot and cold over chocolate: one day in 1671 she saw it as an ideal soporific, two months later 'it is cursed…the source of vapours and palpitations…suddenly lights a continuous fever in you that leads to death'. By October, though, it was the perfect nutritious *digestif.* In 1684, the Parisian physician Joseph Bachot confirmed that chocolate and not nectar or ambrosia was the true food of the gods.

Chocolate, as we have seen, improved sexual prowess; the conquistador Bernal Diaz had noted that the Aztec aristocracy took chocolate 'for success with women'. To the notorious Giacomo Casanova it was as good an icebreaker as champagne and, like Samuel Pepys, he enjoyed a morning draft to set the day off. Louis XVI's mistresses, Mesdames du Barry and Pompadour played their parts in sexing up chocolate, however unwittingly:

du Barry was scurrilously accused of exciting her lovers with chocolate to satisfy her lust. Pompadour, on the other hand, was frigid and, according to Stanley Loomis, used hot chocolate along with 'aphrodisiacs, truffle and celery soup to stir a sensuality that was at best sluggish'.

The paranoid Pope Clement XIV perpetuated chocolate's association with poisoning (facilitated by its strong taste which was sufficient to mask many poisons) when in 1773 he suspected that he had been poisoned with it. This letter from Sir Horace Mann to Horace Walpole tells a version of the story:

> A slow poison was given him by his own confectioner in a dish of chocolate...from the first sip he told the servants it had a bad taste. Nevertheless they both continued to swallow their death...the most alarming of their symptoms was that their arms and legs swelled up and their finger nails fell out.

In the seventeenth century, cocoa was grown intensively by the Portuguese in Brazil. They used slaves, including children and pregnant women, to such a degree that at one point 10 per cent of the whole transatlantic slave trade was employed on their cocoa plantations. Venezuela was another cacoa exporter making use of slave labour, as were the Dutch in Curacao where, between 1650 and 1750, on average 20,000 slaves arrived each year with up to 100,000 thereafter. Spain was still the main importer and consumer: during the reign of Charles III at the end of the eighteenth century, 12 million lbs were consumed every year in Madrid alone. In 1772, there were 150 chocolate grinders operating in the capital and in 1773 a highly professional guild was formed there. John Adams, second president of the USA, was one of the many visitors to Spain who spoke highly of chocolate.

Chocolate Comes to England

By the later seventeenth century, chocolate houses had begun to spring up all over Europe: in Belgium, for example, in 1697, the Mayor of Zurich, Heinrich Escher, had a taste and took the good news back to Switzerland. He thus established a neat link between two of the world's most celebrated chocolate-making nations today. The early association of chocolate with the high arts and with the upper echelons of English politics and society is reflected in its role in the development of the English gentleman's club, by way of the chocolate house.

But England's early encounters with chocolate were far from auspicious. Thomas Gage notes how back in 1579: 'when we have taken a good prize, a ship laden with cocoa, in anger and wrath we have hurled overboard this good commodity not regarding the worth and goodness of it, but calling it in bad Spanish *cagarutta de carnero,* or sheep dung in good English.

Jose de Acosta in his 1590 *Natural and Moral History* tells us that an English corsair burnt 100,000 loads of cacao in the port of Guatulco in New Spain, the equivalent of 2.4 billion beans. Its introduction to England was helped by the capture of Jamaica from Spain in 1655 where cacao walks, or plantations, were already well established.

It took a Parisian shopkeeper to open the first chocolate shop in London, in June 1657. The 23 June 1659 edition of *Needhams Mercurius Politicus* ran the following advertisement:

An excellent West India drink called chocolate, in Bishopsgate Street, in Queen's Head Alley, at a Frenchman's house being the first man who did sell it in England...ready at any time, and also unmade at reasonable rates... it cures and preserves the body of many diseases .

Chocolate makes an appearance in 1658, as a 'compounded Indian drink, whose chief ingredient is a fruit called Cacao', in Edward Phillip's *The New World of English Words, or, A General dictionary Containing the Interpretation of such Hard Words as are derived from other Languages.*

M. Sury's chocolate house pamphlet in Oxford in 1660 describes chocolate as a virtual panacea:

By this pleasing drink health is preserved, sickness diverted. It cures consumptions and Coughs of the Lungs; it expels poison, cleanseth the teeth, and sweetneth the Breath; provoketh Urine; cureth the stone and strangury, maketh Fatt and Corpulent, faire and aimeable.

And when it comes to the benefits to infertile women he is positively poetic: 'Nor need the Women longer grieve, Who spend their oyle yet not Conceive, For 'tis a Help Immediate, If such but Lick of Chocolate.'

Dr Henry Stubbs called it 'Indian nectar' and, although expressing caution on the high fat content, not only admitted that it was more nutritious than a pound of meat, but also calculated dosages for chocolate as a medicine for various ailments.

Chocolate's growing reputation then seems to be built on its apparent medicinal benefits and its supposed aphrodisiac qualities. Stubbs again: 'The great Use of Chocolate in Venery, and for supplying the Testicles with a Balsam, or a Sap' is well known, and

[I]f Rachel had known [about chocolate] she would not have purchased Mandrakes for Jacob. If the amorous and martial Turk should ever taste it, he would despise his Opium. If the Grecians and Arabians had ever tried it, they would have thrown away their Wake-robins and Cuckow pintles; and I do not doubt that you London Gentlemen, do value it above your Cullises and Jellies; your Anchovies, Bononia Sausages…Soys, your Ketchups and Caveares, your Cantharides [Spanish fly] and your Whites of Eggs.

The very word 'confectionery' is derived from the medical term 'confection' which originally meant a sweetened pill.

James Wadsworth wittily declared in his *Curious History of the Nature and Quality of Chocolate*: 'Twill make Old Women Young and Fresh, Create New Motion of the Flesh, And cause them Long for you know what, If they but taste of Chocolate.'

Pepys' diary entries show how it was very much part of his society, thus confirming chocolate as one of the drinks of choice among men of influence and affluence. He received an anonymous gift of chocolate in 1660 and on the morning of 24 April 1661 used it as a cure for a hangover after Charles II's coronation, waking up 'with my head in a sad taking through last night's drink which I am sorry for. So rose and went out with Mr Creede to drink our morning draft, which he did give me chocolate to settle my stomach.' In October 1662, he drank it with Mr Creede and Captain Ferrers in Westminster Hall. The entry for 3 May 1664 finds Pepys 'Up, and being ready went by agreement to Mr Blands and then drank my morning draft in good Chocolatte, and slabbering my band, sent home for another.' On 24 November 1664, he tells us 'Up and to the office, where all the morning busy answering of people. About noon out with Commissioner Pett, and he and I to a coffee house to drink Jocolatte, very good.'

The American Physician, published in London in 1672 by William Hughes, accurately describes how to make and present chocolate. Philippe Dufour around 1685 tells us that 'Chocolate is lately much used in England, as Diet and Phisick with the Gentry', pointing out that the way it is made in England 'loosens the stomach', but also 'causes melancholy'. Chocolate served with lots of sugar was one of the suspects when Martin Lister, echoing Sury, asked in his *Journey to Paris in the Year 1698*, 'Why do Parisians, especially the women, become so corpulent?' E. Veryard, an English traveller, tells in his 1701 *Choice Remarks* how 'The Spaniards being the only people in Europe, that have the Reputation of making Chocolate to perfection', and then goes on to describe the technique in detail. In 1780, Joseph Fry of Bristol won a government contract to supply the Royal Navy with a standard ration of chocolate (to replace rum) on account of its nutritional benefits.

From the eighteenth century, chocolate was featured in the cook books of the day: *The Accomplished Female Instructor* of 1704 tells us how to make the best chocolate and, significantly, how it now includes milk in the recipe; chocolate puffs are included in Mary Kettilby's 1719 pioneering healthy-eating book, *A Collection of Above Three Hundred Receipts in Cookery, Physic and Surgery; For the use of all Good Wives, Tender Mothers and Careful Nurses*. As breakfast developed into a meal in its own right later in the century, chocolate came with it, as we can see from the fine porcelain and silver chocolatieres (complete with holes for the *molinillo*) frequently depicted in many contemporary paintings.

Royal chocolate and Chocolate Houses

The Chocolate Kitchens were built by Christopher Wren in about 1690 as part of William III's (1689–1702) and Queen Mary II's (1689–94) rebuilding of Hampton Court Palace. Its inclusion in the new part of the palace demonstrated the wealth, power and modernity of William and Mary's court.

The king and queen would usually take their chocolate as a drink at breakfast time. It was often served in the bedroom as part of a ritual known as the levee, where the king or queen would get dressed ceremoniously in front of a special chosen few. William, however, was especially fond of chocolate and would drink it throughout the day, often accompanied by his close friend and courtier, the Duke of Portland.

The eighteenth-century Chocolate Kitchen was the domain of Thomas Tosier, personal chocolatier to King George I, whose wife Grace was something of a celebrity in Georgian London, trading on her husband's high station to promote her own renowned chocolate house in Greenwich. Tosier would not have had to roast or grind the cocoa but would have done the delicate flavouring and serving of the chocolate. A privileged and well-paid position, the chocolate maker even had his own bedroom within the palace.

Chocolate houses in London were generally concentrated around Covent Garden and St James's, competing, Lorenzo Magolotti a London resident from 1668 to 1688 tells us, with the ubiquitous coffee houses as somewhere good to eat, play cards and dice, gamble, drink cider, sherbet (a drink then), tea and cock ale (beer with bits of fowl in it) and to converse. And fight: one night at the Royal Chocolate House, the Royal Guards had to be called to restore order with their rifle butts, amongst a group of sword-flashing young bloods who were at each other's throats in a gambling row. Jonathan Swift was less than impressed; he describes White's Chocolate House as a place to be 'fleeced and corrupted by fashionable gamblers and profligates'. But this was untypical; the genteel, aristocratic ambience of White's Chocolate House and the Cocoa Tree was more the norm.

White's was opened in 1693 by the Italian Francis White and by 1709 had achieved such a reputation for fashionability that Richard Steele wrote his pieces for *Tatler* there: 'All accounts of Gallantry, Pleasure and Entertainment shall be under the article of White's Chocolate House Poetry under that of …' White's widow later extended its reputation still further as the place to be. In Alexander Pope's *Dunciad* it was where you went to 'teach oaths to youngsters and to nobles, wit'. In 1733, it was still 'where it was at' when William Hogarth set the gambling scene there for his *The Rake's Progress*.

The Cocoa Tree also enjoyed Steele's patronage; this time along with Joseph Addison who wrote his articles for *The Spectator* from the location, when the paper was launched in 1711. Addison ranked chocolate alongside romances and novels as one of life's great 'inflamers'. On the down side, the Huguenot Dr Daniel Duncan was less enthusiastic in his

1712 piece in the paper: he bewailed the addition of sugar, which while it made the drink 'delicious' totally negated its original medicinal qualities with the water doing damage to the 'protuberant tufts' lining the stomach. Chocolate attained a political reputation too: a paranoid Charles II tried to close the chocolate houses down in 1675 in an attempt to quell the sedition and radical politics they supposedly fostered, and The Cocoa Tree became known as the *Tory Cocoa Tree Club*. By 1746, the year of Culloden, it was the chocolate house of choice for Jacobites and even became their parliamentary headquarters.

By now, chocolate house owners were realising the business opportunities their establishments offered and so rewrote their business plans to convert them into places for the rich, the privileged and the male and, in doing so, forged the origins of the English gentleman's club. To illustrate the money and influence associated with these clubs, Horace Walpole in one of his letters in 1780 tells how £180,000 was gambled in one night at the Cocoa Tree.

Not everyone, though, welcomed the arrival of this divine, medicinal aphrodisiac. Chocolate consumption was, it seems, having a depressing effect on sales of beer in England. In 1763, victuallers and brewers had lobbied for legislation to curb the importation of cocoa beans. But nothing could stop the relentless march of chocolate; chocolate laced cakes 'in the Spanish style' became the vogue in London chocolate houses and in 1826 there were advertisements for chocolate lozenges which were 'a pleasant and nutritious substitute for food while travelling or when unusual fasting is caused by an irregular period of mealtimes' – the first mentions of chocolate as a kind of sweet and as a snack and as something to consume on a road journey.

In 1728, Walter Churchman opened a successful drinking chocolate shop in Bristol and was granted Letters Patent in 1729 by George II, permitting him to make and sell chocolate. This was the shop which the Quaker and chemist Joseph Fry bought in 1761. Churchman was one of many 'cottage industry' manufacturers supplying chocolate to meet growing local markets up and down the country. Another couple were Messrs Berry and Bayldon, established in York in 1767, eventually joining up with Joseph Terry (another chemist) and in 1824, John Cadbury opened his tea, coffee and cocoa shop in Bull Street Birmingham. In 1862, Henry Rowntree acquired William Tuke and Son, a chocolate and cocoa business run by the Quaker Mary Tuke in York.

The English were at the forefront of attempts to make chocolate more palatable. Once the beans are ground the resulting essence produces about 55 per cent cocoa butter. Various efforts to counteract the viscosity and greasiness of the liquid had been made: the English tried arrowroot, potato starch, sago flour and powdered seashells; to darken the colour they added iron rust or brick dust until such practice was made illegal under the Food and Drugs Act 1860 and the Adulteration of Food Act 1872 (dealt with in Chapter 7).

But it was a Dutch chemist and confectioner, Coenraad van Houten, who made the real breakthrough. In 1828, notwithstanding a mention in Diderot's *Encyclopedia* where tablets of chocolate were recommended as a good snack for the busy man who had no time for a real breakfast, he invented a hydraulic press which squeezed out most of the cocoa butter from the liquor, thus reducing the cocoa butter content from over 50 per cent to 27 per cent and leaving chocolate powder or, as we know it, cocoa. Then, in the 1880s, by adding alkalis such as potassium or sodium carbonate in to the liquor (known as Dutching), van Houten was able to render it darker, mellower, more mixable and softer and, with added sugar, sweeter. Much to the dismay of his English competitors at the time, van Houten's new soluble cocoa was winning the approval of eminent scientists at such august institutions as the Pharmaceutical Society of Great Britain and the Society of Public Analysts.

This revolution led the way to the mass production of cheaper chocolate in powder and solid form. In the eighteenth and nineteenth centuries, the Spanish still had a virtual monopoly on cocoa bean cultivation with Venezuela alone still supplying half the world's cocoa in 1810 and the Spanish drinking about a third of the global crop on their own. Casanova, writing at the end of the eighteenth century, tells us that 'The Spaniards offer visitors chocolate so frequently at all hours that if one accepted, one would be choked.' Between 1730 and 1784, 43,000 tonnes of cacao were exported to Spain by one company alone, the Compania Gipuzcoana.

This was all to change though with the political upheaval caused by the Venezuelan Revolution in 1811 and the resulting loss of cheap labour to the warring factions. To maintain supply to meet the ongoing demand, the French developed cocoa plantations in Martinique and Madagascar, the Dutch in Java and Sumatra, the Germans in the Cameroons, the Portuguese on São Tomé and Principe islands off the west coast of Africa, the Spanish on Fernando Po (Bioko) and the British in their colonies in

Gold Coast (Ghana), Ceylon (Sri Lanka) and the West Indies, notably Trinidad and Jamaica. In 1825, Brillat-Savarin tells us that in France chocolate 'had become quite ordinary' and that 'Spanish Ladies of the New World love chocolate to the point of madness.' In fact, so popular had it become that Proust considered it too common to take at teatime.

Along with the squalid deployment of tens of thousands of slaves, mechanisation soon began to help increase production and foster commercialisation. It was Joseph Fry & Sons of Bristol who led the way when in 1761 they bought a water mill and warehouse and established a sales agency network in fifty-three English towns. Companies in France, Germany and Austria followed suit with watermill power, while the Dutch used the windmill, and the Spanish, mules. The advent of steam power in the nineteenth century led to more significant change. In 1776, Doret patented a hydraulic chocolate grinding machine which reduced it to a paste and in 1795, Joseph Fry industrialised chocolate production in England when he started using a James Watt steam engine to grind his beans. In 1834, J.M. Lehmann of Dresden set up a plant specialising in making cocoa processing machinery. Reductions by Gladstone in the punitive duty on chocolate in 1852 from 2*s* to 1*d* per lb also had a profound effect on consumer affordability and demand. This was met not just by grocers and confectioners, but also by chemists; the medicinal properties attributed to chocolate led to a demand for chocolate-coated pills and lozenges, or confectionery.

But the cocoa makers had other things on their minds: what to do with all that discarded cocoa butter which represented up to 30 per cent wastage? The answer was to make it into *eating* chocolate. Joseph Fry & Sons were again the pioneers; they had been making drinking chocolate since 1728 and in 1847 they developed eating chocolate in the shape of bars of chocolate by adding back in some of the cocoa butter to the mix producing a thinner paste that was easier to mould. They thereby went a long way to meeting the massive demand for cocoa beans that resulted largely from a growing number of confectioners, pastry makers and apothecaries all looking for new and innovative product lines.

The Fry launch took place at a Birmingham trade show in 1849 and two years later the new moulded chocolate was on the market – branded as *Chocolat Delicieux à Manger*. This was to exploit the cachet associated with French-sounding food and to counter the popularity of French imports. Cadbury followed: George Cadbury visited van Houten in The Netherlands; he brought back one of his machines thus enabling the firm to start producing their Cocoa Essence from 1866. Sales of chocolate in 1852 were 9 tons rising to 12,000 tons in 1904.

Switzerland then took centre stage: Philip Suchard first came across chocolate when his mother sent him to collect a supply from an apothecary in Neuchâtel; he set up his confectionery business in 1826. Charles-Amedee Kohler introduced hazelnuts into chocolate in 1831 in his Lausanne factory. The high point though was the development of milk chocolate in 1879 by Swiss manufacturer Daniel Peter. Peter was the son-in-law of Francois-Louis Cailler, the owner of Switzerland's first chocolate factory, which he established in Corsier near Vevey in 1819 having worked at Caffarel's chocolate factory in Milan before that. He combined powdered milk – which had recently been developed by Henri Nestlé as an infant food – with chocolate and cocoa butter to produce a solid that was easy to mould and shape. Soon after, in 1876, Rodolphe Lindt introduced conching – a process which resulted in a smoother, more pleasant flavour we now know as fondant chocolate. In 1899, Jean Tobler made the transition from confectioner to manufacturer in Bern, turning out the distinctive bar we still see today. That same year, Lindt merged with Johann Rudolf Sprüngli of Zurich to form Chocoladefabriken Lindt und Sprüngli.

The milk chocolate bar and the chocolate coated sweet were thus born. With the mechanisation that came along, the chocolate industry was totally transformed in England and in the rest of Europe. Chocolate was now being eaten as well as drunk although it would not be until the early years of the twentieth century before sales of eating chocolate outstripped drinking chocolate.

Tobler's Symphony Selection advert in Country Life, October 23, 1958.

Chapter 10

The Quakers and Chocolate

Both the Fry and Cadbury families were Quakers and, like the Quaker Rowntrees in York, they were concerned to provide their workers with clean, safe and pleasant working conditions. In addition, sanitary and comfortable housing, educational, social and recreational facilities were provided. Fry's employed a nurse and a doctor; ran 'continuation classes' (further education) for the girls, provided a gym with instructors, facilities and pitches for football, tennis, cricket and bowls and set up the Operatic Society, the Camera Club, the Debating and Dramatic Societies. Girls leaving to get married received a copy of *Mrs Beeton's Book of Household Management*.

George Cadbury financed the Sweating Exhibition in 1904 to adumbrate the parlous state of British industry where sweat shops were rampant, and payrolled the Anti-Sweating League. As noted, sweating of an altogether different kind was a major problem at R.S. Murray's Clerkenwell, London confectionery factory whose workers went on strike complaining of the sweltering conditions that had to be endured while working there.

Fry's characterises the inextricable connection of chocolate with Quakerism. Friends were excluded from the only teaching universities in England at the time, Oxford and Cambridge, because of the two universities' affiliation to Anglicanism; they were debarred from Parliament; they were restricted in what they could and could not do as lawyers as they did not take oaths and they were disqualified from the guilds and from the armed services because they were pacifists. One of the few alternatives left to a privileged and well-to-do young Quaker men was a life in business. Moreover, cocoa and chocolate were attractive to Fry, Cadbury and Rowntree because of all the attendant social benefits of an alcohol-free beverage.

Early concerns over the intrinsic insincerity of advertising and accusations of price-fixing and a Quaker chocolate cartel were overcome to a greater or lesser degree, allowing the companies to get on with building a largely contented workforce, enlightened industrial relations, fair dealing and pleasant factories with an air of homeliness provided by potted plants and congenial pictures on the factory walls. Managers used workers' Christian names and the extra-curricular provision of housing, entertainment, sport and education was years ahead of its time. In terms of industrial relations generally, Fry and the other chocolate Quakers were at the vanguard providing terms of employment and working conditions introduced in other industries and companies only after legislation made them mandatory. Rules and guidelines were laid down as to how Quakers should conduct themselves in business: the 1738 *Advices* promoted fair dealing and absolute honesty; the 1783 *Book of Extracts* unequivocally banned paper credit; the 1833 *Rules of Discipline* reminded adherents that the root of all evil was money and the 1861 *Doctrine, Practice and Discipline* summarised the whole code: covering debt, seeking advice from other Friends, inappropriate speculation and much more. Paternalism and philanthropy were not of course confined to Quakers, or indeed to England. In the global chocolate industry, Philippe Suchard in Switzerland and the Mennonite Milton Hershey in the US also offered enlightened industrial welfare – but England was exceptional with its Quaker triumvirate.

All the industrial welfare in the world, though, could not eradicate industrial injury or occupational diseases. An example is the boy soldering tins at Clarnico's toffee tin department who presented to his doctor with a headache and a blue rash on his upper torso. The doctor's diagnosis was lead poisoning; verdict (as encouraged by the firm): death by natural causes. In April 1914, 'the very dangerous practice of wearing unprotected hat-pins' was highlighted in Rowntree's staff magazine, *Cocoa Works Magazine*: 'In January during the first few days one girl has had her eye pierced, another her eye badly scratched…since then fourteen accidents have happened in the clock room and corridors through unguarded pins.' Hat pin protectors were made available for sale at 1*d* each. Still in York, Alex Smith, a worker in the Aero plant fell into an 8ft-deep mixer and narrowly escaped being immersed in a boiling hot torrent of liquid peppermint.

The Temperance movement took cocoa up with gusto, establishing British Workman houses to compete with alcohol-serving public houses; they even published a guide instructing how to set up and run these establishments. So began the association of Quakers with chocolate as famously characterised by Messrs Fry, Cadbury and Rowntree. They

A wonderful Fry advertisement which captures the essence of the early sweet shop and the exchange of pocket money for chocolate.

imitated the sweet makers with their conversation lozenges and dragées carrying patriotic and romantic messages: 'Do you love me?'; 'No, I won't ask Mama', but poured sobering cold water on it all by distributing their sweets with such uncompromising messages as 'Misery, sickness and poverty are the effect of drunkenness'.

In addition to his factory site a further 120 acres had been bought by George Cadbury in 1893 and a ground-breaking, life-changing model village built to 'alleviate the evils of more modern cramped living conditions' – inner city slums in other words. This visionary achievement was inspired by what George witnessed all around him: 'It is not easy to describe or imagine the dreary desolation which acre after acre of the very heart of the town presents…hundreds of leaky, damp, wretched houses, wholly unfit for human habitation.' Within seven years, the new village, named Bournville to capture a modish French flavour, comprised 313 sound, clean and sanitary houses complete with front and back gardens on 330 acres of land. Only initially were the houses intended exclusively for Cadbury employees: the later objective was to provide a village of mixed housing for a wide range of inhabitants and thereby establish a mixed community.

Residents were provided with a booklet laying down rules for keeping houses and gardens in good order, abstaining from alcohol on the Sabbath

"CALL ME FUSSY IF YER LIKE," says Mrs. DEE

Mrs. Dee is dirt's worst enemy. She's one of over two hundred people whose job is to keep the factory spotless. "And you could make chocolates in the *passages*" she boasts, "when I've finished work."

Fixing up the vacuum cleaner.

Vacuum or scrubbing brush, she's a demon for "thoroughness." "Men's worse than children for being untidy," she says, "'ow they'd get on without women to clean up after 'em, I don't know."

Here is the redoubtable Mrs Dee featured in the Cadbury staff magazine, '*dirt's worst enemy*' *who boasts that 'you could make chocolates in the corridor when I've finished work...men's worse than children for being untidy*'.

and the advantages of single beds for married couples. The area was alcohol-free until 1940 with no pubs and no alcohol sold in local shops until a licensed members' bar opened in the Rowheath Pavilion. This abstinence was a reflection of John Cadbury's strict temperance beliefs and a manifestation of his work in social reform, which also included campaigns for workhouse reform, and against industrial pollution, child labour, particularly child chimney sweeps, and animal cruelty. He founded the Animals Friend Society which led to the RSPCA. Cadbury's own research showed that 1 in every 30 houses in Birmingham was given over to the sale of alcohol and that 10 per cent of the city's 6,593 alcoholics died of alcohol-related diseases each year. The many gin shops and gin palaces nevertheless provided a ready supply of replacements for these retail casualties, but John and Candia his wife successfully persisted with their Total Abstinence Plan, counting even the moderate Moderation Society amongst their conquests.

Bournville was truly pioneering in all sorts of ways: socially, environmentally and architecturally in particular, but it also had great influence throughout Europe in areas as diverse as housing, urban planning, community health and local education. Visitors included architects from Krupp's in Germany; Dame Henrietta Barnett who went on to inspire the development of Hampstead Garden Suburb; William Hesketh Lever who founded the garden village of Port Sunlight in 1888, and the Rowntrees who established New Earswick garden village just north of their factory in York.

Cadbury was one of the first companies in the UK to introduce half day holidays, at Bridge Street. Philanthropy and paternalism continued in the workplace with ground-breaking pension schemes, a sick club, medical services, outings, in-service education, staff committees (the Works Councils) and decent wages. George and Richard Cadbury had been fervent believers in the value of education – they both taught at the Birmingham Adult Schools – and this was maintained at Bournville where Continuation Classes were set up in 1913 to provide free further education, during working hours, for younger employees from when they left school and joined Cadbury aged 14, until they were 16, later extended to 18. A wide range of apprenticeships were established for the boys and a sewing club for the girls. Employees were, as a matter of course, treated with respect. The Works Councils, segregated until 1964, worked in concert with the trades unions which had also always been encouraged;

the councils were made up of management and shop floor representatives and were primarily responsible for the company's welfare schemes.

In common with other factories of the time male and female workers were segregated with separate entrances, working, rest and dining areas and, as noted, Works Councils. Technicians going in to women's areas of the factory had to wear armbands showing that they had obtained permission to be there. Married women were not employed and betrothed girls had to leave on marriage – but not before they were presented with a bible and a carnation and a talk from one of the directors. It wasn't until the shortage of male workers caused by the Second World War that married women began to be kept on or recruited. During the Second World war, manpower shortages became critical as men joined up: at Cadbury alone 1,700 out of 3,000 men enlisted in the army and navy (218 did not return) with another 700 seconded to munitions work. German submarines blockaded the British Isles, forcing the government to ensure essential foods such as milk and cocoa were in good supply; this helped the chocolate companies.

Social and recreational facilities were a vital part of the Cadbury community: land was bought at Rowheath for football and hockey pitches and a running track; the pavilion opened in 1924 not just as a clubhouse and changing facility for the sportsmen and women, but also as a social venue for dinners and dances. In addition there were bowling greens, a fishing lake and an outdoor lido. An indoor swimming pool was built in Bournville Lane; a boating lake and the cricket pitch, made famous on the Milk Tray boxes, followed – all the sports facilities were free of charge. The Bournville Village Trust, set up in 1900, looked after, amongst other things, the primary and junior school, the School of Art and the Day Continuation School.

Up in York, meanwhile, on the social welfare side, Joseph Rowntree emulated the Cadburys by establishing the Joseph Rowntree Trust and beginning the building of New Earswick, a new and attractive garden village, at the turn of the century. The objective was to provide the worker of even the most modest means with a new type of house that was clean, sanitary and efficient. Rowntree's deep concern for the welfare of his workers, his research findings and those of his son, Seebohm, into the plight of the urban poor, his Quaker beliefs, Cadbury's achievements at Bournville and the pioneering work on garden cities by Ebenezer Howard all combined to drive the establishment of New Earswick just minutes away from the Haxby Road factory.

Chapter 11

The Quaker Triumvirate

Cadbury's of Bournville

The Cadbury story starts in 1824 with John Cadbury, son of a rich Quaker, selling non-alcoholic beverages – tea, coffee and sixteen varieties of drinking chocolate – at 93 Bull Street, Birmingham after an apprenticeship in London at the Sanderson, Fox and Company teahouse. Bull Street featured an eye-catching window filled with Chinese vases and figures and, most strikingly, a Chinese shop assistant, decked out in full Chinese costume, hired to serve behind the counter. Soon after, Cadbury moved to a former malt house in Crooked Lane (where he perfected techniques of cacao-bean grinding to produce cocoa) and then to a factory in Bridge Street. John's brother Benjamin joined and the company became known as Cadbury Brothers of Birmingham. With an office in London and a Royal Warrant under their belt the business benefited from the 1853 tax reduction on cocoa enabling them to reduce retail prices and thus bring cocoa powder to a much wider market. As a consequence the sale of tea was abandoned in 1849 and left to nephew Richard Barrow Cadbury.

John Cadbury's sons, Richard and George, took over the fledgling business in 1861 – with about ten employees and not at all successful. Competition was intense from Rowntree's, Fry's and companies like Taylors in Spitalfields – manufacturers of more than fifty brands of cocoa and mustard; and Dunn and Hewett of Pentonville who sold chocolate sticks and Patent Lentilised Chocolate (made from lentils, tapioca, sago or dried peas) and the unpromising sounding 'Plain Chocolate Sold in Drab Paper'. Richard had joined their father soon after leaving school in 1851, while George followed in 1857 after a three-year apprenticeship with Rowntree's grocery business in Pavement in York. The rules of the shop there were uncompromising and set out in a memorandum written by Joseph Rowntree Snr:

The object of the Pavement establishment is business. The young men who enter it…are expected to contribute…in making it successful… it affords a full opportunity for any painstaking, intelligent young man to obtain a good practical acquaintance with the tea and grocery trades…the place is not suitable for the indolent and wayward.

The 1862 Cadbury catalogue featured such brands as Chocolat du Mexique, Crystal Palace Chocolate, Dietetic Cocoa, Trinidad Rock Cocoa and Churchman's Cocoa. Cadbury produced the first chocolate box in 1868, full of chocolates and featuring a picture on the lid, of Richard's daughter Jessica holding a kitten. Around the same time, the firm produced the first Valentine's Day chocolate assortment. Their first salesman was the top-hatted and punctilious Dixon Hadaway. Travellers' samples were tasted by the trade, and a pledge system was set up at the factory whereby a penny was awarded to any worker who had not succumbed to the temptation of helping him or herself to the manufactured product during the week.

By 1878, it was becoming increasingly urgent to find a factory site which facilitated the importation of cocoa and milk; the 14.5 acre Georgian Bournbrook Hall and Estate 5 miles south of the city centre fitted the bill with its easy access to the Birmingham West Suburban Railway and the Worcester and Birmingham Canal. This was duly purchased and Bournville, with its French (and therefore fashionable) overtones was adopted as the name for the site for the opening in 1879. Cadbury had a fleet of barges working the canal, in Cadbury livery, and was the first company to use powered canal boats. By the turn of the century, sidings had been built to link the factory with the national railway network and Cadbury rolling stock was being manufactured. Horse-drawn vans were the earliest mode of road transport. In the 1920s, the factory was reconstructed and the site expanded to cope with demand and new production techniques. Until the 1960s, all the affiliated crafts and trades required to run a chocolate manufacturing plant were carried out on site – these included the manufacture of boxes, cartons and tin cans, machine-making, sheet metal production, printing, joinery, advertising and marketing.

Meanwhile, back on the production line things were not going well, that is until George's 1866 visit to van Houten in the Netherlands to acquire a press; this visit was pivotal and eventually led the way for a company on the verge of failure to the successful company it soon became. Eschewing Quaker reservations about advertising, the Cadburys set about gaining medical testimonials and establishing the health-giving credentials of their products – no doubt with an eye on the soap manufacturers Pears' pioneering work in slogans and eye-catching posters featuring glamorous women, and children exuding healthiness. Both the *British Medical Journal* and the *Lancet* lent their approval to Cocoa Essence when it was launched in late 1866, the former asserting it to be 'one of the most nutritious, digestible and restorative drinks'. *Grocer* magazine joined in the praise, emphasising the absence of adulteration. The advertising campaign devised to capitalise on these endorsements featured the slogan 'Absolutely Pure, Therefore Best. No Chemicals Used'. The early 1870s saw the launch of the exotic and luxurious, decidedly un-Quakerly French-influenced Fancy Box, complete with silk lining and mirror – the *Chemist & Druggist* described it as 'Divine. The most exquisite chocolate ever to come under our notice.' Easter eggs were introduced in 1875 and Cadbury Fingers in 1897.

The renowned chocolatier Frederic Kinchelman joined the company, bringing with him his successful recipes and production techniques for Nougat-Dragées, Paté Duchesse and Avelines. One of its new brands was named The Model Parish Cocoa in anticipation of the model village to be built at Bournville. Another was Iceland Moss which contained lichen – believed to be highly nutritious – and launched with an early instance of the Cadbury's enthusiasm for advertising and branding: bright yellow packaging with black typography, and a reindeer. Taking the fight to the enemy they opened a shop in Paris and sales outposts were established in Ireland, Canada, Chile and Australasia.

The new technology and expertise in recipes led to the successful and revolutionary production of chocolate bars and, in 1898, *milk* chocolate bars made by Daniel Peter's powdered-milk technique, soon to be replaced in 1905 with fresh milk. This manifested itself in Cadbury's Dairy Milk – a successful challenge to the popular Swiss milk chocolate bars. The original plan was to call it Dairy Maid, but the name was changed at the last minute after the daughter of a customer in Plymouth happened to remark that Dairy Milk was a 'much daintier name'. Bournville Cocoa was launched a year later.

From 1905, the roll call of new Cadbury chocolate products is nothing short of breathtaking. Dairy Milk on its launch contained more milk than any other chocolate bar ('a glass and a half of fresh milk') and became the top-selling brand by 1913. Cadbury had overtaken Fry as the biggest UK manufacturer in 1910 with sales of £1,670,221 compared with Fry's £1,642.715 and Rowntree's £1,200,598. Milk Tray made its debut in 1915 – originally presented in open boxes on wooden trays (hence the name) and Flake, made from folds of milk chocolate, was introduced in 1920: 'the crumbliest, flakiest milk chocolate in the world'. Milk Tray packaging has changed almost imperceptibly over the last 106 years and still sells over 8 million boxes every year.

As we have seen, in 1918 Cadbury merged with Fry, overseen by the British Cocoa and Chocolate Company to ensure the survival of both companies' identities and brands. In the 1920s, the factory was reconstructed and the site expanded to cope with demand. New products and new mass-production techniques were also developed at the Fry's Somerdale plant. The familiar purple packaging was introduced on Dairy Milk in 1920, chosen to reflect the noble connotations of the colour, which was reminiscent and emblematic of the Roman senatorial classes and the emperors. The famous Cadbury signature started life in 1921.

Creme Eggs came in 1923 – today 66,000 eggs are 'laid' every hour; Crunchie and Fruit & Nut arrived in 1929 – Crunchies were turned out at the rate of 5mph at the Somerdale factory; Whole Nut hit the market in 1933 when Cadbury's became the biggest selling chocolate company in Britain. Cadbury's Roses Selection arrived in 1938 with its distinctive 'Dorothy Bag' carton; annual production today exceeds 13,000 tonnes.

Cadbury's, in the face of all the austerity of the 1940s and 1950s, launched Fudge in 1949. To meet the surge in demand for confectionery after 1953 and the end of rationing, more factory space was needed at Cadbury, and the move away from selling biscuits loose in tins to packets – triggered by self-service shops, meant that for Cadbury a new factory was opened on 17 September 1954 at Moreton on the Wirral to turn out 3 million chocolate biscuits every day; Somerdale was extended in 1958 to cater for Picnic. Cadbury's Buttons came in 1960 followed by Bar Six to compete with KitKat. The launch of Aztec in 1967 was the most significant event of the post-war period. Aimed squarely at the Mars Bar market it benefited from a merchandising campaign that included in store displays in over 100,000 shops and a TV ad campaign filmed on the steps of the Aztec temples in Teotihuacan, no less. The anomalies involved in both Fry and Cadbury representatives calling on shops and fighting each other for display space were ended in 1967 when the two companies formed a full merger.

In 1969, Cadbury joined up with Schweppes – a firm founded in Geneva in 1783 by Jean Jacob Schweppe who had perfected a method of carbonating water. This was despite Cadbury's reservations about Schweppes' association with alcohol (their drinks were used as mixers) and the impact this would have on the Quakers' temperance – one of the original *raison d'etres* for cocoa manufacture and promotion in the previous century. Curly Wurly, Double Decker, Star Bar and Caramel were next to come off the production lines. In 1978, Chunky Dairy Milk was developed to counter Rowntree's highly successful Yorkie. In 1981, Wispa (codename P46) was successfully launched as a competitor to Aero, tactically withdrawn and then relaunched in 1983, backed by Cadbury's biggest ever campaign. The size of Wispa's bubbles are controlled to within 0.2–0.3mm and the specially designed £12 million plant, constructed in great secrecy, produces 1,680 bars per minute.

In 1988, Cadbury purchased first the Lion Confectionery Company of Cleckheaton, West Yorkshire (famous for Midget Gems) and then Trebor Bassett, which led to the development of Cadbury's Mini Cream Egg – 700 million of which are laid each year.

Fry's of Bristol

We have seen how Fry's was at the forefront of developments in chocolate production in England in the eighteenth and nineteenth centuries. It started in 1728 with Walter Churchman's shop and the granting of Letters Patent from George II. Seven monarchs subsequently appointed Fry's to the Royal Household as cocoa and chocolate manufacturers. It accelerated in 1761 when Joseph Fry, a Quaker physician – entrepreneur, industrialist and businessman *par excellence* – with John Vaughan – bought Walter Churchman's chocolate business which then became Fry, Vaughan & Co. The coffee and chocolate houses in nearby fashionable Bath soon became a lucrative cocoa market. At the same time, they acquired patent rights and recipes for the manufacture of drinking chocolate. The company moved in 1777 from Newgate Street to upmarket Union Street to tap the wealthy clientele strolling there; two years later, on Joseph's death, Anna Fry took over and renamed the company Anna Fry & Son. That son was Joseph Storrs Fry who was in charge from 1795; it was he who industrialised and revolutionised chocolate manufacture when he introduced the Watt steam engine into the manufacturing process. On Anna's death in 1803, a Dr Hunt joined the company thus leading to another rebadging as Fry & Hunt; on Hunt's retirement Joseph Storr's sons (Joseph II, Francis and Richard) became partners and the company was renamed J. S. Fry & Sons – by then England's largest chocolate producer. In 1835, Fry's was using 40 per cent of the cocoa imported into Britain with sales of £12,000 per annum.

Up until 1853 it was French chocolate that enjoyed the best reputation in Britain and the belief was that anything British simply could not compete. But then Fry's produced its Cream Stick – the first chocolate confectionery to be produced on an industrial scale. Hitherto chocolate had been a luxury beyond the budgets of most people, but this was a 'value for money bar'. The popularity of French chocolate receded to the extent that Fry's even received a *brevet* appointing the company as manufacturers of cocoa and chocolate to the Imperial House of Napoleon III.

So, having mechanised chocolate production with steam power, and pioneering eating chocolate in 1847, Fry's can claim another first when in 1866 it started production of the direct descendant of Fry's Cream Stick, Fry's Chocolate Cream – a fondant cream-filled chocolate bar which was remoulded in 1875 to the shape it still has today. In 1902, Fry's Milk Chocolate was launched – later rechristened Fry's Five Boys. Orange Cream and Peppermint Cream followed with Fry's Five Centre in 1934 (orange, raspberry, lime, strawberry and pineapple). Output of the cream bar exceeded half a million units per day at one point; the iconic foil wrapping and blue label came in 1925.

Chocolate Cream was the first of many 'Specialties of the House', to be followed by Crunchie; Punch (which came in four flavours: Full Cream, Milk Chocolate, Delicious Caramel and Milky Fudge – output was millions per month); Caramets – produced in a pack 'ideal for both pocket and handbag'; Crunch Block; Turkish delight 'exquisitely flavoured with genuine Otto of Roses'; Five Boys: the iconic label featured sequential expressions ranging from Desperation, Pacification, Expectation, Acclamation and Realisation.

In 1868, Fry's highly decorated chocolate boxes were launched, full of assorted chocolates: very popular at Christmas and sporting a vast array

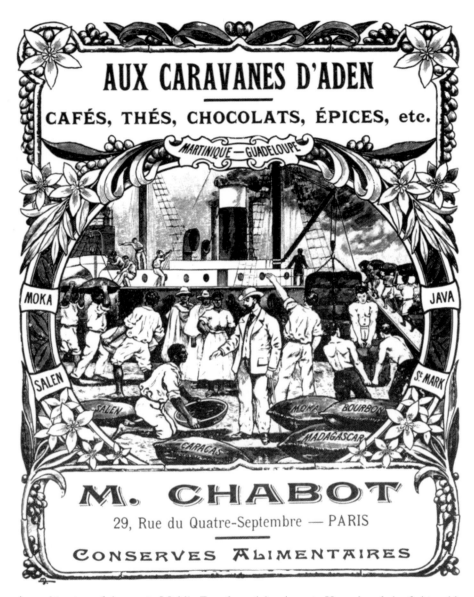

A combination of the exotic Middle East from Aden (now in Yemen) and the fashionable French was provided in this intriguing advertisement for M. Chabot, Parisienne confectioners.

of different coloured designs. The most sought after were double Milk Assortment: eleven different chocolates with a double milk chocolate coating; Sandwich Assortment: separated layers of milk and dark chocolate in one block; Silver Lining Assortment: this contained Cherry in Fondant; Hazelnut Fudge and Fruit Nougatine. Market research was an important facet of Fry's marketing right from the start: the colour of the cups for these chocolates was chosen by 85 per cent of respondents. The chocolate assortment was boosted in 1913 by Jules Sechaud who invented the technology for making moulded chocolate shells into which the fondant could be poured.

By the 1870s, Fry's could boast 220 different products, including the first British Easter egg in 1873; in 1902 it launched its first milk chocolate bar, five years after Cadbury's; the popular and enduring Fry's Turkish Bar came in 1914. In 1910, Fry's supported Captain Scott's expedition to the Antarctica with a £1,000 donation, an early shrewd marketing move which elicited the following testimonial from Captain Scott: 'Messrs. J.S. Fry and Sons supplied our Cocoa, sledging and fancy chocolate, delicious comforts excellently packed and always in good condition…Crunching those elaborate chocolates brought one nearer to civilisation than anything we experienced sledging.'

In the years leading up to the First World War, Fry's suffered badly from a lack of investment and its reputation suffered as a result. In 1918, as noted, the company merged with Cadbury, overseen by The British Cocoa and Chocolate Company to ensure the survival of both companies' identities and brands; Cadbury's value had been assessed as three times that of Fry's so illustrating very clearly the relative strengths of the two companies. Egbert (Bertie) Cadbury joined the Fry part of the business and he and Cecil Fry engineered the move to a purpose built factory on 222 rural acres in Somerdale, Keynsham in 1923, in between the River Avon and the London-Bristol main line. Both companies retained their individual identities, marketing and branding of products. The 1920s saw the development of mass production – the mechanised production of fewer brands at lower costs. The new factory allowed them to do this successfully. Somerdale had its own power station, and a railway station serving a siding linked to the Great Western Railway line.

The move from Union Street was a gradual affair lasting twelve years until 1934, when 6,000 women and men were on the payroll. The factory itself was set in parkland with poplar and chestnut trees, flower beds and lawns. *Fry's of Bristol*, an early corporate booklet, tells us that 'The Cocoa department looks on to woodland slopes and sunlit meadows', giving us a flavour of the bucolic setting of Somerdale.

Another early booklet, *Into the Open Country*, gives the company's mission statement and an insight into the corporate ethos back then:

An eye-catching Fry's advertisement.

'Fry's have kept before them two guiding principles; one, giving the public the best possible value in cocoa and chocolate manufactured under the best possible conditions; the other, of giving the workpeople the best facilities for recreation and happiness.' However, this extract from the Fry Bicentenary Number – patronisingly and offensively by today's standards – describes the radical changes which were taking place though:

> the sweeping changes which took place in the Offices ... made it necessary for the Firm not only to retain the ladies they had but to engage a large number of others. And so Eve came to our offices ... at first we were inclined not to take her very seriously. We thought that after a few days' steady work Eve would be probably knocked up and absent with an attack of hysteria, the megrims or the vapours. Eve had nothing of the sort. She did her work well and kept on doing it ... her smile, her shingle and her stockings, have caused the commercial desert to blossom as the rose.

Rowntree's of York

The Rowntree story starts with the tenacious, enterprising and Quaker Mary Tuke. In 1725, age 30, Mary opened a grocery business first in Walmgate, then Castlegate, and, after a number of legal wrangles with the exclusive and intransigent York Merchant Adventurers Company, finally won the right to trade as a grocer in 1732. Her nephew William joined the firm in 1746 and inherited the business, now specialising in the sale of coffee, chicory and drinking chocolate, on Mary's death in 1752. His son Henry came on board in 1785 and they began to sell tea and to manufacture cocoa and chocolate themselves.

Henry's grandson, Samuel Tuke, was a good friend of fellow Quaker Joseph Rowntree I, and was related to him through marriage; we have seen that Joseph, too, ran a grocer's shop, in Pavement. Samuel's sons, meanwhile, were more interested in banking and teamed up with their relatives the Barclays; they had no interest in the York cocoa business.

In July 1862, Joseph's son, Henry Isaac Rowntree, who had served his apprenticeship both at the family shop in Pavement and at Tuke's, made one of the most prescient and significant decisions in British industrial history when he bought the Tukes' business. The firm was small, with twelve staff and sales of about £3,000 – 10 per cent of Cadbury sales and 5 per cent of Fry sales at the time. The best-performing brand was Tukes's Superior Cocoa, later to become Rowntree's Prize Medal Rock Cocoa.

Henry relocated the firm to an old foundry at Tanner's Moat in 1864. However, the combination of Henry's preoccupation with his Quaker activities, old technology and short run manufacturing techniques stifled any real progress; in short, the business was soon ailing. Help was at hand, though: in 1869 he was joined by his brother, Joseph Rowntree II, and the firm H. I. Rowntree & Co was established. Joseph injected much-needed business sense by focusing on the financial and sales side, leaving manufacturing to Henry; in effect he probably saved the 'hopelessly embarrassed' company from (a very un-Quakerly) bankruptcy, bailing out a brother who 'knew next to nothing of the business'.

The Claude Gaget Effect

A routine sales call by Claude Gaget in 1879 had a major impact on Rowntree's. Gaget was working for Compagnie Française, Parisian confectioners, in London. The samples of gums and pastilles he presented that day eventually led to Rowntree's manufacture, in 1881 (but only when the product was perfected and of the highest quality), of their famous Crystallised Gum Pastilles. An immediate success, sales of the pastilles galvanised the company and they expanded into nearby North Street. By 1885, 4 tons were being produced weekly. Staff numbers increased to 182 in 1883 and sales more than doubled from 1880 (£44,000) to 1889 (£99,000); net profits increased five-fold from around £372 in 1879 to £1,649 in 1889. These sweets were of course the precursors of Rowntree's famous Fruit Gums and Fruit Pastilles.

This success also enabled Joseph to invest in new machinery in 1880, notably a van Houten press for the production in York of cocoa essence – Rowntree's Elect, 'more than a drink, a food' and made from top quality cocoa. Overall output remained low. Notwithstanding, Joseph bought a 20-acre site on Haxby Road in 1890 for a more efficient and ergonomic factory which would enable the firm to meet the anticipated growing demand for their products. The factory had its own railway line and halt, and by 1898 all production was on the new site; the number of employees in 1884 was 182, by 1899 this had rocketed to 1,613.

It was the appointment and rise of sales manager, marketing director and future chairman George Harris, a friend of Forrest Mars, which began to make a real difference. Harris' experience of American marketing methods, product development, branding and advertising eventually led to the change from a conservative, production-led company to a market-driven one, ultimately resulting in the launch of KitKat, Black Magic, Aero, Dairy Box, Smarties and Polo in the 1930s. It was Aero, an aerated rather than a solid chocolate, which provided Rowntree's first real success, in 1935. Aero was originally to be called Airways to reflect the increase in jet travel in the 1930s; in the end it was branded Aero, a name originally registered with Cadbury, but transferred over to Rowntree. Aero soon started to eat into the massively successful Cadbury Dairy Milk's market share.

March 1902 saw the publication of the inaugural issue of the *Cocoa Works Magazine*, or *CWM*; the final issue was in May 1986. For eighty-four years it provided an intriguing and detailed record of life at Rowntree from the board to the shop floor. Subtitled *A Journal in the Interest of the Employees of Rowntree & Co Ltd, York*, its purpose was to keep everyone informed about what was going on at all levels.

At Rowntree's, Munchies were reintroduced; the Fawdon factory, Newcastle, opened in 1958 and in 1959 Caramac was launched. Nux

A Rowntree traveller selling into a sweetshop in the 1950s.

was brought to market in 1959, but lost the battle against Fry's Picnic. Peppermint, and orange Aeros came in 1959 and 1960 respectively. In 1962 After Eight was launched, with its apparently sophisticated dinner party market, followed by Toffee Crisp a year later. Motoring Bar was renamed Fruit and Nut in 1963, but could not compete with its namesake down at Cadbury and was scrapped in 1965. In 1967 Golden Cup was introduced and Matchmakers in 1968, before Rowntrees acquired Chocolat Menier in 1969.

Rowntree merged with Mackintosh in 1969, bringing such famous brands as Rolo, Toffee Crisp, Toffo, Weekend and Quality Street to the fold. Aimed at, unusually, the male market rather than the traditional female market, Yorkie was launched in 1976 to compete with Cadbury's Dairy Milk and to meet the demand for a chunkier alternative to the much thinner Dairy Milk bars. Yorkie, despite, or because of, its unashamedly sexist marketing, was soon a major success with sales of 13,000 tons by 1978.

KitKat though continued to dominate. A corporate advertisement in 1987 asserted that enough KitKats were produced every hour to reach to the top of the Empire State Building four times over, and 30 million KitKats were sold in 100 countries every week. In 1988, Rowntree Mackintosh was the world's fourth largest confectionery manufacturer after Hershey, Mars and Cadbury; turnover was £1.4 billion in 25 subsidiaries with 33,000 employees. A takeover bid by Jacobs Suchard in 1988 failed (Suchard had already acquired Cote d'Or and van Houten), but that same year Rowntree Mackintosh was acquired by Nestlé, despite unsuccessful attempts by Cadbury to keep Rowntree British by appealing to the Department of Trade & Industry to relax competition rules and allow them to acquire Rowntree Mackintosh.

A 1950s Rowntree advert.

Chapter 12

Chocolate Manufacturers in the United Kingdom

Bendicks, Winchester

Bendicks is a chocolate brand currently owned by August Storck KG and famed for its 'quintessentially British' Bittermints: dark mint chocolates, still manufactured to the original 1931 recipe and the ultimate posh chocolate.

In 1930, Oscar Benson and Colonel 'Bertie' Dickson bought a small confectionery business at 164 Church Street in Kensington, London, making the chocolates in a tiny basement below the shop. They used the first syllable of each of their surnames to arrive at the name Bendicks.

The flagship Bittermints were the happy combination of two unpalatable ingredients: in 1931, Benson's sister-in-law, Lucia Benson, produced a dark chocolate so bitter that it was virtually inedible on its own, so she mixed it with a mint fondant that was so strongly flavoured with mint oil that it was too was a struggle to eat on its own. When she combined these two troublesome constituents she hit on a winning recipe which resulted in a very palatable chocolate and named it Bendicks Bittermints. The chocolate coating contains 95 per cent cocoa solids.

By 1933, Bendicks had won a reputation for quality and a new store opened in the heart of London's Mayfair. In 1946, the business was sold to Edgar Lawley and by 1952 Bendicks had moved to Winchester in a building from 1890 which had been used as The Winchester Temperance Billiards Hall. The firm acquired William Cox & Son, manufacturers of Royal Winchester Chocolates.

Though expensive, the products were all made with the highest quality ingredients. The main chocolate-coated confectionery products were all hand dipped, giving a much thicker layer of chocolate. The company also produced nougat and chocolate bars.

Since 1988, Bendicks has been a subsidiary of the German sweet producer, August Storck founded in 1903 and headquartered in Berlin.

A. J. Caley & Sons Ltd, Norwich

Caley was originally a manufacturer of mineral waters founded in 1863; its entry into the confectionery market was a strategic move to balance out the seasonal water market. In 1857, Albert Jarman Caley opened a chemist's business in London Street, Norwich; in 1883 he started manufacturing drinking chocolate as a winter drink as part of his product-balancing act, followed in 1886 by eating chocolate, all made at the Fleur-de-Lys factory. In 1898, Christmas cracker manufacture began, to keep the girls who wrapped and decorated the chocolate boxes busy all year round; A.J. Caley & Sons Ltd was formed at this time. In 1918, the African and Eastern Trade Corporation – a Liverpool company with interests in a number of African colonies – bought Caley; it later became a Unilever subsidiary.

In 1932, John Mackintosh & Sons Ltd of Halifax paid £138,000 for Caley, although the Caley's brand name continued to be used until the early 1960s. In 1935, mineral water production dried up; in 1936, Double Six was successfully launched – a chocolate bar filled with six different centres. The public's response was described by Eric Mackintosh as 'a little frightening'. Miners' wives in South Wales were giving their husbands Double Six sandwiches in their pack-ups. Marketing was excellent with some of the wonderful Caley advertisements and posters drawn by Sir Alfred Mullins.

The Second World War saw the first production of sustaining 'cocoa rich' Milk Marching Chocolate. In 1942, Caley's factory was destroyed by the Luftwaffe in the Baedeker Raid; Eric Mackintosh described the scene: 'a smouldering, smelling, twisted jumble of steel and concrete… [watched] by a crowd of tired, dirty, heart-broken colleagues…a thousand or so employees stood around, dazed and unable to believe their eyes'.

The factory reopened after rebuilding work in 1956; production of Caley lines had been moved to Halifax in the interim. Mackintosh merged with Rowntree in 1969 to form Rowntree Mackintosh. Norwich took on production of Weekend, Good News, Rolo, Munchies, Mintola, Caramac, Golden Cup and Easter eggs, and, paradoxically, Yorkie. The Norwich factory closed in 1994; in 1996, three former executives acquired Caley's brands and production equipment from Nestlé and formed Caley's of Norwich Ltd. In 1997, Caley's Plain Marching Chocolate was relaunched and in 1998 Caley's Milk Marching Chocolate was reintroduced. In 2002, a Caley's Cocoa Cafe opened in Norwich Guildhall while the company started working with Fair Trade and Help for Heroes.

W. & M. Duncan and Company, Edinburgh

W & M Duncan and Company, better known as 'Duncan's of Edinburgh', was a Scottish confectioner whose most popular and enduring product was the Walnut Whip, launched in 1910 and now manufactured by Nestlé Rowntree.

Mary Duncan started if off when, with her son William, she established a cake business in Dundee in 1861. In 1884 the company moved to Edinburgh, and started making chocolate confectionery moving in 1896 to the Regent Confectionery Works in Beaverhall Road, Edinburgh.

The business was acquired by Rowntree in 1947. Rowntree closed the factory in 1987, but it was reopened immediately by new owners trading as 'Duncan's of Scotland'. By 1987, the new Duncan's business moved to Bellshill, Lanarkshire, and passed through several owners before becoming part of J. E. Wilson & Sons (Kendal).

Terry's of York

As we have already described, Joseph Terry started making cocoa and chocolate in 1886 and had become the market leader of chocolate assortments by the end of the 1920s.

Terry's wasted no time in going national; by 1840 their products were reaching seventy-five towns all over England. They included candied eringo, coltsfoot rock, gum balls, and lozenges made from squill, camphor and horehound. Apart from boiled sweets, production included marmalade, marzipan, mushroom ketchup and calves' jelly. Conversation Lozenges, precursors of Love Hearts, with risqué slogans such as 'Can you polka?', 'I want a wife', 'Do you love me?' and 'How do you flirt?' were particularly popular.

When he died in 1850, Joseph left the business to his son, Joseph Junior, then aged 22. In 1864, Joseph leased a riverside factory at Clementhorpe on the River Ouse. St Helen's Square was retained and converted into a shop, ballroom and restaurant; you can still see the Terry name on the building's façade. Joseph Jnr died in 1898 and was succeeded by his sons

Thomas Walker Leaper Terry and Frank Terry. The famous Neapolitans brand was launched in 1899.

In 1926, the company moved again to the purpose-built Chocolate Works in Bishopthorpe Road. Between the years 1918 and 1938, revenues doubled as did tonnage sold rising from 2,332 tons in 1925 to 4,836. Employees stood at 2,500 in 1937, 60 per cent of whom were women. These increases were due in part to the launch in 1932 of All Gold and Chocolate Orange. Up to the Second World War, Theatre Chocolates were available with their unique rustle-proof wrappers.

By an amazing act of metamorphosis, Chocolate Orange started life as Chocolate Apple (phased out in 1954) and before that the equally unsuccessful Chocolate Lemon in 1979; 1 in 10 Christmas stockings reputedly contained a Terry's Chocolate Orange at one time.

A replica Terry's chocolate shop was opened in the Castle Museum in York in the 1950s. The Forte Group bought Terry's in 1963; Forte already owned the Hammersmith-based Fullers confectioners and cake manufacturers. The then Lord Mayor, Mona Armitage, questioned whether Terry's had been fortified or Forte had been terrified. Another takeover by Colgate Palmolive in 1978 was soon followed by another by United Biscuits in the early 1980s. In 1980 the elegant restaurant in St Helen's Square closed after 150 years.

In the 1990s annual sales of All Gold were seven million boxes; All Gold revenue was £11 million in 1981, doubling by 1990. At its zenith Terry was selling 23,000 tons of chocolate, 56 million Chocolate Oranges and Easter eggs weighing 650 tons. Moments were launched in 1991 with a new £7m moulding plant.

The company was taken over by Kraft in 2003; for the time being chocolate stayed in York with sugar confectionery concentrated in Bridgend. In 2004 Kraft made 6,000 redundancies across all of their operations. Terry's York closure was announced with the loss of 316 jobs. When the factory closed in 2005, over 400 objects including photographs, packaging, catalogues and chocolates were donated to the Castle Museum.

Lazenby & Son (York) Ltd and Backhouse & Marb

When we think of York's rich chocolate and confectionery history we automatically think of Rowntree, Terry and Craven. However, there were others: York Confectionery Company was run by a man called Henderson who suffered from dyspnoea, laboured breathing, and thereby won for his firm the nickname 'Puffy's'. Puffy started in Fossgate in 1867 before moving to Fenwick Street just off Bishopthorpe Road; he did a good line in candied peel and mint rock which was all the rage and shipped out to seaside resorts around the country. The firm finally ran out of breath in 1909 and Henderson was declared bankrupt. When chocolate became readily available, candied peel lost its popularity.

Nunthorpe Peel Works was the name of the factory. When production ended, the site was used as a storage warehouse for some years. It is now in residential use.

The *York Herald* of 10 June 1876 reported a fire at the Nunthorpe Peel Works. This gives us a description of the premises, as follows:

> The works... consist of three large blocks of buildings running parallel with each other, and contain lemon peel, bags of sugar, sweets, and confectionery of almost every description. It was in the centre block of buildings, known as the lemon peel and lozenge departments, at one end of which are a couple of inhabited cottages belonging to Mr Keswick builder, and at the other the offices of the [York Confectionery] Company.

By the time that the fire was extinguished 'nothing but the bare and blackened walls of the building remaining. Several tons of lemon peel, lozenges, sugar, etc., were destroyed.'

Cook's York Directory of 1900 lists some of York's main cocoa and chocolate manufacturers. Not only are the usual suspects there but we also discover H. Backhouse & Co. of Clementhorpe.

Herbert Backhouse and his colleague, who delighted in the wonderful name of Xavier Marb, ran the Criterion Cocoa Works on Walmgate with a subsidiary business in Ogleforth. They ran these operations until around 1900, trading as Backhouse & Marb, when they went into liquidation. Parts of the business continued as separate entities including 'Backhouses' of River Street, Clementhorpe, which survived until 1935, when it too was liquidated.

Backhouse & Marb was mentioned in the local press down the years:

- *Yorkshire Post,* 14 November 1900 wanted – 'An experienced moulder, H. Backhouse & Co., Clementhorpe'.

- *Yorkshire Evening Post,* 27 October 1899 wanted – 'Experienced starch hand well up in fondants, creams and chocolate centres. H. Backhouse and Co., Clementhorpe'.
- *Leeds Mercury,* 27 September 1898 described a meeting of creditors of Backhouse and Marb, listing all the known liabilities and assets.
- The *Manchester Evening News* of 22 January 1901 ran an advertisement for staff placed by H. Backhouse and Co. The company was looking for skilled chocolate moulders.

The 1914 edition of *Who's Who in Business* included the following entry:

'Backhouse, H. & Company Limited. Chocolate Manufacturers, Clementhorpe, York. Hours of Business: 8 a.m. to 6 p.m.; Saturdays 8 a.m. to 12.30 p.m. Established in 1899 by H. Backhouse, the present Managing Director. Incorporated as a Private Limited Company in 1911. Speciality: Fine Chocolate.'

The *Yorkshire Post and Leeds Intelligencer* of 24 November 1930 had an advertisement for sales representatives at Backhouse and Co. Ltd's chocolate and toffee house. Applicants needed to demonstrate good connections, and preferably to own a car. Payment would be by commission only.

The *Yorkshire Post and Leeds Intelligencer* of 18 June 1934 featured an advertisement for Backhouse's chocolate and fruit dessert 'only the purest ingredients.'

The *Leeds Mercury* of 18 June 1934 had an advertisement which read:

'Backhouses Chocolate Fruit Dessert 4d Per Qr. The MOST DELICIOUS SWEETMEAT YOU CAN BUY. Delicious fruit jellies with real fruit flavours covered with that rich, smooth chocolate for which BACKHOUSES have been famous since 1898. Only the best and purest ingredients are used for all BACKHOUSE lines…Backhouses Ltd., Makers of Good Chocolate since 1839.'

On 23 February 1935 the *Yorkshire Post and Leeds Intelligencer* reported the liquidation and sale of Backhouses Ltd. of River Street. The same edition contained a notice announcing the sale by public auction of the

Backhouse premises in River Street, Clementhorpe. The sale included all manner of chocolate making machinery and equipment.

The owner, Herbert E. P. Backhouse was born in Ilfracombe, North Devon, in 1865. He lived at 110 Bishopthorpe Road in 1911, but by 1939 he was retired and living at Pine Crest, 100 Acomb Road with his wife Florence. He was then described as a retired cocoa and chocolate manufacturer. He died in 1950. The house still stands, opposite the Mormon Church.

And then there was Lazenby & Son (York) Ltd on the Hull Road which, despite the 200 employees on its books, seems to have vanished into a black hole in industrial and York history generally.

In the early 1900s, Percy Lazenby set up as a 50:50 partner with Harold Needler in Hull; however, Needler ploughed more equity into the business and so a financially diluted Percy left and the business became part of Needler's. Percy's appointment in 1915, as Head of the Chocolate Department, had coincided with Needler's decision to invest in and expand chocolate confectionery to complement the lower margin sugar confectionery already up and running.

According to Raymond Needler in his definitive *Needlers of Hull* (1993), the minute book of February 1915 tells how Percy had been headhunted from Carson's Chocolates and Confectionery Ltd of Shortwood near Bristol. They were originally a Glasgow firm which had been bought by Packer's of Bristol in 1912 with a share capital of £50,000. Trading at the highest end of the chocolate market, Carson's had been the first company to introduce tray chocolates. In the early 1960s Carson's became famous as Britain's biggest producers of chocolate liqueurs. H.J. Packer's was established in 1881 by Edward Packer (1848–87), a Quaker and a former employee of Fry's. Packer's focused on products for the cheaper end of the market; they headed upmarket, though, in 1912 with a new subsidiary company, Charles Bond Ltd based in London. The new range was an instant success, and Charles Bond, or Bonds', survived until the 1960s.

In 1927, Percy moved on to York where he built his own factory on the Hull Road, 'The Works', and established his own chocolate manufacturing company, complete with all the modern machinery, including massive conches. A conche is a surface-scraping mixer and agitator that evenly distributes cocoa butter within chocolate; it also enhances flavour development through frictional heat, release of volatiles and acids, and oxidation. The conche is named after the shell whose shape it resembles. Richard Lazenby joined his father in the early 1940s, along with Lottie Lazenby as directors.

At its height, Lazenby employed 200 or so people. It produced couverture for food and biscuit makers. Couverture is chocolate made with extra cocoa butter to give a high gloss. The company also went under the name of Ellanson Couverture. Contracts were won with Carrs, MacFarlanes, Foxes, Huntley & Palmers and Craven's as well as supplying liquid couverture to Rowntree's. During the Second World War the company produced and stored tens of thousands of block couverture – an essential foodstuff which was issued to the Royal and Merchant navies to provision their lifeboats on the Arctic convoys. The Lazenby engineering shops were busy making tensioners for British army tank tracks.

Given the nature of contract supply, Lazenby was unable to advertise its products so, for example, the fleet of Commer vans it used were simply sprayed brown with no branding.

Tunnock's, Uddingston

Thomas Tunnock established Tunnock's in 1890 when he bought a baker's shop in Uddingston, south of Glasgow, for £80. The firm quickly became a Scottish institution and today still enjoys something of a cult market. Its famous teacakes, Tunnock's Chocolate Caramel Wafer, Caramel Logs and Snowballs have been produced since the 1950s. The Tunnock's Teacake is of course not really a tea cake: it is in fact a round shortbread biscuit covered in a marshmallow-like mixture, itself covered in milk or dark chocolate. The Caramel Wafer is a bar consisting of five layers of wafer, interlayed with four layers of caramel and all coated in chocolate made from condensed milk. The wrappers of the milk chocolate version boast that 'more than 5,000,000 of these biscuits are made and sold every week'. The Snowball is similar to the Tea Cake, with the addition of grated coconut to the exterior of a soft chocolate shell, but with no biscuit base.

Tunnock's can count amongst its fan club the wife of the Sultan of Brunei who came with her entourage to the factory to enjoy one of the regular tours. St Andrew's University runs a Tunnock's Caramel Wafer

Appreciation Society, which is one of the oldest student societies at the university. The trademark face of the Tunnock's Boy was chosen by Thomas Tunnock because of the fresh, friendly image his face brought to the business.

Indeed, 'You can't top a Tunnock's!'

Packer & Co, Bristol and Elizabeth Shaw

H.J. Packer, a former Fry's employee and a Quaker, began trading in 1881, making chocolate from his house in Armoury Square, Bristol, under the name of Packer & Co. The workforce was Packer's sister and brother, and a Miss Lily Brown who was paid 2s 6d a week; the plant comprised a kitchen fire and a paraffin lamp, two saucepans and a small pan for making the chocolate and the cream centres. Sugar was bought in 14lb loads and the finished chocolates were delivered by hand. In 1884, Packer took on H.J. Burrows – another ex-Fry's employee – and when the partnership was dissolved in 1885, it was Burrows who became owner of the business. The next year saw the 24-year-old Bruce Cole pay Burrows £950 for all plant, stock, debts and goodwill. Business began to boom from 1896, and in 1901 the company moved to a specially commissioned, high-specification factory at Greenbank. The business grew and between 1903 and 1912 sales increased by 250 per cent. Their strategy to sell 'Two Ounces a Penny' chocolate – good quality chocolates at a low price a child could afford – had taken off and paid off. Packer's Chocolate Mixtures was one of their main lines.

Around 1908 they purchased Carson's Ltd, a high quality confectionery firm based in Glasgow. To extend its range, the company launched a new subsidiary to produce high-class chocolates like the 'walnut whirl': Bond's of Bristol (formerly of London) chocolate products began to be made on new production lines in the high-spec Greenbank factory, alongside the Packer's brands. Success continued into the early 1920s, with the company employing 2,500 workers at its peak.

The end of the First World War saw a return of the low cost Packer's brand at a penny an ounce. One of the new lines, Milk Crispets, was particularly popular and went on to become the company's most enduring product. By 1922, Packer's had become the fourth largest chocolate manufacturer in Britain and was the most popular low cost brand in the country. But the company was in decline from the mid-1920s through the Second World War.

In 1955, despite losing money, it was decided to reenter the low cost market with the relaunch of the Packer's brand, featuring Summit milk chocolate bars and penny sweets in the shape of white mice, coconut squares, sweet cigarettes, and zoo bars, along with a relaunch of Milk Crispets. By 1961, all production had been moved to the Greenbank factory; Carson's products had become the company's best selling brand and in 1962 the company was renamed Carson's Ltd. Carson's was by now the UK's biggest producer of chocolate liqueurs; it used leading brands such as Courvoisier, Grants, Harvey's Bristol Cream, Sandeman Port and Tia Maria as fillings and thus marketed the liqueurs under Famous Names. A new liqueur production line was constructed – almost 200ft long and operated by only eight workers to produce 20,000 chocolates an hour. All to no avail: in 1963 the company was still making losses of around £39,000 a year. It was then bought by James Goldsmith in 1964 and renamed Cavenham Confectionery.

Elizabeth Shaw was acquired in 1968 and added to the products produced in Bristol. Elizabeth Shaw started as a cottage confectionery business in 1937, run by Elizabeth and Patrick Joyce with Elizabeth turning out chocolates made from mint-flavoured honeycomb crisp. These were soon to be marketed as Mint Crisps and Langes de Chat. Success led to a new factory – The Mint House – in 1939 in Brentford – and in 1953 to larger premises still, in Camberley. Other products now included Digestive Mint Creams, which were granted a Royal Warrant in 1963 that is still held today.

In 1968, Elizabeth Shaw production was moved to Bristol. A 1981 management buyout saw the company name change to Famous Names to reflect their number one liqueur chocolate brand in the UK. Famous Names held 44 per cent of the chocolate liqueurs' market and Elizabeth Shaw 50 per cent of the chocolate crisp market. The Famous Names brand was dropped in 1988 with the chocolate liqueurs rebranded as an Elizabeth Shaw product, and the company renamed Elizabeth Shaw Ltd.

The early 1990s saw Elizabeth Shaw Mint Crisp alone take a 10 per cent share of the UK mint market, and the launch of Elizabeth Shaw Liqueur Truffles. In the early 2000s, new products such as Vodka Shots and Mint Crisp Truffles were launched and Orange Crisp and Coffee Crisp were relaunched.

Meltis, Bedford

Meltis was set up by Peek Frean & Co in 1913 to produce peppermints, glacé fruits and the chocolate coverings for its biscuits; it soon expanded into a manufacturer of chocolates in its own right. In 1931, Meltis began to make chocolate for Suchard, an alliance which lasted into the 1980s, producing a wide range of products including prestige selections of chocolates in elaborate packaging. In 1933, the Duchess of York range of assorted chocolates was launched, and the top of the range 4lbs de-luxe box of Assorted Superfine Chocolates entered the market at 17s 6d.

Meltis continued to develop new products, and in the 1950s chocolate liqueurs were introduced, becoming a leading product line up to the 1970s. In 1961, a new chocolate plant was installed to produce 100 tonnes of liquid chocolate per week. Meltis was now the largest producer of Turkish delight and crystallised fruit in Britain, and the second largest producer of liqueurs. In 1975, Interfood, the owners of Suchard, took over Tobler Meltis; Jacobs purchased Interfood in 1982 and Jacob Suchard was formed. The company went into receivership in 1996.

Stockley Sweets Ltd, Blackburn and Chocley's Ltd, Hull

Stockley's was established in 1918 when Malcolm Stockley returned to his native Accrington to start again in the craft he had pursued as a younger man – toffee making. Stockley's became recognised as quality sweet manufacturers from these humble beginnings in a garden shed in High Street, Rileys Hill. The name of Stockley's was soon to be seen from market stalls in Lancashire and retail stands at Blackpool Pleasure Beach, to the World Exhibition in San Francisco in 1939.

Stockley's produced confectionery from the gamut of sugar confectionery: medicated winter nips, herbal candy, cinder toffee, bronchial lozenges, sarsaparilla sticks, pear drops, barley sugar, fudges, lemon sherbets, caramels and coltsfoot rock.

The Blackburn factory has now been the home of high quality traditional sugar confectionery for over 100 years. The Chocley's factory in Hull is where the firm manufactures high quality chocolate-based confectionery products ranging from, the website tells us: 'novelty moulded chocolate lollipops through to exquisitely finished premium chocolate coated fruits, nuts and confectionery centres'. Both ranges include sugar and sugar-free confectionery.

Stockley's is the sole manufacturer of coltsfoot rock worldwide; whilst many companies sell this product with their own branding and apply their label to its packaging, all of the production comes out of the factory in Blackburn.

In 2018, Stockley announced the acquisition of Maxilin, manufacturer of the famous Maxilin Flyers liquorice range of products.

Divine Chocolate Limited, London and Ghana

Originally known as the Day Chocolate Company, this ethical manufacturer of Fairtrade chocolate products was established in the UK in 1998 as a partnership between the Kuapa Kokoo cocoa growers' collective in Ghana and the alternative trading organisation Twin Trading; other supporters included The Body Shop, Christian Aid and Comic Relief. From the start, the farmers owned the biggest share in the company, which has since grown to 44 per cent. Divine's first product, launched in 1998, was a milk chocolate bar. White and dark chocolate, with a wide

Ethical chocolate company Divine designed this brand-new bar to celebrate International Women's Day. As the UK's only chocolate company co-owned by the men and women who grow the cocoa beans that go into their bars, Divine has seen first-hand how its dynamic programme of empowering women and supporting gender equality all over the world has made for better chocolate and stronger communities.

variety of flavours, and in many gift and seasonal formats as well as bars have since followed.

This is the remarkable Divine Chocolate story:

> In the early 1990s, structural changes in the cocoa market in Ghana prompted Nana Frimpong Abebrese to begin creating a farmer-owned company to help farmers sell their own cocoa. Nana was a visionary farmer representative and independent representative of COCOBOD (a Ghanaian government-controlled institution that fixes the buying price for cocoa in Ghana). With the support of Twin Trading, a Fairtrade company aiming to support cocoa farmers, Nana and a group of other farmers found ways to ensure the net gains of the company would belong to farmers, farmers could be paid in cash, and fair trade premiums could be invested in social programmes.
>
> (www.divinechocolate.com/divine-story)

The empowerment of women is central to everything the company does. Divine Chocolate and Kuapa Kokoo, both led by women, are driving progress toward Sustainable Development Goal 5 – this goal aims to achieve gender equality and women's empowerment; they 'support women in cocoa farming so they may develop the skills and confidence to grow better cocoa, build better communities, and thrive in business'.

Today Divine Chocolate is still the only Fairtrade chocolate company co-owned by cocoa farmers: of the 100,000 Kuapa Kokoo farmers who co-own the company, more than a third are women. Divine also works with farmers in other West African countries, for example CECAQ-11, the farmer co-op in São Tomé which produces the cocoa in the Divine Organic range. It has 1,135 members of which more than a third are women, and Divine is directly investing in their key women's projects too – particularly focusing on training and access to land titles.

Prestat, London

Prestat Ltd is one of London's oldest and most revered chocolate manufacturers' shops. It can boast two Royal Warrants: one from Her Majesty the Queen (1975) and the other from Her Late Majesty, Queen Elizabeth the Queen Mother in 1999.

Prestat Ltd was established in 1902 by French émigré Antoine Dufour; the Dufour family created the chocolate truffle in Chambéry in France in 1895. This exquisite chocolate only became widely available when Antoine brought the recipe to England and opened the first Prestat shop in London's South Molton Street.

Dufour, for whatever reason, named his business Prestat after Pierre Prestat who was his wife's first cousin; and some of the earlier packaging has the company's name as P. Prestat. Dufour opened two more shops, one at 405 Oxford Street and a second at 28 St Swithin's Lane, in the City.

Antoine passed the business on to his son Tony Dufour who ran Prestat through to the late 1950s. The difficulties of trading during the Second World War forced him to close the Oxford Street and St Swithin's Lane stores before he sold the business to brothers Neville and Maxwell Croft.

Prestat was rated as one of the world's top three chocolate shops by *The Economist* in 2003; Prestat's current flagship store is at 14 Princes Arcade, Piccadilly, and in March 2009, Prestat opened in the Chocolate Hall at Harrods. Its current range of packaging is the work of designer and artist Kitty Arden, who, in 2000, collaborated with Lulu Guinness, the handbag designer, to create a limited edition handbag in the design of the Prestat shop.

Prestat has had a long history of celebrity customers; from the actress Sarah Bernhardt in the 1910s through to Sir John Gielgud and Dame Peggy Ashcroft in the 1950s.

All Prestat's chocolates are handcrafted and manufactured on the premises at Park Royal, West London.

Whitaker's, Skipton

Whitaker's began as a grocery and drapery shop in Crosshills, North Yorkshire, run by John and Rebecca Whitaker in around 1889. Their daughter Ida, a trained baker, persuaded her father to specialise as a baker and confectioner. He did, and produce was made in a room behind the shop and sold in the front, while the family lived above. They moved to the High Street, Skipton in 1926, and opened a restaurant above the shop. Claire, after whom the shop was named, was the mother of John Whitaker, who was chairman and grandmother of William, the current managing director.

Among their bestsellers are Mint Wafer, Mint Cremes and Mint Crisp made with an old family recipe; these are currently the world's best selling after dinner mint chocolates and are to be found in hotels (usually on your pillow), in restaurants, on airplanes and in supermarkets as own brands, as well as in the usual sweet shops. In 1999, Chocolate Neapolitan was successfully launched: half a million of these are made every day out of an average daily production total of 1,500,000 chocolates. Today the firm converts highly refined liquid chocolate, delivered by tanker in 24 ton lots every week.

Other Yorkshire confectionery companies include Pickles & Co, 6 Boar Lane, Leeds, established 1874, specialising in chocolate and sweets for dessert; Royd's of Drighlington; Swan Confectionery Works Hull; Toffee Smiths, Halifax; Evans & Priestman, Hull; Goldsborough Toffees Ltd, Brewerton Street, Knaresborough – wound up in 1929; Harlow's Mintoes, Leeds; Bertie Runton's Confectionery Works, Leeds; Waterhouses Sweets, Elland; and RK Confectionery, Hull.

Foreign Chocolate Companies in Britain

We have already met a number of US and continental European chocolate manufacturers exporting to and operating in the UK over the years. As we will see, some of these maintained a strong presence here and eventually, in the case of Nestlé, became a major force in the industry; competing with companies such as Mars, Cadbury and Fry – the latter two of which have been taken over by the US Kraft Foods. Chocolat Menier established a factory in Southwark in 1870 and by 1873 was turning out 500 tonnes a year. The Boisselier Chocolate Company was founded by Henri Conrad Boisselier who in 1900 was working for the Watford Vi-Cocoa Company. He later bought the company and renamed it Boisselier's Chocolates. At the end of the nineteenth century, Swiss companies were selling 30 tonnes of milk chocolate a week in the UK, while Cadbury, for example sold barely one tonne. In 1911, over half the chocolate eaten in the world was still made in Switzerland. Pralines (invented by one of the chefs employed by the French Marechal du Plessis Praslin in the seventeenth century) came over from Brussels in 1912 through Jean Neuhaus and paved the way for Leonidas (founded 1910) and Godiva (1912). They were usually packed in high-end chocolate boxes called *ballotins*.

van Houten, The Netherlands

Most famous, of course, for his revolutionary press, Coenraad Johannes van Houten was also a significant exporter of cocoa to the UK for many years from his factory in Weesp. He patented an inexpensive method for pressing the fat from roasted cocoa beans. The middle of the bean, the 'nib', contains an average of 54 per cent cocoa butter, which is a natural fat. Van Houten's machine – a hydraulic press – reduced the cocoa butter content by nearly half. This created a 'cake' that could be pulverised into cocoa powder, which was to become the basis of all chocolate products.

Amongst its products was Rova, launched in 1911 and a competitor to Rowntree's Elect and Fry's products. Like Cadbury, van Houten was an innovative and aggressive advertiser and this, along with technical innovations in the shape of the eponymous Press and Dutching, ensured the company was a major irritation to the UK companies, particularly Rowntree, for many years. The van Houten business was sold in 1962,

Mr. PICKWICK GOES A JOURNEY.

'. . . Mr. Pickwick once more drew his head into the chaise and pulled up the glass; but he had scarcely resumed the conversation which Mr. Bob Sawyer had interrupted, when he was somewhat startled by the apparition of a small dark body, of an oblong form, on the outside of the window, which gave sundry taps against it, as if impatient of admission.
"Wat 's this?" exclaimed Mr. Pickwick.
"It looks like a case-bottle," remarked Ben Allen, eyeing the object in question through his spectacles with some interest; "I rather think it belongs to Bob."
The impression was perfectly accurate; for Mr. Bob Sawyer having attached the case-bottle to the end of the walking-stick, was battering the window with it, in token of his wish that his friends inside would partake of its contents, in all good fellowship and harmony.'

P. T. O.

One of a series of Mr Pickwick adverts from Dutch firm Van Houten. This one is titled 'Mr Pickwick goes on a journey' and like all the others features some related text from Dickens' *The Posthumous Papers of the Pickwick Club* (1836).

and the brand name has changed hands several times: in 1990 from the German chocolate manufacturer Jacobs Suchard to Philip Morris and currently to the Barry Callebaut chocolate manufacturing company.

Mars Food UK Limited, Slough

Franklin Clarence Mars' mother started it all: she taught him to hand dip candy and he was selling candy by the time he was 19. He established the Mars Candy Factory in 1911 with Ethel V. Mars, his second wife, in Tacoma, Washington. This factory produced and sold fresh candy wholesale, but ultimately the venture failed due to the presence of a better-established business, Brown & Haley, also operating in Tacoma. By 1920, Mars had gone home to Minnesota, where the earliest incarnation of the present day Mars company was founded that year as Mar-O-Bar Co. in Minneapolis, and later incorporated there as Mars, Incorporated. Frank C. Mars launched the Mar-O-Bar in 1922; initially it was not a great success, mainly on account of its fragility. Mars' Milky Way followed in 1923 – an immediate hit promoted as 'chocolate malted milk in a candy bar'. In 1929, the company moved to Chicago, and Frank's son, Forrest E. Mars Snr, joined the company. The Snickers bar was launched in 1930.

Forrest arrived in England in 1932 with £5,000, and set up Mars Ltd in a rented factory in Slough with twelve staff; he launched the Mars Bar as a sweeter version of the US Milky Way which itself is quite different from the Milky Way produced for the European market.

The US variety of Mars Bar is again quite different from its European counterpart. Initially the bars were coated in chocolate as supplied by Cadbury ('why ever did we do that?' Sir Adrian Cadbury wryly asked recently) and they were such a success that staff increased from twelve to over a hundred within a year. Today, over 2 million Mars Bars are produced every day in Britain alone.

Maltesers appeared in 1935 and Mars Bars were supplied in 1940 for the troops and for POWs in Germany. In 1960, the iconic 'A Mars a day helps you work, rest and play' was heard for the first time. That same year, Galaxy hit the streets in competition to Dairy Milk with the UK's biggest ever TV advertising campaign. In 1982, M&Ms were the first sweets to be taken into outer space, when the crew of the first space shuttle included them in their food packs; 3 million Mars Bars were taken with the task force to the Falklands.

M&Ms (named after the company's founders) had been launched in the US in 1941 as a cheaper alternative to Smarties. Forrest Mars Snr got the idea when he saw soldiers in the Spanish Civil War eating chocolate pellets with a hard shell of tempered chocolate surrounding the inside, preventing the candies from melting. A black 'M' first appeared on each sweet in 1950, later changed to white in 1954.

The two-bar Bounty was launched in 1951, Treets in 1955, Galaxy 1958, Topic in 1962 and, in 1967 Twix, Revels and Marathon – later reverting to Snickers in 1990 in the UK, France, Germany and the Netherlands. Chocolate and peanut M&Ms were introduced in 1990.

Apart from the Milky Way-Mars Bar-Milky Way mid-Atlantic triangle confusion mentioned above, there is much more opportunity for disorientation. Milky Way in Europe and worldwide is known as the 3 Musketeers in the US; Galaxy in the Middle East is known as Dove in America and worldwide; and Starburst was known in the UK and Ireland as Opal Fruits until 1998.

Mars Ltd is an incredibly secretive company; a 1993 *Washington Post Magazine* article momentarily took the lid off, as the reporter was able to see the 'M's being applied to the M&M's, something that 'no out-sider had ever before been invited to observe'. Moreover, in 1999, for example, the company did not acknowledge that Forrest Mars Snr had died or that he had even worked for the company.

Despite this commercial paranoia, Mars demonstrated many of the philanthropic industrial welfare initiatives of our indigenous Quaker companies: these included a pension plan, an in-house doctor, a cafeteria and a company newsletter. Mars paid well and in return demanded long hours and the highest quality in their products. This arrangement is enshrined in its *Principles in Action* communication published in September 2011, which traces the history of Mars, its legacy as a business committed to its Five Principles, and the company's goal of putting its principles into action to make a difference to people and the planet through performance. It embraces health and nutrition, supply chain, operations, products, and working at Mars. It also describes its businesses, including petcare, chocolate, Wrigley, food, drinks, and symbioscience.

A giant M&M outside the M&M shop in Times Square, New York.

Nestlé, Switzerland

Henri Nestlé was born in Frankfurt in 1814; in 1875, twenty-two years after moving to Vevey on Lake Geneva in 1843, the chemist started making *farine lactée,* an infant formula (*Kindermehl*) made from Alpine milk in powder form and ground cereal, for babies who had difficulty breastfeeding. Henri Nestlé with Daniel Peter and Jean-Jacques Kohler, his chocolate manufacturing neighbours, then went on to develop the first real milk chocolate when the three businessmen combined their products to produce Chocolat au Lait Gala Peter – 'The Original Milk Chocolate' – in 1874.

Henri opened a sales office in London in 1883 for the Farine Lactée Henri Nestlé Company and in 1901 its first UK factory began production. Nestlé merged with the 1866 established Anglo–Swiss Condensed Milk Company in 1905 to form the Nestlé and Anglo-Swiss Milk Company. Sales were boosted by Nestlé's extensive use of the new-fangled vending machines which were springing up everywhere and which, in this case, dispensed 1*d* chocolate bars. In 1904, the company made an agreement with Kohler & Cailler to import their chocolate product and thus strengthened their position in the UK market. In 1913, chocolate production began at Hayes. The white chocolate Milky Bar was launched in 1937 and soon gained a reputation for being good for children because it contained only cocoa butter, sugar and milk; it is made entirely from natural ingredients without artificial colours or flavours. Nearly half a pint of milk is poured into every 100g of chocolate.

In 1988, Nestlé acquired Rowntree Mackintosh after a bid by Jacobs Suchard for the York company was rejected. The seventy-fifth anniversary of KitKat was celebrated by Nestlé in 2010; the Nestlé UK website gives us the following statistics:

Over 1 billion products are eaten in the UK every year equal to 564 fingers every second; 17.6 billion fingers are eaten across the world every year; the largest single retail outlet for KitKat is Dubai Duty Free, which sells over 1 tonne per day. Three million KitKats are made every day in York.

More generally,

[S]ince Nestlé took over Rowntree's we have invested over £200 million into the York site alone and we've invested £100 million in our Tutbury factory. In fact, between 2006 and 2011 Nestlé have invested £224 million in our UK sites. Nestlé is a major UK employer, we employ 6,500 employees across 20 sites. We are one of the UK food industry's major exporters, exporting in excess of £260m worth of products each year to 50 countries around the world.

KitKat

This is what we say in Europe: 'Have a break...Have a KitKat!' – punchy and precise. In the US and elsewhere it's 'Gimme a break, Gimme a break, Break me off a piece of that KitKat Bar!, Break time, anytime'. Not quite so precise.

In the mid-1930s, Wafer Crisp, was rebranded as Chocolate Crisp, later KitKat Chocolate Crisp, and then launched as just KitKat. It sold (from 1939) with the slogan 'give yourself a break at teatime', and was launched on a meagre budget of £1,750.

Other tags included 'the biggest little meal' and 'the best companion to a cup of tea.' The simple, enduring rationale behind it was to produce 'a chocolate bar that a man could take to work in his pack up' – a concept which came from a Rowntree's employee via *CWM*'s suggestions columns. The KitKat name first appeared on a box of assorted chocolates in the 1920s (it had been trademarked in 1911), was derived from the eighteenth-century Whig literary club and featured its proprietor, pie-shop owner Christopher Catling (aka Kit Cat), on the box. In 1931, the old KitKat assortment became a casualty of a product review. Profit forecasts for 1935 were revised upwards from £80,000 to £200,000, although this was tempered slightly by a rise in advertising costs from 10 per cent of sales in 1930 to 13 per cent.

One of the team involved in the KitKat research and subsequent launch was Thomas Thompson. His retirement notice in *Cocoa Works Magazine* in 1965 highlights the key role he played in bringing it to market:

He is, of course, best remembered for his contribution to the development of lines which have been established and are now household names throughout the world. It would be impracticable to mention all of the new lines with which he was concerned, but perhaps Kit Kat requires special mention for here his personal efforts probably tipped the scales in the right direction when its very future was in the balance. Thomas Thompson worked in Cream Manufacturing Experimental (later to be known as Product

Development) where he used the experience that he had gained in Time Study Sales Department, of which he was a founder member, to estimate the probable future outputs for lines which were then in their very early stages and enabled very accurate assessments of costs and value to be made.

His nephew, Peter Stanhope, adds:

> It seems that the Directors of the Company were not at all sure in the early stages of the future success of their Rowntree's Chocolate Crisp new line and were ready to abandon it. It was Tom who did the research into manufacturing costs set against his predictions of future sales potential, that finally persuaded the Board to give it a second chance and, out of the ashes of 'Chocolate Crisp' rose KitKat which is now renowned and enjoyed around the world.

Early press advertisement copy was nothing, if not didactic. No one after reading this virtual essay could go away ill informed about KitKat – what it lacks in the pithiness of the later 'have a break…' slogan, it more than makes up for with this long-winded, almost technical, copy:

> When you have a break in your work, there's nothing else quite like a KitKat. Crisp, golden-baked wafer biscuit, moulded into a block with delicious milk chocolate. The wafer and the chocolate are a pair – not a mixture. You can see them, quite separate, when you snap off a piece from your Kit Kat – feel them, quite separate, in your mouth. You can taste them, still quite separate, as you crunch them up. Two splendid foods, with two wonderful flavours, each doubling the enjoyment of the other. Crisp wafer – milk chocolate – KitKat Chocolate Crisp made by Rowntree's and sold by confectioners and cafes. Price 2d.

In the United States, KitKat it is made under license by H.B. Reese Candy Company, a division of The Hershey Company.

Toblerone, Berne, Switzerland

In 1868, Jean Tobler was running a confectionery shop called Confiserie Speciale in Bern, Switzerland, producing chocolate sweets from products supplied by other manufacturers. By 1899, Tobler's chocolates were so successful that Tobler set up his own factory with his sons: the Fabrique de Chocolat Berne, Tobler & Cie. In 1900, Theodor Tobler took over the business, and exports to countries including Britain began that year. In 1908, with his cousin Emil Baumann, he invented the unique milk chocolate bar that is Toblerone. Emil Baumann created the recipe consisting of milk chocolate including nougat, almonds and honey; Theodor Tobler came up with the distinctive triangular shape and packaging. A new factory was built in 1985, with every Toblerone ever produced manufactured there. Dark Toblerone was launched in 1969 with White Toblerone following in 1973. The 1990s saw rapid product expansion with Minis in 1995, Blue in 1996 (the first filled Toblerone) and Praline in 1997. In 2007, Toblerone Fruit & Nut entered the market with a half purple triangular cardboard box.

Other brands include: Honeycomb Crisp with a half white box with honeycomb pieces pictured on it (2009); Tobelles – Toblerone thins in a beige triangular box; Snowtop editions with white chocolate peaks, also in a white/silver triangular box; Filled editions – milk chocolate with a white chocolate centre (blue triangular box); OneByOne – individually wrapped triangular chunks; Toblerone Pralines released in 1997, a single peaked version in the distinctive beige packaging; Crunchy Salted Almond with honey and almond nougat and salted caramelised almonds; Berner Bär – a 500g milk chocolate bar, with a relief portrait of the Bernese Bear and the coat of arms of Bern on its face – the only non-triangular Toblerone; Crispy Coconut with honey and almond nougat and coconut.

A very similar product is the Croatian Kolumbo, made by Kraš in Zagreb. Kraš produced Toblerone under licence during the 1970s and 1980s. There is also Mahony, produced by the company Chocolat-Frey AG in Switzerland. In July 2017, in response to Toblerone's 2016 highly controversial size reduction, the UK store chain Poundland launched its own version called Twin Peaks, which was larger than the modified Toblerone bar.

The name Toblerone is derived from the chocolatier's family name Tobler and *torrone*, the Italian for nougat. It is commonly believed that

Theodor Tobler fashioned the shape of his unique and iconic chocolate on the beautiful Alpine scenery of Switzerland, and on the Matterhorn in particular. But the truth is much more exotic, erotic even: according to Theodor's sons, the bar was inspired by the red and cream-frilled line of dancers at the Folies Bergères in Paris, which formed a shapely pyramid at the finale of each show.

Prudently, Theodor Tobler and Tobler AG applied for a patent in Bern in 1909 to cover the manufacture and shape of the bar, and Toblerone thus became the first patented milk chocolate bar. The official who gave the authorising signature was one Albert Einstein who was working in the Swiss Federal Institute of Intellectual Property in Bern Patent Office at the time. A picture of a bear – the civic symbol of Bern – lurks in the Matterhorn mountain image on the packaging. In 2000, after cigarettes, the biggest selling line in airport duty-free shops was Toblerone.

Over the years Toblerone has enjoyed some prodigious linguistic and political influence. The distinct pyramidal shape of the bar has given its name to the Toblerone line, a series of anti-tank emplacements in Switzerland's frontier areas. In 1995, we found out that the Swedish politician Mona Sahlin had misused her government-issued credit card for unauthorised purchases. Because she had bought, among many other more expensive items, two bars of Toblerone, pro-Sahlin journalists attempted to downplay her abuse of parliamentary financial privileges as the 'Toblerone affair'. Unsuccessful as they were, Sahlin was forced to step down as a candidate for the post as prime minister. She returned to politics in 1998. A triangular set of student residences on Oxford Road, Manchester, for the University of Manchester built in 1975 and resembling the chocolate bar are known as the Toblerones. Finally, the small, plastic composite triangular, cylinder-shaped boundary ropes in cricket are apparently referred to as Toblerones, because their shape is the same.

In 1970, Toblerone merged with Suchard to become Interfood and then with Jacobs in 1982 to create Jacobs Suchard. Kraft acquired Jacobs Suchard in 1990; it is currently owned by US confectionery company Mondelēz International, Inc., which was formerly Kraft Foods.

Chocolat Menier, Noisiel, France

Chocolat Menier was a chocolate manufacturing business founded in 1816 by Antoine Brutus Menier (1795–1853), initially as a pharmaceutical manufacturer in Paris, at a time when chocolate was vaunted as a medicinal product. Chocolate was just one part of the overall business; its main use was as a medicinal powder and for coating bitter-tasting pills.

Under the founder's son, Emile-Justin Menier, the company concentrated solely on the chocolate products. In 1864 he sold off the pharmaceuticals and began a period of expansion that made the Menier Chocolate company the largest chocolate manufacturer in France. Menier purchased cocoa-growing estates in Nicaragua along with sugar beet fields and a sugar refinery at Roye in the Somme in France. By 1893, Menier was the world's largest manufacturer of chocolate; it opened its London office in 1870 in Southwark Street.

In the 1880s, production capacity at the Noisiel plant was 125,000 tonnes per annum and the company employed 2,000 people. In 1874, Menier built 312 houses for its workers near the factory, and a school, followed in 1904 with a home for retired workers. The company pioneered developments in industrial refrigeration and factory design. Its famous chocolate graffiti posters designed by Firmin Bouisset showed a girl scrawling 'Chocolate Menier' on a wall or window. The old Menier Chocolate Factory building in south London is today a thriving arts complex, comprising an art gallery, restaurant, and theatre.

Ferrero SpA, Alba, Italy

Ferrero Rocher is produced by Ferrero SpA, makers of Nutella chocolate spread and Tic Tacs. The company was established in Alba, Piedmont, by Pietro Ferrero, a confectioner and pastry maker, when in 1946 he developed a cream of hazelnuts and cocoa, derived from gianduja and called it Pasta Gianduja. It came in solid loaves wrapped in aluminium foil which had to be sliced with a knife; this was succeeded by a spreadable version Supercrema. The hazelnut was added to save money on chocolate. It was eventually relaunched as Nutella. The production of Nutella uses one-quarter of the world's annual hazelnut supply.

As with Toblerone the early establishment of a strong brand and an effective international sales network were keys to its success. Ferrero SpA is now the second biggest chocolate producer and confectionery company in the world.

Based in Watford, the UK company was opened in 1966 and launched the famous chocolates, with their distinctive gold wrapping, in 1982; the hazelnut in every Ferrero Rocher is specially selected for its size to ensure the best possible flavour. With a production volume of 3.6 billion a year, Ferrero Rochers are sold in more than forty countries. An almond and coconut alternative, Raffaello, was introduced in 1989. Ferrero Rondnoir is a dark chocolate version.

For many, Ferrero Rochers are Christmas and New Year. In 2009, Ferrero suspended three 15m tall, golden Ferrero Rocher Christmas trees in Westfield, London, Bullring, Birmingham and the Trafford Centre, Manchester shopping centres. In 2010, Meadowhall, Sheffield and the MetroCentre in Gateshead were added. Figures for 2015 show that 61 per cent of Ferrero Rochers were sold between October and December.

Ferrero also makes Kinder Chocolate, launched in the 1950s and aimed, as the name suggests, at children and their mothers looking for a chocolate bar that contains nutritious, quality ingredients.

Ferrero Rocher chocolates and baby formula are the top items smuggled across the border from Hong Kong into mainland China. In an article explaining how the name Ferrero Rocher was inspired by the Virgin Mary, Zelda Caldwell reveals how Michele Ferrero in 1982 named them 'Rocher' after the craggy rock grotto, called the Rocher de Massabielle, which is where Mary appeared to St Bernadette in Lourdes, France. At the celebration of the fiftieth anniversary of the founding of his company, he said, 'The success of Ferrero we owe to Our Lady of Lourdes; without her we can do little'.

(https://aleteia.org/2018/05/08/how-ferrero-rocher-chocolates-were-inspired-by-the-virgin-mary/ May 08, 2018)

Ferrero is intensely secretive: it has never held a press conference and does not allow media visits to its plants. Ferrero's products are made with machines designed by an in-house engineering department.

The company acquired the British chocolate retailer Thorntons in June 2015 for £112 million.

Barry Callebaut, Banbury

Formed in 1996 by the merger of Belgian chocolate producer Callebaut and the French chocolate company Cacao Barry, today Barry Callebaut is the world leader in high quality cocoa and chocolate products and the only fully integrated global chocolate company. The company has evolved to become a provider to multinational and national branded manufacturers, chocolatiers, pastry chefs, bakeries and caterers, and food retailers for whom it makes private label as well as branded products.

Consumer products include Sarotti, Jacques and Alprose. The company has an ongoing programme of important research into chocolate recipes: it has launched tooth-friendly chocolate, probiotic chocolate, chocolate with a high level of antioxidants (branded Acticoa), and 'rebalanced' chocolate, which boasts an improved nutritional profile.

The UK Chocolate Academy™ is based in Banbury, and 'is a "state of the art" purpose-built training environment with eight individual work stations, allowing for one-to-one, hands-on tuition. The Academy is situated adjacent to the factory, allowing easy access for tours of the Barry Callebaut plant.'

(https://en.wikipedia.org/wiki/Category:Confectionery_companies_ of_the United_Kingdom)

Ferrero Christmas decorations by Anna Anichkova (2013). (*Licensed under the Creative Commons Attribution-Share Alike 3.0. Unported license*) Scary?

Chapter 13

Marketing Chocolate and Sweets

Chocolate always had an advantage over other confectionery when it came to the wooing/placating/ pleasing of women. A box of chocolates usually went down well, whereas a gobstopper, humbug or a dolly mixture seemed to lack the caché and bonhomie that usually came with the giving of chocolate. Indeed, a 1910 advertisement in *Confectionery Journal* agreed about its powers of seduction: 'If he understands women he will take her to the confectioner's and when she is chock full of candy she will be a very agreeable young woman'.

We have seen how from earliest days chocolate has been closely associated with aphrodisiacs, romance, erectile dysfunction and the pursuit of women. This, like other themes, has been endlessly exploited by the chocolate companies and their advertising agencies in the marketing of chocolate products. Early market research had found that 60 per cent of all chocolate boxes were bought by men as gifts for women. It extends of course from early advertisements and posters through television and, today, on corporate and product websites. You only have to think of the mildly erotic ('Be yourself, enjoy yourself') Flake TV adverts of the 1970s, 'The lady loves Milk Tray', the coy girl on the Caley's Monarch Assortment, and 'Caley's Fortune makes the heart grow fonder' …to get the picture, literally.

Black Magic, which combines the occult with the erotic, launched by Rowntree's in 1933, captured the mood in their 1939 trade catalogue:

Caught me under the misletoe! I was just about to give the wretch a piece of my mind when he whipped out a box of Black Magic. So what could I do? Those chocs would soften the hardest heart.

Perhaps their most explicit advertising copy though was this from 1934:

We silly creatures are always so thrilled when a man thinks us worth the very best. Imagine it, a big box of these new Black Magic chocolates on my dressing table. My dear, each choc's an orgy!

The distinctive black box endured more or less for sixty years, and the twelve chocolates (which were market researched before selection) until 2007; they were relaunched in 2009 by popular demand. After Eight sent a similar message: 'According to Cynthia, the Squeeze is what happens in taxis with an admirer, and the Freeze is when he forgets to buy her After Eight'.

Confectionery generally had long harboured such claims for romance, with Terry's, for example, presenting their Fairy Kisses in a highly romantic pre-Raphaelite-esque wrapper and a few select verses from Tennyson: 'A touch, a kiss! The charm was snapp'd…' In Italy, Giovanni Buitoni, one of the founders of Perugina, the Perugia pasta and chocolate company, branded his chocolates *bacio* – a kiss – and so the famous Baci were born in the 1930s. Unique to Baci though is the love note that comes with each box, the famous love-themed sayings conceived by Federico Seneca. Perugina's website tells us that these billets doux are 'like an invisible embrace…integral to enjoying all of the magic of Baci'. They soon became a cult object and collector's item. Hershey had launched their Kisses in 1907 in the US.

The introduction of wrappers, of course facilitated branding, giving it endless more opportunity; before that, up to the end of the nineteenth century, chocolates were sold loose in wooden boxes. One of the earliest examples of successful wrapper branding was Fry's Five Boys launched in 1886 for Fry's Milk Chocolate, showing a range of emotions excited by eating Fry's chocolate: Desperation, Pacification, Expectation, Acclamation and… the Realisation that it's Fry's. A matching poster appeared in 1905 telling us that 'The "Five Girls" want Fry's "Five Boys" Milk Chocolate and will have no other.' To make Desperation appear tearful, ammonia was sprayed close to his face.

At the same time these adverts demonstrated another universal and enduring theme – that chocolate is quite simply exceedingly good to eat. 'Pascall Chocolate Eggs are good to eat, Pascall Novelties complete the treat' delivered the message. A 1927 Cadbury poster tells us that its chocolate has 'tastes that thrill'; Terry's took no prisoners when it launched its Theobroma – food of the gods – assortment, Theobroma being the Linnaean classification name for the cacao tree, with the added slogan 'Wait until she sees inside'. 'Mars are marvellous' and Fry's Caramets were 'sweet bliss'. Bounty was 'far and away the most exotic chocolate treat'. The Crunchie ('Crunchie makes exciting biting!') was always associated with striking gold or orange foil wrappers. We all know that everybody is a (Cadbury's) fruit and nut case. Cellophane was introduced in the 1920s which, to some extent, took over from paper wrappers and provided much the same opportunities for powerful branding.

Chocolate boxes too, for assortments, offered another vehicle for impact branding and eye-catching illustration. From 1862, Fry's and Cadbury's were selling chocolates in boxes, particularly at Easter and Christmas; in 1882 Rowntree's had no fewer than 150 different boxes on offer. Sentimentality was the order of the day in artwork and, apart from their primary, immediate use as a box for chocolates – that box was often repurposed as a useful long-term repository for odds and ends, photos, postcards and other keepsakes – long fuse, slow drip advertising. Cadbury's indeed produced some very lavish boxes, plush-lined with silk and satin and designed to hold jewellery, handkerchiefs or gloves – long after the chocolates were eaten.

The very product names themselves were designed to work hard and contribute to the selling effort: Mackintosh's Egg & Cream Toffee Deluxe, for example – an early version of us getting precisely what it says on the tin. In the 1990s, Terry's redesigned its All Gold and Moonlight boxes to target the 15–24-year-old market which made up 24 per cent of sales: the former were shaped into ingots, the latter into dinner jacket shape boxes with art nouveau illustrations. Tins followed and these too produced vivid and colourful designs with immediate and long-term functions as many a cupboard and loft will attest.

Associations with royalty: weddings, coronations and jubilees, and with patriotic events such as the Festival of Britain were exploited on wrappers, boxes and tins. More mundanely, but just as influential, was the association of chocolates with everyday life, often nagging us into worrying that if we don't have this or that we are somehow failing: Caley's Marching Chocolate was aimed at the military; Rowntree's Motoring Chocolate from 1928, just as essential as petrol and aimed at the glovebox ('You can't go without it!'); Cadbury's Holiday Chocolate and Excursion Chocolate aimed at the increasing number of motorists, day trippers and holiday makers; Payne's Poppets: 'stop at the shop that has Poppets' and 'add that touch of surprise that makes the holiday...make this a real Poppet of a holiday'.

Rowntree's indulged in some outstanding advertising stunts in the late 1890s, perhaps the company from whom you would least expect them given their early advertising-averse marketing. Joseph Rowntree's nephew Arnold organised one of those new-fangled motor cars to tour the country with a giant Elect Cocoa tin on the back; he later went on to have a barge covered in Elect posters cross the Thames on the course of the 1897 Oxford and Cambridge boat race. Less dramatically, the need to win repeat business was developed through the use of coupons, prizes and collecting cards on all manner of subjects by all the main UK companies and by Nestlé. In 1976, Terry's launched its 56,000 cubic feet All Gold hot air balloon, the only gold balloon in the world at that time.

Christmas and Easter have always been peak times: seasonal catalogues offering their special ranges were produced from the 1920s. Selection boxes were aggressively promoted with up to sixteen lines, and with games and puzzles on the boxes. Examples are Caley's Xmas Tuck Box and Needler's Xmas Gift Box. Easter eggs were first laid in the 1870s by Fry's and Cadbury's; sweets were soon filling them; free gifts were popular in the 1930s with toys such as quacking ducks imprisoned inside and packaging inspired by light bulb carton designers. Innovative, and by today's standards decidedly odd, receptacles were used as containers for chocolates: Rowntree's had a chrome teapot (with a special ebonite heat-resistant base) for 5s 6d; Nestlé a Royal Winton teapot; Fry's a brass coal scuttle (21s) or a pickle jar (2s 6d); and Needler's the knitcraft case: 'a useful and attractive container for your work, wool, needles &c' all with 4s worth of County Chocolates, for 5 shillings.

By the beginning of the Second World War, the UK market alone was huge and the stakes were high – there were around over 300,000 shops selling sweets and chocolates supplied by around 350 confectionery and/ or chocolate producers. Advertising hoardings and shop windows, show cards and point of sale, as well as newspaper and magazine advertisements were also crucial to the promotion of a seemingly endless stream of new products. In the 1950s, Cadbury's had sixty permanent display men, responsible for window displays and point of sale, working the length and

You can make almost anything out of chocolate; here's a tool set from Walker's of London on the Treasure Island Sweets, Bristol website: https://www.treasureislandsweets.co.uk/

breadth of the country, all backed up by 200 representatives. Postcards – often featuring the images from the show cards – were extremely popular and collected by avid collectors from the earliest times right up to the present day where they are still much sought after.

Cadbury's was quick to recognise the value of good public relations. It set up a Visitors' Department in 1902 and was receiving 150,000 people a day up to 1939 – many of them on organised bus or rail excursions. A 2-mile tour of the factory and Bournville was their offer, with refreshments and a film. This all had to stop though for the war, and again in 1970, when health and safety regulations demanded compliance with the same rigorous hygiene procedures for visitors as for production line workers. But Health and Safety were not going to get away with it. Popular demand led to the establishment of the £6 million Cadbury World in 1990, with 420,000 visitors going through the doors within a short period after opening. Research had shown that visitors were more likely to buy Cadbury products for up to twenty years after their visit.

Children, of course, were targeted mercilessly and were seduced with sly word association by such brands as Dolly Dymple, Bunny Bon, Tiny

Tots Cachous, Zoo Mixture, Sea Shore Pebbles and Toyplane Toffees. Simply daft, not to say puerile, names had the same effect: Curly Wurlies, Fairy Crystals, Midget Gems. As we have seen, what we today would describe as racist names were much in evidence, for example: Black Boys, Black Jacks, and 'Nigger' Babies.

Even child death was accepted as a valid and presumably valuable marketing tool when Kelly-in-a-Coffin was launched – unbelievably, a small sweet fashioned into the shape of a coffin with a black or pink candy baby inside. At least we can't fault their attention to diversity.

Barratt's seems to have been obsessed with ophthalmology. Apart from the perennial Bullseyes it had in its range: Cat's Eyes, Hippopotamus Eyes and the mystifying Ogo-Pogo Eyes – and then there were Laughing Irish Eyes.

The letter 'k' seems to have been a magic letter when it came to marketing sweets, originating perhaps with Sharp's Toffees' introduction of Sir Kreemy Knut to an unsuspecting world. He was followed by a whole lexicon of k words, including Koff-Nips, Stop Kof, Toffee U-Neek, Kreema, Maskots, Krispie and Klix, all eklipsed by Kinema Krunchie. The English language – particularly poor letter 'c' was similarly murdered by such misspellings as Swon by Swan which descended further with brands such as Swon Nuga and Swonkenda.

Chocolate and 'Health'

If the romantic qualities of chocolate were aimed mostly at the middle classes then the nutritional and energy characteristics were somewhat less class bound. Health benefits – physical and psychological – were a factor in the expansion of sales of milk chocolate in the early twentieth century, aided by claims of high nutritional values afforded by rich, pure milk content. This, of course, chimed with the traditional claims surrounding so-called medicinal confectionery: lozenges, voice ju-jubes and barley sugar, for example, all claimed medical benefits as indeed did Mackintosh's toffee – good for sore throats. Bettys Tea Rooms, who produced their own chocolate for sale in their York and Harrogate cafes, convinced us that eating chocolate actually leads to weight loss.

Posters and adverts were populated with healthy, rubescent children. Cadbury's Dairy Milk Chocolate (or CDM) was 'rich in cream'.

Here it is – the greatest cough and voice lozenge on earth.

'Overflowing with goodness' was trotted out by both Mackintosh and Nestlé, while Pascall's Ambrosia Devonshire Chocolate was 'the glory of Devon in a packet'. Fry's famous churn-shaped showcard from 1925 announced that its milk chocolate contained 'full cream milk from west of England farms'. In 1955, Mars was still telling us that not only was a Mars Bar good for your work-life balance, but it also 'feeds you goodness 3 good ways: milk, chocolate, glucose'. There has been a glass and a half of milk in every bar of Cadbury's Dairy Milk since 1928. Rowntree's Milk Chocolate contained 'delight in every bite' in 1928. The *British Medical Journal* of 26 December 1891 endorsed Bovril Chocolate – Bovril Caramels containing 10 per cent Bovril; Oxo Chocolate was manufactured on a similar basis – 'a stand-by between meals'. Bovril's claim was that 'it contained 300 per cent more actual nourishment than any other chocolate extant'. Moreover, it was particularly suitable for children and the sick, as well as being good for sportsmen and travellers: 'a food by the way'; 'a perfect food in itself'. Oxo also marketed Oxo Toffee (containing fluid beef and fresh cream milk) as did Boots – Vitamalt Toffee – while Horlicks produced a malted milk toffee. Terry's Snack was ideal for walkers as it contained raisins and 'nutritive' cereals. Mars initially launched Maltesers as low-fat 'energy balls', a description which did not travel very well.

The children eating Radium Schokolade may have been rubescent for an entirely different reason. Before the effects of radiation exposure were fully understood, radium found itself in all manner of products keen to benefit from its purported magical healing properties and its glow-in-the-dark fascination. Radium and thorium were contained in toothpaste (courtesy of Alfred Curie – no relation to Marie), skin cream, Vita Radium Suppositories ('for restoring sex power'), baby blankets, and Hippman-Blach bakery's Radium Bread, for example. Its wide use in cosmetics in the popular Tho-Radia brand of make-up included radioactive powders and creams that promised to rejuvenate and brighten the skin. The wonderful German 'wunder bar', Radium Schokolade, sold by Burk & Braun from 1931 to 1936, could claim among its contents not just cocoa and milk, but also an unhealthy dose of radium salts, endowing it with a half-life as well as the more usual shelf life. To really make you better there was always Heidelberger Radium-Pastillen and, if you fancied a change to your radioactive fix, then you could try Snowflake uranium ice cream.

On a related note, Victory Vs were enlisted to help win the Cold War while Harlow's of Birstall, Leeds, manufactured Anti Fall-Out Sweets

Radium Chocolate containing real radium. You could also get uranium ice cream for your own personal nuclear winter.

– a sugar coated confection packed full of something called ashodine – a concentrate invented by a Professor Cripps and certain to protect you from your own personal nuclear winter by blocking any insidious absorption of nuclear fallout. You washed the sweets down with a swig of radioactive iodine.

Closely associated with health-giving were the themes of quality and purity, key elements in chocolate production, particularly as we have seen, amongst the Quaker manufacturers. Cadbury's end of century slogan was 'Absolutely Pure, Therefore Best'. To the Mackintoshs it was all very simple: 'always quality first, publicity second, as advertising alone can only sell a poor article once'. For Quality Street the slogan for shopkeepers was 'Put your shop in Quality Street by putting Quality Street in your shop'. It must have rung out as a siren warning, or threat, in the ears of many a shopkeeper. Sell Quality Street or go bust.

In the 1930s, Rowntree's would have had you believe that chocolate was a solution to social anxiety disorder when one of their advertisements proclaimed that 'it contains extra cream which specially feeds the nerves'.

It is no surprise that confectionery companies were amongst the first advertisers on commercial television on its launch in 1955. By 1958, 60 per cent of chocolate advertising budget was spent on TV commercials. Some of their more memorable slogans include: Murraymints – 'the too-good-to-hurry-mints' and Fruit Gums: 'don't forget the fruit gums, mum'. Polar cool Polos were 'the mint with the hole'. In 1957, we were invited to 'have a break…have a KitKat'. The Milky Bar Kid first rode into town in 1961

You could even soothe your sore throat with these pastilles full of radium salts – not just a shelf life but a half-life too.

and the Bond-like Milk Tray hero overcame almost insurmountable odds most nights from 1968 to get that box to his intended – 'all because the lady loves Milk Tray'; he made his last surreptitious delivery in 2003 to the strains of Cliff Adams' Night Rider, as usual. Milky Way was the 'the sweet you can eat between meals' – I know, for years my mother used to give my brother and I one every school day to eat at morning break – but only Milky Way, as nothing else fitted her non-appetite-spoiling agenda. In the 1970s, Fry's Turkish delight was 'full of Eastern promise' (more music by Adams); 'A finger of Fudge is just enough to give your kids a treat', and Flake proved that 'Only the crumbliest, flakiest chocolate, tastes like chocolate never tasted before'. Terry's Chocolate Orange is famous for its striking marketing; slogans included: 'When you whack a Terry's Chocolate Orange, Good Things Happen'; 'tap it and unwrap it'; 'It's not Terry's, it's mine', or 'Don't tap it... Whack it!' Recent TV advertising campaigns carry the slogan 'Smash it to pieces, love it to bits'. Ferrero Rocher's ambassadors' reception advertising campaign from the 1970s was recently revived to great effect. The original still features in the top twenty advertisement recall lists.

In 1988, the Cadbury brand – as opposed to individual lines – was relaunched, mainly through television advertising and with the slogan: 'Cadbury's. The Chocolate. The Taste'. Cadbury's Dairy Milk was the vehicle, focusing on the four instantly recognisable pillars of brand Cadbury: the colour purple, a swirl of chocolate, a glass and half... and the Cadbury signature. The seductive refrain of the popular song, 'Show Me Heaven', could be heard in the background. Perhaps, though, the most significant move in television advertising was in 1996 when Cadbury became sponsors of Coronation Street – Britain's longest running soap opera, now more than fifty years old. The initial cost was £10 million for one year, but this ensured that the Cadbury name and associated icons were on our screens at the beginning and end of each episode and at every commercial break. In 2010–11, Mars sponsored Harry Hill's programmes.

Changes in the retail landscape obviously influenced chocolate marketing. Self-service grocers and supermarkets gradually replaced the traditional confectioners-tobacconist-newsagents; their eye-catching window displays gradually gave way to display units and point of sale. A move towards the use of wholesalers as opposed to the company traveller or representative had a similar impact on how chocolate was

1996 saw Cadbury become sponsors of *Coronation Street*.

displayed in shops: merchandising had arrived and impulse buying – pioneered by Mars – was the way forward. Retail price maintenance was lifted on confectionery in the early 1960s allowing cut price chocolates, multipacks and minipacks containing 'fun-size' bars. The effect of this is exemplified by KitKat: 20 per cent of sales were in multipacks by 1970. Voucher schemes, personalities hosting lavish prize competitions, the famous philanthropic C.D.M. award for Cadbury's Dairy Milk all added to the marketing mix at one time or another. Cadbury's Cococub Club was an enormously successful children's magazine which had 300,000 members at its peak and was centred on the activities of a character named Jonathan. It grew out of an equally successful campaign in 1936 featuring a special tin of cocoa targeted at children and containing highly collectible free miniature animals such as Nutty Squirrel, Dan Crow and Monty Monkey.

After completing three years of painstaking research, Cadbury bid for and won the contract in 1992 to site hundreds of vending machines in railway and underground stations. Each machine holds 800 units, is made from seemingly indestructible polycarbonate with unblockable slots and is refrigerated.

Celebrated artists were sometimes employed to great effect: Caley, Bovril Chocolate and Fry's used John Hassall; Fry's commissioned Tom Browne and Chas Pears. Alfred Leete drew Rowntree's Mr York in 1928. Mackintosh used Jean d' Ylen for their Toffee de Luxe in 1929 as well as Heath Robinson and Mabel Lucie Atwell for Toffee Town as used in national newspaper advertisements. Peynet worked on Dairy Box, and Sir Alfred Mullins painted and drew Caley's famous Marquee and Lady posters. G.M. Elwood designed some of Caley's chocolate boxes around 1922. Richard Cadbury, an accomplished artist in his own right, worked on some of his own chocolate boxes. The Bauhaus Italian painter Federico Seneca produced a number of posters for Perugina. Cadbury used Arthur Rackham on its chocolate boxes and a team of top comic illustrators for its popular Cococub Club in 1935. Cococubs also featured comic strips in the national press drawn by top artists of the day.

In 2010, Cadbury made plans to drop the 80-year-old 'glass and a half' slogan from Dairy Milk wrappers in response to European Union rules that all weights and measures must be in metric. The somewhat less pithy 'the equivalent of 426ml of fresh liquid milk in every 227g of milk chocolate' will probably never be used as a replacement although the memorable image of the glass and a half of milk lives on.

Today, if all Cadbury's Easter eggs for one year were stood next to each other they would stretch from London to Australia; if all its Creme eggs were piled on top of each other they would reach a height of 26,126,100ft or 900 times the height of Mt Everest; 2 million bars of Cadbury chocolate are bought every year and a year's production of Crunchies would extend from Bournville to Bangkok and back. Cadbury wrapping machines can wrap 800 bars per minute. Microprocessors monitor over 1,000 temperature points in the making of Wispa bars. The 2009 relaunch of Wispa was celebrated by the production of a bar covered in edible gold leaf and costing £961.48 (normal price about 55*p*).

On 3 April 2007, Thorntons set up what is thought to be the world's first edible advertising hoarding. The 14.5ft by 9.5ft and 860lb sign was erected outside its Covent Garden shop, and was eaten by passers-by within three hours; it included 10 chocolate bunnies, 72 giant chocolate eggs and 128 chocolate panels.

Chapter 14

Dulce et decorum est pro patria mori

This famous line of poetry – 'it is sweet and fitting to die for one's country…' was written by Horace in the early first century AD in his *Odes* 3, 2, 13; the words have not always been the patriotic rallying call to arms that many think them always to be; rather it has had ironic, sardonic overtones, particularly when Wilfred Owen borrowed it in his celebrated poem published in 1920. This chapter will show how something as small and simple as sweets and their manufactories played a crucial role in twentieth-century conflict and was frequently used to boost morale amongst combat troops fighting for their country.

Chocolate played an important role either as rations for servicemen and women, as a gift to liberated civilians or as a peace offering to the vanquished. In 1780, as we have seen, Fry was commissioned to supply the Royal Navy with a ration of chocolate in cocoa slab form for its sailors – to replace the daily tot of rum and to provide them with something a little more nutritious to go with their ship's biscuit. In the 1850s, Fry's tins were sent to the troops fighting in the Crimean War. Chocolate played a role during the Boer War when in 1900, Queen Victoria instructed George Cadbury to send 120,000 tins of chocolate to the troops. At first he refused, citing his Quakerly aversion to war as a reason; Victoria tartly responded that this was not a request, but a royal command. The issue was resolved by sharing the regal order with Fry and Rowntree and the tins were sent out unbranded to obscure their origin: each tin contained a half block of vanilla chocolate. George Cadbury then salved his conscience by producing and sending out over one million anti-war pamphlets.

The importance of chocolate in military circles was highlighted by the 1905 issue of *War Office Times and Naval Review:* 'Now chocolate is… the sweetmeat of the Services: on the march, at manoeuvres, or on any special occasion where staying power is needed'. Fourteen years after the Boer War, confectionery tins were sent to the troops in the trenches of the First World War; they contained sweets, chocolates and, in a compartment at the base of Rowntree's tins, a set of postcards. Cadbury's also provided books and clothing for the troops.

Initially at least, the fall off in demand caused by the privations of the First World War had little impact on sales and profits – it was amply compensated for by huge government orders. Nevertheless, tariffs on cocoa and sugar increased and postal charges and general taxation went up. Serious manpower shortages occurred as men left for the front in droves: at Cadbury alone 1,700 out of 3,000 men departed to the army and navy (218 did not return) with another 700 leaving for munitions work. The naval blockade by German submarines focused the government on providing essential foods such as milk and cocoa, which also helped the chocolate companies. Sugar shortages, though, led to the suspension of many brands and the adaptation of recipes for others.

Caley's Marching Chocolate was issued to British troops under the name of 'Marcho'. Special wrappers were produced showing soldiers presenting arms (but unfortunately the rifles were drawn on the wrong shoulder). After the war, it was marketed at, and became popular with, sportsmen and outdoor enthusiasts receiving plaudits from such popular heroes as Jack Hobbs, the Surrey and England batsman.

In the Second World War, chocolate was of course rationed, in 1942, with 3oz allowed per person per week – half the average pre-war consumption – with supply being shared between no fewer than 181 firms. Chocolate companies, or parts of them, were either transformed completely to help the war effort or else hosted other war manufacturers. Importation of raw materials was seriously compromised; the subsequent shortages which developed as a result, and the diversion of the domestic supply of milk, had a serious effect on the quality of major brands. Rowntree's, for example, responded by manufacturing a kind of ersatz KitKat (then called Chocolate Crisp) and changing the distinctive red wrapper to a blue one denoting which key ingredients were missing. The strategy was that if any adverse public reaction came from this debasement then the original name and wrapper could be restored when normal production was resumed. Dairy Milk disappeared from the shops when milk was prohibited for priority manufacturing use in 1941; Ration Chocolate replaced it, made from skimmed milk powder.

The day rationing ended for sweets and chocolates in 1953 was the signal for Mars to send out 7,000 Mars Bars: one to each Barnardo's child.

But it wasn't just chocolate; sugar confectionery and liquorice too were enlisted to help king, queen and country. In the First World War, liquorice found itself fashioned into lifebelts, chains, telephones, cartridge belts, handcuffs (for PoWs and deserters) and tyres.

The names of sweets took on a military air with Royal Navy Monster Screws, Military Braid, Telegraph Wires, Tommy Talkers and Dr Jim's Rifles. Back in the Crimean War we had Inkerman Balls, Alma Drops and Sebastopol Balls. The Boer War inflicted Buller's Bullets, Kruger's Favourites, Khaki Toffees and Transvaal Toffee on us.

The services were not the only casualties, though: William Maynard, of wine gum fame, was so depressed by his son away serving in the Boer War that, after pinning his will to his chest, mixed a concoction of peppermint, chlorodyne and beer, drank it down and died. Verdict: suicide while insane.

Requisitioning

Army and Navy Lozenges – liquorice-and-herb-flavoured lozenges – were issued to servicemen during the First World War, hence the name. They supposedly contained tincture of opium.

In the Second World War, factories up and down the country were requisitioned to focus on essential war work: for example, the manufacture of sweets and chocolate might be replaced by the making of aircraft cockpits, machine-gun parts or artillery shells. Alternatively, the factories might host other war manufacturers: for example, Rowntree's 'became' County Industries Ltd and they manufactured Oxford Marmalade on behalf of Frank Cooper Ltd.

The brief for County Industries Ltd was mainly to produce shell and mine fuses in the Smarties block. In addition, 300 clerks of the Royal Army Pay Corps moved in, as did York firm Cooke, Troughton & Simms, for the manufacture of military optical instruments. Out of the Cream Department came National Milk Cocoa, Ryvita, Household Milk and dried egg. The Card Box Mill swapped production of fancy boxes for supplies for the RASC, Northern Command. Part of the Dining Block became a refuge for blitzed families, notably in the aftermath of the 1942 Baedeker Raid; a VAD hospital with a hundred or so beds occupied the rest of the building. There was also a nursery to allow mothers of young children to come to work. At any one time sixty children were in occupation; cots were made by the factory's joiners and the orchard became the playground.

The raids on York, Norwich, Bath, Canterbury and Exeter became known as Baedeker Raids because Göring's staff allegedly used the famous travel guide to select their *Vergeltungsangriffe* (retaliatory) targets – namely 3 Star *** English cities – in retaliation for the RAF's destruction of Lübeck and Rostock. On 28 April 1942, seventy German bombers, largely unopposed, bombed York for two hours: eighty-six people died including fourteen children, and ninety-eight were seriously injured (not including undisclosed army and RAF fatalities). Around 9,500 houses (30 per cent of the city's stock) were damaged or destroyed leaving 2,000 people homeless. The Guildhall and St Martin le Grand Church in Coney Street were badly damaged. The Bar Convent School collapsed, killing five nuns including the headmistress, Mother Vincent. The following day the *Daily Mail* reported: 'The gates of York still stand high, like the spirit of its people who, after nearly two hours of intense bombing and machine-gunning, were clearing up today.' Rowntree's survived unscathed; Caley's in Norwich was completely destroyed.

To support the war effort, Cadbury turned out aircraft seats; part of the Bournville factory was let to Austin for the production of aircraft gun magazines and helmets, and to Lucas to enable them to increase rotating gun turret and Sten gun magazine production. Bournville Utilities Ltd was established in 1940 and 2,000 employees were transferred to the new company: the Moulding Department produced gun doors for Spitfires, air-intake and super-charger controls for Stirlings and flare cases for other aeroplanes; Packing made gas masks while Metals turned out pilots' seats for Defiants, junction boxes for Wellingtons and upper-mid gun turrets for Stirlings, with other departments churning out jerry cans, fuel tanks for Spitfires, Beaufighters, Lancasters, and Vosper motor torpedo boats. Anti-aircraft rockets were filled with explosives and 600 workers turned out over 5 million gas masks and 6 million canisters. Only 15 of this 600 were men – the work requiring the 'nimble fingers' of women. Sheep grazed on the green, Bournville was shrouded in wire camouflage netting, 'mercy vans' carrying hot cocoa were sent into the Birmingham city centre during raids, the recreation fields were dug for Victory and the Cadbury Home Guard was formed.

Fry's was able to make a positive contribution to the war effort by giving up factory floor space to the production of Rolls Royce Merlin engines and aircraft propellors. Somerdale became the Bristol Aeroplane Company. The US Hershey Company was asked to produce a chocolate ration for its troops in Europe and promptly started turning out a billion bars of Ration D and Ration K – a 600-calorie 4oz chunk of sustenance in your pocket. Pobjoy Airmotors and Aircraft Limited took over part of the Meltis factory and many staff were moved to war work, making aeroplane parts and helping with the Admiralty Stores. Meltis was also licensed to produce vitaminised chocolate for prisoners of war.

The tower at Terry's factory in York was used as a look-out post for the prisoner of war camp on nearby Knavesmire. F. Hills & Sons, manufacturers of Jablo propeller blades from Manchester, took over part of the Bishopthorpe factory, while Chivers & Sons requisitioned part of the Clementhorpe factory until 1954.

Part of the Packer factory in Bristol was borrowed by the US army for the preparation and packaging of field ration packs and Mars Bars were supplied as rations for the troops and for prisoners of war.

Branding and packaging reflected the conditions and times: on the confectionery front in the 1940s there was Mackay's ARP toffee whose wrappers showed barrage balloons and anti-aircraft guns, while Cadbury's had its Ration Chocolate. Indeed, because of the shortage of full cream milk, separated milk was used to produce blended chocolate, as manufactured by Nestlé and Cadbury. Apart from its obvious nutritional and energy benefits the chocolate sent out to the troops had other uses, not least as civilising gifts and peace offerings to liberated populations and as 'romantic gestures' to local girls and women.

VE Day in Europe saw Cadbury's, in a marvellous humanitarian gesture, send 35,840,000 2oz bars of chocolate to British troops in Germany for them to hand out to civilians in the bomb-wrecked towns and cities – 25 per cent of a 9,000 ton order from the Ministry of Food. At roughly the same time, $1m worth of Cadbury's chocolate went the other way to the USA under the CARE Scheme (Co-operative for American Remittances to Europe) where the chocolates were repackaged and sent back to Bournville to be handed out to the poor children of Birmingham.

Orbit gum – a play on the artificial sweetener Sorbitol – is among the most popular brands, managed by the Mars subsidiary brand Wrigley.

During the Second World War, Wrigley was selling its eponymous gum only to soldiers, while Orbit was sold to the public. Though abandoned shortly after the war, about thirty years later Orbit made a comeback in America during the chewing gum craze.

On 8 August 1942, the Ewbanks' factory in Pontefract was torched by German incendiaries. The pan, gum and liquorice rooms were all badly damaged, and the factory was put out of action. During this time other Pontefract sweet manufacturers produced some Ewbanks sweets while Ewbanks' workers made parachutes. A new gum department was officially opened on 6 February 1948.

During the Second World War, the Robinson and Wordsworth factory in Pontefract was diverted to aero-engine renovation. WR Wikinson carried on sweet-making at a low level throughout the Second World War, but the factory was also used to machine tank parts.

Toffee was called up to assist in naval warfare during the First World War when it was enlisted to help with the perilous activity of mine laying. The Royal Navy was having a problem with its mine laying: mines dropped into the sea kept bobbing back to the surface before the mine layers could retire to a safe distance. Enter toffee: globs of toffee were applied to the chains securing the mines as a slow-release mechanism with a bonding strength of a ton. By the time the toffee had dissolved, the ships were well out of the danger zone and the mines bobbed back to the surface to do their deadly job.

The Defence of the Realm Act (DORA) imposed a curfew on shopkeepers who were obliged to close by 8.00 pm during the Second World War. A number of grocers and sweetshops fell foul of this; they must have wondered why selling a gobstopper or two at 8.15 pm was going to lose us the war. Did the Germans know something they didn't? Furthermore, vending machines were exempt, so theatres and music halls could sell their sweets while sweet shops could not. The (admittedly biased) London Confectionery Protection Association claimed that one theatre they knew of had 2,000 machines.

The influx of white-hatted, white coat wearing, wounded and disabled veterans onto the streets of our cities, in desperate need to make some money, did little to help sweet shops. One of their trades was sweets and chocolates sold on trays; shell-shocked survivors were recognisable by their signs indicating that by buying the chocolates the public was doing their bit just as the veterans had done theirs. But pleasing all the people all of the time is, of course, impossible, as war widows left to run the family sweet shop on their own were quick to point out: they too needed and deserved help. Fry's did what it could by hiring blind former soldiers as typists, trained at St Dunstan's.

We have noted how in 1982, M&Ms were the first sweets to be taken into outer space when the crew of the first space shuttle included them in their food packs. More recently Mars provided 3 million Mars Bars for the Falklands Task Force in 1982. At the end of 2010, Caley was busy maintaining chocolate manufacturers' century-old tradition of sustaining the UK's armed forces with their support of the *Help for Heroes* campaign, for wounded soldiers mainly from the Iraq and Afghanistan campaigns.

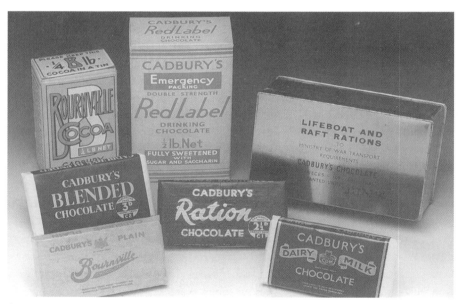

A selection of Cadbury Second World War products.

Chapter 15

The Dark Side of the Sweet: Obesity, Diabetes, Bad Teeth, and Choking to Death

It is well documented that sugar has been linked in developed countries to diabetes, obesity and cancer. Credit Suisse Equity Research conducted a survey and found that 86 per cent of medical professionals link obesity with high sugar intake. *The New York Times* reports that:

> If it is killing all of us, it is killing black people faster. Over the last 30 years, the rate of Americans who are obese or overweight grew 27 per cent among all adults, to 71 per cent from 56 per cent, according to the Centers for Disease Control, with African-Americans overrepresented in the national figures. During the same period, diabetes rates generally nearly tripled. Among black non-Hispanic women, they are nearly double those of white non-Hispanic women, and one and a half times higher for black men than white men.
>
> (www.nytimes.com/interactive/2019/08/14/
> magazine/sugar-slave-trade-slavery.html by
> Khalil Gibran Muhammad 14 August 2019)

The perils, and benefits, of chewing gum

Chewing gum, defined elegantly and damningly by the Food and Drug Administration base as a 'nonnutritive masticatory substance', has been the subject of many a myth over the years; we all believed them, some of us still do. Perhaps the most famous, and disturbing, maintains that if you swallow your gum it will fester in your stomach for up to seven years, as it is not digestible, an enduring legacy of your devotion to Wrigley's. Not true, you will be relieved to know: according to paediatric gastroenterologist David Milov of the Nemours Children's Clinic in Orlando, Florida, in most cases, swallowed gum will pass through your system, maybe not as swiftly as other foods, but with no sticky consequences.

There have, however, been cases where chronic gum swallowing in conjunction with other indigestible matter has resulted in uncomfortable gastrointestinal blockages in young children. The report describes three children, two of whom were in the habit of winning their gum as a routine reward for good behaviour. One of them was found to have always swallowed his gum after chewing five to seven pieces each day. In both cases the children became constipated and the gum snowballed into a mass that required surgical removal. In the case of the third patient, a girl just a year-and- a-half old, four coins were found lodged in her oesophagus, fused into a single lump, a bezoar, by a ball of chewing gum.

Milov relates another case in which a patient swallowed sunflower seeds – and the shells. Milov found 'all these very prickly seeds that were congealed around gum', forming a body that he describes as 'like a porcupine'.

Adults have actually choked to death on chewing gum. A 2012 report describes a 42-year-old woman who fell on the stairs while chewing gum. Due to the impact, the gum fell into her pharynx and was inhaled into the larynx, causing complete blockage and resulting in the woman's death by choking. Darren Toop, a 22-year-old tennis coach from Dorset, choked on his gum in May 1996.

On the positive side, sugar-free gum sweetened with xylitol has been shown to reduce cavities and plaque. Gum chewing is also a good way to cure or reduce halitosis. Chewing gum not only helps to add freshness to breath, but can aid in removing food particles and bacteria, associated with bad breath, from teeth. It does this by stimulating saliva, which essentially washes out the mouth.

There are some medical benefits to chewing gum. Chewing gum after colon surgery expedites patient recovery, according to research published in the Archives of Surgery (Purkayastha, Sanjay et al.; (2008). 'Meta-analysis of Randomized Studies Evaluating Chewing Gum to Enhance Postoperative Recovery Following Colectomy'. Archives of Surgery. 143 (8): 788–93). If the patient chews gum for fifteen minutes for at least four times per day, it will reduce recovery time by a day and a half. The average patient took 0.66 fewer days to pass gas and 1.10 fewer days to have a bowel movement. Saliva flow and production is stimulated when gum is chewed. Gum also gets digestive juices flowing – a form of 'sham feeding'. Sham feeding is the role of the central nervous system in the regulation of gastric secretion.

Type 2 diabetes

Most sweets have a high glycemic index (GI), which means they cause a rapid rise in blood sugar levels after ingestion. This is a concern for people with diabetes, but could also be dangerous to the health of non-diabetics. With type 2 diabetes, we know that sugar, and therefore most sweets that are not sugar-free, does not directly cause type 2 diabetes, but it is a serious contributory factor. Obesity is a risk factor for type 2 diabetes and you are more likely to develop type 2 diabetes if you are overweight. You gain weight when you take in more calories than your body needs, and sugary foods and drinks contain a lot of calories. So, if consuming too much sugar – or, put another way, eating too many sweets – is making you put on weight, then you are increasing your risk of developing type 2 diabetes.

Rates of type 2 diabetes have increased significantly since 1960 in parallel with obesity. In 2015, there were approximately 392 million people diagnosed with the disease compared to around 30 million in 1985. It typically begins in middle or older age, although rates of type 2

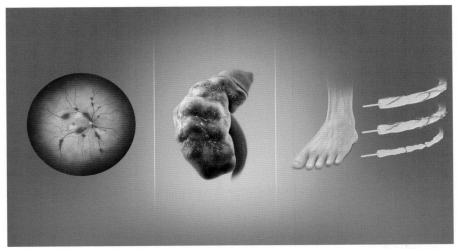

Complications of Diabetes (from L–R): Retinopathy, Nephropathy and Neuropathy. 2018. (*Source :http://www.scientificanimations.com/wiki-images/*)

diabetes are increasing in younger people. Type 2 diabetes can deliver a ten-year-shorter life expectancy.

Cardiovascular Disease (CVD)

Research published in 2014 linked excessive sugar consumption to an increased risk of death from cardiovascular disease (CVD). People who derived more than 25 per cent of their daily calories from sugar were more than twice as likely to die from heart disease as participants who got 10 per cent or fewer of their calories from sugar.

Choking to death

Lychee Mini Fruity Gels are sweets made with konjac, a gummy binding agent made from the tubers of the konnyaku root. They are manufactured by AP Frozen Foods Ltd, Thailand and have been implicated in a number of deaths and choking injuries in the US and Pacific Rim countries: the gel used means that these sweets can totally block the airway; konnyaku gel is ten times stronger than gelatin and can resist attempts to dislodge with the Heimlich manoeuvre. Lychee Mini Fruit Gels have been banned due to choking hazards in the US by the FDA and the European Union.

Introducing toys into chocolate products, for example chocolate eggs, comes with its hazards and is banned in the US. In the EU if the material attached to the confectionery has a function and will not cause any injury to the consumer, it is allowed. In the EU, however, the Toy Safety Directive 2009/48/EC specifies that toys contained in food only need separate packaging that cannot be swallowed.

The Sweet Tooth

In 1959, a Swedish dental health campaign encouraged people to reduce the risk of poor dental health by limiting eating sweets to once a week. The slogan, 'All the sweets you want, but only once a week', started a tradition of buying sweets every Saturday, called *lördagsgodis* – 'Saturday candy'.

Regular sweets contain sugar, which is a key factor in the formation of dental caries (cavities). Tooth decay, or dental caries, occurs when acid from within the mouth attacks the enamel and dentine of the teeth causing cavities to form. Several types of bacteria commonly found in the mouth feed on sugar, particularly *Streptococcus mutans*. Bacteria within the plaque use the sugar as energy and release acid as a waste product, which gradually dissolves the enamel in the teeth. Heavy or frequent consumption of high-sugar foods, especially lollipops, sugary cough drops, and other sugar-based sweets that stay in the mouth for a long time, obviously increases the risk of tooth decay. Sweets that also contain enamel-dissolving acids, such as acid drops, increase the risk. It is estimated that 1 in 3 adults suffers from dental caries and close to 1 in 4 children equally suffer from some form of tooth decay.

The *Action on Sugar* website tells us that:

Free sugars are now found in almost all food and are the most important factor in the deterioration of oral health. It is especially problematic in children who have become accustomed to sugar at an early age. Tooth decay is the leading cause for hospitalisation among 5–9 year olds in the UK, with 26,000 children being hospitalised each year due to tooth decay – in other words, 500 each week… We currently consume far too much sugar in our diets. The report published by the WHO (October 2017) and by the SACN highlight the need for a reduction in sugars intake to 5% of our energy intake. This is the equivalent of 7 teaspoons/cubes or 30g of sugar per day for an adult. The recommendation for children is 24g for children aged 5–11 and 19g for children aged 4–6. This 5% limit is far below the current intake which is of 11.9% in children aged 1.5 to 3; 14.7% in children aged 4 to 10; and 15.6% in children 11 to 18. It is also thought that adherence to the 5% recommended sugar intake would halt the increase in obesity.

(www.actiononsugar.org/sugar-and-health/
sugars-and-tooth-decay)
(www.who.int/nutrition/publications/nutrientrequirements/
sugars-dental-caries-keyfacts/en)

Interestingly, in the 1950s the Medical Research Council undertook a two-year study in which children were given maximum allowable sweet rations and went to bed without brushing their teeth. The findings, as reported in *The Lancet*, found no evidence of caries in the sample population. Lemons got the blame, apparently.

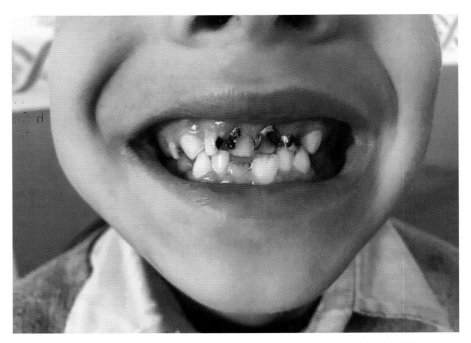

Too many sweets will damage your health – and not just your dental health. This image was used to illustrate an article reporting on a Dentaid dental team trip to Chefchaouen in northern Morocco. The team comprised seven dentists, five nurses and a hygienist, along with an experienced team of local translators and assistants relieving pain and promoting oral health and prevention to school children. 'The dental team worked hard over the course of the week treating 931 patients and providing 1,059 extractions. More than 4,000 children received tooth brushing instruction and 4,000 toothbrushes were distributed along with many tubes of paste. Fluoride treatments were applied to 1,450 children in the classrooms and clinics'. (*https://www.dentaid.org/morocco-blog/*)

Chocolate dermatitis

Research has shown that diet can exacerbate eczema (atopic dermatitis) or cause dermatitis due to systemic contact dermatitis. Other studies have found that compliance with a low-nickel diet leads to skin improvement. Sources of dietary nickel include chocolate, nuts, seeds, black tea, and canned foods in general; these triggers should, of course, be avoided.

Chapter 16

Twenty-one Sweets from Around the World

This twenty-one sweet tour around the world shows the rich diversity of sweets and sweet making, from Argentina to Japan, to Israel, Georgia, to Scotland…

Botan Rice Candy – a soft, chewy, slightly lemon-orange flavoured sweet with an outer layer of rice paper or Oblaat. The rice paper is clear and plastic-like when dry, but it is edible and dissolves in the mouth. It is a traditional Japanese sweet. Botan Rice Candies come in a small cardboard box which contains 3/4 oz (21 grams) of candy. Each box contains six individual pieces and a child's sticker. The candy's name, Botan (ぼたん),

Konpeitō (金平糖, コンペイトー), is a Japanese sugar confection. It comes in a variety of colours and flavours. (*Photographer: Midori GFDL, cc–by–sa–*)

means flower blossom in Japanese. A peony blossom is depicted on the label, next to an *inu-hariko*, a dog-shaped traditional toy for Japanese children.

Churchkhela (ჩურჩხელა) is a traditional Georgian candle-shaped sweet, the main ingredients are grape must, nuts, and flour. Almonds, walnuts, hazelnuts, and chocolate and sometimes raisins are threaded onto a string, dipped in thickened grape juice or fruit juices and dried in the shape of a sausage. Churchkhela has a wide fan base outside Georgia, such as Iran, Armenia, Cyprus, Greece, Russia, Ukraine, and Turkey. In Persian, it is known as باسلوق شیره انگور. In Armenian, Greek, and Turkish it is *sujuk*, which is actually a dry sausage. It is known in Cypriot Greek as shoushoukos (σιουσιούκκος) and as soutzouki (σουτζούκι) in Greece. The Cypriot variety is made by dipping strings of almonds into jelly, called palouzes (παλουζές).

Georgian Churchkhela from Kakheti. (*CC BY-SA 2.0 File:Kakheti, Georgia – Churchkhela.jpg Levan Gokadze*)

Coucougnette – a French confection made with almonds, marzipan and chocolate. The sweet consists of a whole roasted almond coated in dark chocolate, rolled in a mix of crushed almonds, cane sugar, ginger brandy and Armagnac. Each coucougnette is dipped in raspberry juice, resulting in the familiar pink colour.

Dalgona (달고나) or **ppopgi (뽑기)** is a Korean sweet made with melted sugar and baking soda. It was a popular street snack in the 1970s and 1980s.

Deuk Deuk Tong 叮叮糖 – commonly known as Ding Ding Tong, it is a type of traditional sweet popular in Hong Kong. It is a hard maltose candy with sesame and ginger flavours. In Cantonese, *deuk* means chiselling, breaking things into pieces. When street hawkers sold it they had to break it up with a pair of flat chisels called deuk. Chiselling makes a noise which draws the children in to buy. *Tŏng* means candy in Cantonese. Today, in order to cater to young people's tastes, different flavours of Deuk Deuk Tong are made, including coconut, chocolate, mango, banana, and strawberry.

Gulab jamun – a milk-solid-based sweet from the Indian subcontinent, popular in India, Nepal, Pakistan, the Maldives and Bangladesh as well as Myanmar. It is made mainly from milk solids, traditionally from Khoya, which is milk reduced to the consistency of a soft dough. It is often garnished with dried nuts such as almonds to enhance flavour.

Hanukkah gelt – Hebrew: הכונה ימד, meaning Hanukkah money, also known as gelt, are chocolate coins traditionally given to Jewish children during the festival of Hanukkah. The custom had its origin in the seventeenth-century practice of Polish Jewry to give money to their small children to hand over to their teachers. In time, as children demanded their share of the loot, money was also given to children to keep for themselves.

Hematogen Гематоген – sounding like something you'd find in a test tube in a medical research laboratory, this nutrition bar is produced in Russia and is made of sugar, milk and black food albumin taken from processed (defibrinated) cow's blood.

Irish potatoes – sweet confections made of sugar, butter, coconut, vanilla, and cinnamon that are a traditional St. Patrick's Day treat in Pennsylvania.

Mantecol – peanut butter nougat from Argentina. It was originally created in the 1940s by the confectionery company Georgalos which was founded by a Greek immigrant family. Miguel Georgalos was inspired by halva, the Greek dessert.

Modak मोदक – an Indian sweet; the filling consists of freshly grated coconut and jaggery while the outer soft shell is made from rice flour or wheat flour mixed with khava or maida flour.

Meiji – from Japan, these chocolates have a range of flavours which include cheese, black pepper, jasmine, basil, and lemon salt. It is made by Meiji Co., Ltd. (株式会社明治 Kabushiki-gaisha Meiji). On 6 December 2011, radioactive caesium was found in Meiji baby formula. The level of contamination was lower than the Japanese government's allowable limit of 200 becquerels per kilogram, which is 50 becquerels higher than the limit applied in the aftermath of the Chernobyl disaster. The company made the controversial claim that the infant milk was 'within safety limits' and that it 'didn't pose a health risk', despite a potentially large number of infants suffering from internal radiation. Meiji Dairies voluntarily recalled 400,000 cans of formula.

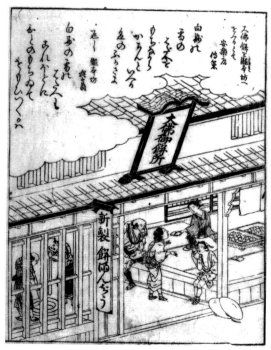

A Japanese confectionery store as shown in 'The Great Buddha Sweetshop' from Akisato Ritō's Miyako meisho zue (都 名所 圖 會; An Illustrated Guide to the Capital), illustrated by Shunchosai Takehara Nobushige. The store benefited from being situated near the Great Buddha built by Toyotomi Hideyoshi, one of Kyoto's most popular tourist attractions. (Berry, Mary Elizabeth. Japan in Print Information and Nation in the Early Modern Period. Berkeley, Calif): U of California, 2006. (*Original source: Akizato Ritō. Illus. Shunchōsai Takehara Nobushige. Miyako meisho zue. 6 fascicles. Kyoto: Yoshinoya Tamehachi, 1787. East Asian Library, University of California, Berkeley*)

Negro – This Serbian product's slogan is 'the chimney sweep of the throat'. A chimney sweep features on its wrapper depicted while sweeping a chimney. It gets its originally black colour from active carbon and anise, which is similar in taste to liquorice, and its flavour from menthol. Its recipe is apparently an industrial secret. The name Negro has sometimes been labelled as racist, but it refers to its inventor, Pietro Negro. (*Photographer: Metsavend. This file is licensed under the Creative Commons Attribution-Share Alike 3.0 Unported license.*)

PEZ – first marketed as a compressed peppermint sweet in Vienna in 1927 by Eduard Haas III. The name PEZ is an abbreviation of PfeffErminZ (German for peppermint). The original products were round peppermint lozenges called PEZ drops. Over time, a new manufacturing process evolved and the hard pressed brick shape known today was created. The first PEZ mint dispensers, known as 'regulars', were similar in shape to a cigarette lighter, and dispensed an adult breath mint marketed as an alternative to tobacco. They were invented by Oscar Uxa.

Queijadinha – this sweet originated in Portugal, and is also popular in Brazil. It is traditionally made with grated coconut, cheese, sweetened condensed milk, sugar, butter and egg yolks.

Saladitos – a Mexican sweet; Saladitos are salted plums, which can also be sweetened with sugar and anise or coated in chilli and lime. They originated in China.

Salmiakki – a salty liquorice originating in Finland as a pastille; flavoured with salmiak salt (sal ammoniac; ammonium chloride) it is a common confectionery in the Nordic countries, Benelux, and northern Germany. Sal ammoniac (ammonium chloride) has long been used in cough medicines, as it works as an expectorant; salty liquorice probably then has its origins in pharmacies that manufactured their own cough medicine. In 2012, there was a European Union proposal to limit the amount of ammonium chloride to 0.3 per cent, which was met with some opposition. Although the European Union now regulates the use of ammonium chloride to 0.3 per cent in most foodstuffs, there is no specific restriction for it in liquorice or ice cream. With a level of up to 7.99 per cent ammonium chloride, salmiak pastilles are considered a 'traditionally-applied medicine to assist expectoration in the airways'.

German legislation required that a content of above 2 per cent ammonium chloride in salty liquorice had to carry the label 'Adult Liquorice – Not Children's Liquorice' (Erwachsenenlakritz – Kein Kinderlakritz) on packaging. When the content was between 4.49 and 7.99 per cent, the declaration 'extra stark' (extra strong) was also required on packaging. Products containing more than 7.99 per cent of ammonium chloride are illegal in Germany.

Tablet – a medium-hard, sugary confection from Scotland. Tablet is made from sugar, condensed milk, and butter, boiled to a soft-ball stage and allowed to crystallise. It is often flavoured with vanilla, and sometimes has nut pieces in it. It is first recorded in *The Household Book of Lady Grisell Baillie 1692–1733*. Tablet is very like *Québécois sucre à la crème* and the South American *tableta de leche*. Another close relative can be found in the Netherlands called *borstplaat*, eaten during the Sinterklaas celebrations. A similar sweet, often with nuts or raisins added, is known as *kiri aluwa* or 'milk toffee' in Sri Lanka.

Vanparys – essentially chocolate dragée: a Belgian dark chocolate, coated with thin layers of sugar, and delivered in a spectacular range of fifty colours in three finishes: matt, glossy or pearlescent.

Vichy pastilles – a French sweet produced in the spa town of Vichy in France; they were invented in 1825 and are recognisable as a white, octagonal pastille bearing the word 'Vichy' in caps. They were originally made purely from bicarbonate of soda and taken for their digestive properties. Doña María Eugenia Ignacia Augustina de Palafox y Kirkpatrick, sixteenth Countess of Teba, fifteenth Marchioness of Ardales, known as Eugénie de Montijo, was a fan; she was the last Empress of the French as wife to Napoleon III. Later, they were made with mineral salts extracted from the local spring water. Today they include sugar and are flavoured with mint, lemon, or aniseed.

During the Second World War, the sweets were used as 'branding and marketing' by the authorities in Vichy France. By August 1942, shops in Vichy were giving Vichy pastilles away to customers, while other foods and drinks were rationed. The propaganda failed in the long term, though, with some French still uneasy today with the connotations the name has; this has affected sales.

Zaotang 灶糖; – these sweets are made of maltose; the Chinese use them as a sacrifice to the Kitchen God around the twenty-third day of the twelfth lunar month just before Chinese New Year. The Kitchen God is despatched to earth by the Jade Emperor to supervise the domestic life of every household and returns to heaven to report the activities of every one of those households over the past year on the Kitchen God Festival or the Little New Year. People offer the Zaotang to Kitchen God to sweeten his words to the Jade Emperor or to stick his teeth together to prevent him delivering a bad report.

Early 20th century box of Vichy Pastilles: sweet collaborators?

Chapter 17

Some UK Sweet Manufacturers

The UK has had, over the years, a breathtaking number of confectionery manufacturers; here are some of them with their histories and stories, past and present.

Yorkshire, for example, has been home to more confectionery companies than any other region of Britain – and it's by no means just Rowntree's, Terry's and Mackintosh; there is a lot more to Yorkshire than just York or Halifax or Hull. Thornton's and Bassett's of Sheffield and Thorne's of Leeds have all been significant forces in the industry – the two Sheffield companies still are. Indeed, Dobson's of Elland, Riley of Halifax, Whitaker's of Skipton and Simpkin in Sheffield have nineteenth or early twentieth-century origins and, along with Lion Confectionery in Cleckheaton, are still trading successfully today, the first two with retail

A selection of Yorkshire confectionery.

outlets. Add to this the liquorice companies clustered around Pontefract; Doncaster, the home of butterscotch, and land-locked Dewsbury where Slade & Bullock perfected seaside rock.

Barker & Dobson, Liverpool

Founded in 1834, this was originally a husband and wife team, Barker was his surname and Dobson was her maiden name. They opened a sweet shop in Paradise Street, stocking sweets and chocolates manufactured by other companies including some from Europe.

It was the two grandsons of the founders, Henry and Percy Jacobson, who scaled the business into a large company. They were the first to introduce individually wrapped sweets; by 1939 the company was manufacturing around 450 different types of sweets. Quality control was very important, so much so that to ensure that their sweets met their exacting quality standards Henry and Percy personally sampled sweets every morning until their deaths in 1961 aged 95 and 90 respectively. Proof, then, that sweets are good for you?

One of their 1960s' slogans was somewhat ill judged. BSD=LSD was read by some mischievously as BSD = lysergic acid, rather than as the innocuous £sd intended.

Barratt's, London and York

Founded in Shoreditch in 1848 by George Osborne Barratt, Barratt's became market leaders in the 'children's own-purchase' market, making an extensive range of 1d sweets including Sherbet Fountains and Black Jacks. One day, George left the toffee on the boil for too long and inadvertently produced Stickjaw Toffee and access to the working class market with rock bottom prices. After a move to Wood Green in north London, Barratt's was soon the biggest jam and confectionery company in London, employing 2,000 people by 1899; a fire that same year was devastating, causing £1,000 worth of damage.

However, by 1906 it was the largest confectionery company in the world turning out 300 tonnes of sweets every week. In 1907, E.W. Barratt gifted a 14-carat gold watch to all of the employees in honour of his late father, G.O. Barratt.

The company was taken over by Bassett in 1966; its brands are now manufactured by Tangerine Confectionery of York.

Products include Black Jacks, Bruiser, Sherbet Fountain (remember the liquorice straw?), Dip Dab, Catherine Wheels, Dolly Mixture, Jungle Mix, Dew Drops, Flumps, Frosties and Fizzy Frosties, Fruit Salad, Gums, Jelly Babies, Milk Bottles, Milk Teeth, Refreshers, Refreshers Gums. In the 1980s, Wham Bars were selling 30 million bars per year at their peak.

Bassett, Sheffield

Founded in 1842 by George Bassett, Sheffield, 'wholesale confectioner, lozenge maker and British wine dealer', the company opened its first factory in Portland Street in 1852 before moving to larger premises in Owlerton around 1900. Bassett's partner was Samuel Meggitt Johnson (his future son-in-law); they employed around 200 workers in what was the world's biggest sweet manufactory at the time. The Sheffield factory is today Cadbury's centre for sugar confectionery in the UK. Bassett's three most important brands are: Liquorice Allsorts, Jelly Babies, and Wine Gums.

Geo. Bassett & Co Ltd bought Wilkinson's of Pontefract, famous for their Pontefract cakes, Barratt's in 1966 (sherbet fountains and sweet cigarettes) and Trebor (of the eponymous mints) before being bought themselves by Cadbury's in 1989.

Jelly Babies were originally conceived by an Austrian confectioner, a Herr Steinboch, working for Fryers of Lancashire in the 1860s (makers of Victory Vs) and, with a nod towards the parlous situation relating to foundlings at the time, were branded as Unclaimed Babies. As we have seen, Bassett's Jelly Babies were launched in 1918 to celebrate the end of the First World War; then they were called Peace Babies. Production was halted during the Second World War, resuming in 1953 when rationing finally ended; they were then rechristened as the less disturbing Jelly Babies. The Beatles were often pelted with them and successive Dr Whos have used them as a negotiating tool to take the steam out of tense intergalactic situations. Screaming Jelly Babies are the dramatic result of a school experiment when the sweets are immersed in a strong oxidising agent.

The origin of Liquorice Allsorts is also intriguing. In 1899, Charlie Thompson, a sales representative, was on a call in Leicester when he dropped a tray of samples all over the floor. These had already been rejected as individual purchases, but the resulting colourful, random mix so impressed the shopkeeper that he placed an order for what was soon to become the Allsorts. Bertie Bassett is the Bassett company mascot, a man made entirely from liquorice allsorts, created by John (Jack) McEwan and introduced to the sweet-buying public on 1 January 1929. He was obviously inspired by the highly successful and contemporary Michelin Man. Today, the allsorts mix honours Bertie's heritage: it contains a son of Bertie: a diminutive aniseed and liquorice figure in Bertie's image.

The Doctor Who serial *The Happiness Patrol* featured the evil Kandy Man, a villain who bore an uncanny likeness to Bertie Bassett who, of course, was as honest as the day. Bertie, however, triumphed: an out-of-court settlement led to oblivion for Kandy Man, sentenced to eternal exile. To celebrate his eightieth birthday in 2009, Bertie married his '*sweet*heart' Betty Bassett (no relation we hope, the laws of bigamy apply even to the world of sweets) in the Sheffield factory with workers enjoying the ceremony as wedding guests, including even a best man.

By 1966, Bassett was the largest sugar confectionery manufacturer in Britain employing 1,300 people. Bassett's now also produces varieties of allsorts devoid of all liquorice: fruit allsorts feature mixed-fruit flavours; dessert allsorts include apple tart and lemon cheesecake. There is also a red liquorice Betty Bassett.

RS Brownhill & Sons, Leeds

Brownhill made feculina, a flavoured flour used in making cakes of different flavours, butterscotch, peppermint rock, lozenges, fruit pastilles, Turkish delight and other sweets. They were active in the Wellington Works from the 1890s and described themselves as wholesale druggists, dry-salters and manufacturing confectioners. They also operated from Stand No. 10 at the Grocery Exchange, every Tuesday in the Corn Exchange, Leeds and became known as Brownhill-White Ltd, noted for their Crestona Butterscotch.

Callard & Bowser, London and York

The company was founded by two Scottish brothers, Richard Callard and John Bowser, in 1779 in Maryhill, Glasgow. Others say that Finchley was the original home of this firm established in 1837 by Callard and his brother-in-law, Bowser. Their speciality was Creamline Toffee. They bought William Nuttall of Doncaster and were themselves bought by Terry's of York in 1982.

The company's best known product is its traditional mints, available in peppermint, wintergreen, cinnamon, and spearmint flavours, packed in a distinctive rectangular tin box. Callard & Bowser formerly marketed a popular line of English toffees, which was discontinued between 2001 and 2003.

Craven, York

Craven dates back to 1803 when Joseph Hick, aged 29, set up in York as Kilner & Hick, confectioners. Kilner left the business to Hick, which he relocated to 47 Coney Street, next door to what was then the Leopard Inn and opposite St Martin's Church. Hick's youngest daughter, Mary Ann, was born in 1829. In 1833 Thomas Craven, son of an East Acklam farmer, arrived in York aged 16, as apprentice to Thomas Hide, his brother-in-law. Hide was running a confectionery business established in the mid to late 1820s under the name George Berry & Thomas Hide after the joint owners, and located at 20 High Ousegate. Thomas Craven bought the

When you think of York and sweets you automatically assume Rowntree's and Terry's. However, there was a lesser known but highly productive and successful company called Craven which still trades today on the outskirts of the city.

right to trade in York, never easy due to the tight hold the guilds had on commerce in the city, when he became a Freeman in 1840; on Hide's death in 1843 he set up his own business next door at 19 High Ousegate.

On 1 May 1845, Craven moved the business to 31 Pavement, not far from the Rowntree's grocery shop and in 1851 he married Mary Ann Hick – she was 22, he 34. In 1860 Joseph Hick died; then in 1862 Mary Ann's husband died leaving her with three young children (one boy and two girls aged 8, 6 and 4) to raise, and two businesses to run. Mary Ann was equal to the challenge: she amalgamated the two businesses, changed the name of the company to MA Craven, and ran it until 1902. Production was in Coppergate – roughly where the Jorvik Viking Centre is now – along with additional properties in Coney Street and Foss Islands Road; staff numbers had increased to 800 by 1908 – a sizeable business by York standards. There were four Craven's retail shops in the city one of which, Craven's Mary Ann Sweet Shop, was in the Shambles and featured a sweet museum on the first floor where visitors could see 150 years of the 'Art, Trade, Mystery and Business of the Confectioner'.

In 1920, the Coppergate factory was named The French Almond Works in recognition of the importance of that product line and the vogue for anything French. In 1992, Craven's bought Crusader, Barker & Dobson, Keillers & Bensons and Milady; the company was subsequently

Making the sweets at Craven's in the 1960s in what looks very like a cement mixer. The pictures come courtesy of Carol Partington and show her father.

renamed Craven Keiller in 1995. Trebor Bassett bought Craven in 1996 and in 1999 the York and Pontefract factories combined to form Monkhill Confectionery, later owned by Cadbury Schweppes. In 2004, Monkhill relaunched the entire Sharps of York range with the monocled cartoon aristocrat named Sir Kreemy Knut who had featured in Sharp's marketing at launch in 1911. In February 2008, Tangerine Confectionery bought Monkhill from Cadbury Schweppes for £58 million.

J. Dobson & Son, Elland

One of the largest privately owned confectionery manufacturers in Yorkshire. Joseph Dobson came to Elland in 1850 with his young bride, Eleanor, from York. The 21-year-old Joseph had come fully expecting to collect his inheritance, only to find that his solicitor had absconded with it. Notwithstanding, Joseph and Eleanor set up business, catering mainly for Victorian family occasions producing wedding cakes and funeral biscuits.

By the time he was 10, both Joseph's parents had died from plague and he was raised by his grandparents. As a boy he worked for Craven's in York. Eleanor was the sister of William Charles Berry, confectioner and Freeman of the city of York. The Berrys, as we know, were joint founders of Terry's.

In the very early 1900s, Joseph Dobson launched Conversation Lozenges, some of which promoted sound Victorian values such as 'Take Ye Not To Strong Drink' and 'Honour Your Parents'. London sweet maker F. Allen's followed a similar line in their cocoa advertisements: they depict contrasting domestic scenes where the cocoa drinkers are paragons of temperance and prosperity while their less abstemious and feckless neighbours are drowning in intemperance and poverty. George Cadbury and Joseph Rowntree would surely have endorsed these sentiments. The Conversation Lozenges were the precursors of the famous Love Heart which, as noted above, Joseph Terry was making about the same time with such risqué messages as 'Can you polka?', 'I want a wife', 'Do you love me?' and 'How do you flirt?'

The company has always been owned and managed by direct descendants of Joseph Dobson. Joseph, who died in 1885 at the age of 56, left three sons, Robert Henry, William Charles and Thomas John, each of whom ran the company at one time or another. Dobson's has always enjoyed a reputation as the local Elland 'sweetie man', ever active in local events, carnival processions, and mounting displays centred around the giant antique glass jars in shops, supermarkets and museums.

The famous Yorkshire Mixtures were, like Liquorice Allsorts, named entirely by accident. One day Joseph's son, Thomas John, was carrying some sweets downstairs when he slipped and the eighteen varieties of sweets cascaded down. The resulting jumbled-up mixture was then named Yorkshire Mixtures. Other vintage brands which have stood the test of time include Butter Mintoes made with real butter and flavoured with natural oil of peppermint; Menthol Mixtures, an assortment of four strong menthol and eucalyptus sweets; and Bonfire Toffee, a toffee made with lots of black treacle and real butter. Big in early November.

Don Confectionery Co, Sheffield

Somewhat unfairly, the Don Confectionery Co is best remembered as the company which Joseph Thornton left in 1911 to set up on his own. Don Confectionery was established by Samuel Meggitt Johnson in 1878; Johnson was managing director of Bassett, but he needed somewhere for George Bassett's two sons to work, apparently, because he did not want them in the Bassett's business. The company was bought by Bassett in 1933.

Farrah's, Harrogate

John Farrah founded the business in 1840; his shop was originally on Royal Parade, but this closed in the mid-1990s and the retail outlet now stands on Montpellier Parade as the Palm Court Café Fine Chocolate Shop.

The purpose of Farrah's Original Harrogate Toffee was to cleanse the palate of the notoriously putrid taste of Harrogate's sulphur water. Original Harrogate Toffee is similar to both butterscotch and barley sugar and uses three different types of sugar, butter and lemon to give a unique texture and flavour. It is still made in copper pans and packaged in the recognisable trademark blue and silver embossed tins.

Fox's Confectionery, Braunstone, Leicester

Founded in 1890, the company was established by Walter Richard Fox as a wholesale grocery and confectionery business starting in a Victorian warehouse in Leicester. By 1897, son Eric was on board having tired of selling Olivetti typewriters and the Foxes were turning out over 100 different confectionery lines. Eric it was who invented the famous Glacier Mint, originally saddled with the less than snappy Clear Mint Fingers. Eric's wife chipped in with the all important glacier and the rest is sweet history after registration of the brand in 1919 – 'the Finest Peppermint in the World'. Cool was now cool and gave rise to me-toos such as Bebson's Arctic and Needler's Niagara Mints.

In 1969, the company was acquired by Mackintosh's, a year before Mackintosh merged with Rowntree's of York. After purchasing Rowntree-Mackintosh in 1988 Nestlé sold the Fox's Brand and its Leicester site to Northern Foods in 2001. The company was then sold to Big Bear Ltd in 2003, with sites in Blackburn and Leicester.

Peppy the polar bear is the original trademark for Fox's Glacier Mints; he or she was created by Leicester-based artist C. Reginald Dalby, better known for illustrating *The Railway Series* books by the Rev. W. Awdry. Fox's Confectionery was acquired by Valeo Foods in 2015.

Haribo, Bonn

Haribo, or more properly HARIBO, is a family-owned German company founded in 1920 by Hans Riegel; he trained as a confectioner and before establishing his own company, worked for a number of German sweet makers.

The first Haribo sweets were made in his small backyard laundry-kitchen. In 1921, Hans' wife Gertrud became the first member of staff. The first liquorice products were introduced in 1925 including a stick on which the Haribo logo was stamped.

HARIBO grew rapidly after the Second World War swallowing up confectionery companies across Germany and elsewhere including the Netherlands, France, Sweden and Austria. The company started its presence in the UK through the acquisition of Dunhills Ltd. The company continued to make Pontefract cakes under the Dunhills name as well as a variety of other sweets.

By 2011, the brand had established sixteen factories around the world and its sweets were available in more than a hundred countries. The company continued to lead the gums and jellies market and to develop new, innovative products. To celebrate the royal wedding of Prince William to Kate Middleton (a known HARIBO fan) in 2011, the company launched a Hearts and Rings range.

In 2012, HARIBO announced that its Pontefract site was operating to capacity and unveiled plans for a new a new multi-million pound factory in Castleford with the creation of almost 300 jobs.

Haribo opened its second UK retail outlet in 2018 in York, to complement the existing store in Pontefract.

Wm Jackson, Hull

William Jackson opened his first shop at 28 Scale Lane in September 1851 on the afternoon of his wedding. Parsimony, or value for money, has been an abiding principle: the Jacksons were known locally as Mr & Mrs Split Currant. Under William's son, George, the firm moved to 127 Spring Bank. By 1912, there were seventeen shops, a bakery in Derringham Street, a jam factory, warehousing and stables. By 1916, there were thirteen stores rising to eighty-five in 1939.

Today Wm Jackson Food Group owns a number of companies including Jackson's Bakery on the Derringham Street site.

RK Confectionery, another Hull firm, exploited the popularity of *Felix the Cat* films which were very popular around 1920. Not to be confused with RK Confectionery Works in the main bazaar in Kathua, India.

Lion Confectionery, Cleckheaton

Lion has been synonymous with Midget Gems since they opened its factory in Westgate in 1902. The company is still in Cleckheaton turning out thousands of tonnes of gum-based products every year and still using a steam boiler, called Helen, from 1926. Lion is now owned by Tangerine.

Mackintosh, Halifax

John and Violet Mackintosh set up their business in a pastry shop in King Cross Lane in 1890, financing the company with the £100 they had saved between them. Their first launch was Mackintosh's Celebrated Toffee, a winning mixture of English butterscotch and American caramel.

Mackintosh was nothing if not innovative – he exploited sampling to the full: one week he was inviting customers to come and taste a sample for free, the next he was urging them to come again and 'eat it at your expense'; you pay for it this time. Modest too: by 1896 Mackintosh was styling himself 'Toffee King'. A great believer in product advertising and self-promotion, one of Mackintosh's most celebrated ads was a magnificent 1921 Heath Robinson advertisement published in *Punch*; the strap at the bottom boasted: 'in every Town and Village in the Kingdom … obtainable in every country in the World'.

Another of his catchy slogans was 'Early to bed, early to rise; never get drunk – and advertise!' He also knew very well how to win friends and influence the right people, as exemplified by his sending every MP in 1905 a mackintosh and a tin of coffee.

Mackintosh was keen to develop his export trade, but this was not without its problems: in mainland Europe, potential customers confused toffee with coffee and poured boiling water on it 'with unsatisfactory results'. In the US, the extreme variations in climate across the country wreaked havoc and, depending on the time of year, toffee was melting in some states while it was rock hard in others. Notwithstanding, this is how he modestly heralded his entry into the US market:

I am John Mackintosh, the Toffee King, Sovereign of Pleasure, Emperor of Joy. My old English candy tickles my millions of subjects…I was crowned by the lovers of good things to eat…I am the world's largest consumer of butter, my own herd of prize cattle graze on the Yorkshire hills. I buy sugar by the trainload. I am John Mackintosh, Toffee King of England and I rule alone.

His eloquence and industry were rewarded with ample success, even in intractable markets like China where the toffee he supplied was pink.

In 1927, chocolate-coated Toffee Deluxe was launched followed by Mackintosh Chocolate in 1924. John's son, Harold Mackintosh, later 1st Viscount Mackintosh of Halifax, took over in 1920. He developed the Methodist principles on which the firm had been founded, notably enlightened management and sympathetic labour relations. In 1932 he bought the A.J. Caley Norwich confectionery company from Unilever; this expanded the range of products and led to the launch of blockbuster products such as Quality Street in 1936 and Rolo in 1938. According to Mackintosh 'Quality Street 'tis the Most Momentous thing that has yet Happened in the World of Sweetness'.

The Quality Street name was inspired by the play by Peter Pan author J. M. Barrie. 'Major Quality' and 'Miss Sweetly' owe their lives to the play's protagonists – Captain Valentine Brown and Phoebe – and appeared on all Regency-style Quality Street packaging and advertising until 2000. They in turn were originally modelled by Iris and Tony Coles, the children of Sydney Coles who created the brand's image. Mackintosh took an advertisement on the front page of the Daily Mail, on 2 May 1936: 'An introduction to Quality Street'. It shows Miss Sweetly tempting Major Quality with a tin of the sweets.

'Sweets to the sweet, Miss Sweetly?' asks the Major, to which she coyly replies: 'Spare my blushes Major Quality, feast your eyes rather on this sumptuous array of toffees and chocolates … 'tis the most momentous thing that has yet happened in the world of sweetness.' She gives him a 'toffee creme brazil' which he declares 'a veritable triumph!'

Some 7 million Quality Street chocolates are now produced every day, the most popular out of the seventeen being 'The Purple One'. Heath Robinson and Mabel Lucie Atwell were among the artists commissioned to draw for Mackintosh, most famously for the Toffee Town advertisements.

The purchase of Bellamy's and then Fox's brought liquorice allsorts and Fox's Glacier Mints respectively into the catalogues. Other products included Beehive Toffee and Creamy Rolls in the 1920s, Cresta in 1950 – Caramac in 1959 – Cracknel Bon-Bons, Toffo, Toffee Crisp, Golden Toffee Wafers, Munchies, the Weekend assortment in 1957 and Good News in 1960.

Maynards, London & Sheffield

Tom and Charles Riley Maynard began making sweets in 1880 in their kitchen in Stamford Hill, London. Next door, Charles's wife, Sarah Ann, looked after the sweet shop which sold their products. In 1896, the Maynards sweet company was established. It was Charles Gordon Maynard who suggested to his Methodist and teetotal father that they make wine gums. Initially incandescent at the thought, Charles Riley eventually relented, comforted in the knowledge that the gums would contain no alcoholic wine. Maynard's Original Wine Gums were launched in 1909. By 1930, the company owned 250 shops, 18 of which were bombed out in the war (17 reopened) and a warehouse was built in York in 1937, followed by a new one in 1976. In 1959 there were 300 shops, the largest specialist confectionery chain in Europe. Maynard's merged with Bassett's in 1990 and in 1998 were bought by Cadbury who continue to manufacture their lines in Sheffield.

R. S. Murray & Co, London

R. S. Murray & Co goes down in confectionery history for introducing American-style caramels to Britain, and for Murray Mints.

Robert Stuart Murray (1854–1912), a confectionery salesman from Chicago, identified a ready trade for his caramels, made from milk or cream and sugar, in England, and so established a factory at 67 Turnmill Street, Clerkenwell, London in 1882. He was joined in partnership by Charles Hubbard and Walter Michael Price (1826–1919). The three shipped over £8,000 worth of caramel-producing machinery from America and initially employed 300 workers, producing 5 to 6 tons of confectionery every day.

The company had diversified into chocolate manufacturing by 1906. As we have noted, 1911 saw a strike at the firm when the largely female strikers were supported by the women's rights campaigner Mary Macarthur (1880–1921). The workers eventually won and received a pay rise and better working conditions.

The works extended over 3 acres and by 1914, had a staff of 1,500 to 2,000. Murray Mints, a mint-flavoured caramel, were introduced from 1944. It soon became the best known R. S. Murray product. Murray Mints are still sold in Britain by Mondelēz under the Maynards Bassetts brand. Murray Butter Mints are also available as part of a mint assortment.

Needler's, Hull

Needler's was a significant force in the industry in the early twentieth century. Frederick Needler, a Methodist from Arnold, Skirlaugh near

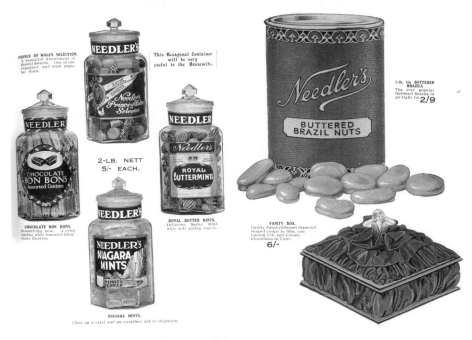

A page from the Needler's catalogue in 1926.

Hull, was working in a Hull tea and coffee warehouse at 14. He was later with Buckton's Confectionery opposite paragon Station before, at the age of 22, in 1886 he bought a small manufacturing confectionery business comprising two stoves, slabs, rollers and other basic plant with £100 of his mother's savings and set up in Anne Street near Paragon Station. Staff then was a sugar boiler and a boy called Watson, assisted by a delivery horse, with cart.

In 1900, he employed ten female and twenty-three male workers producing a variety of lines: thirty-eight different boiled sweets, forty types of toffees, thirty-five health sweets, fourteen pralines and fifteen different labelled sticks of rock.

The company was also a wholesaler for other firms, such as the German Quaker company Stollwerk, Cadbury's, Fry's, Craven's, Taverner's and Rowntree's. This ended in 1912 when the own brand product range was 576 lines of which 74 were chocolate, 106 were caramels and toffees, 79 pastilles and lozenges, 34 tins of assortments, 33 rocks and cracknels, and 224 kinds of boiled sweets. In 1906, a new five-storey chocolate plant was built in Lotus Avenue off Bournemouth Street to cater for this.

Percy Lazenby was hired from Carsons of Bristol; he went on to found confectioners Lazenby and Son (York) Ltd.

Some of the names were just as outrageous as the range: Floral Tablets, Clove Cushions, Army Rock, Bon Bon Kali, Hothouse Grapes, Moonstone Assorted, Trinidad Candy, Alabama Coons (!), Town Hall Gums and Berlin Mixture, Caramel Bullets, Choc Cream Dots, Dolly Pears, Tom Tit Mix, Little Yorkshire Girls (?), San Toy Mixture (!?).

By 1920, turnover was £570,000, comprising 650 tons of chocolate and 1,500 tons of sweets, with a range now including Christmas boxes and Easter eggs. There were 1,700 employees, mostly women. In 1929, the catalogue featured twelve different assortment boxes and numerous chocolate bars. The boxes gloried in such names as Wilberforce (a local hero), Minaret, Lido, Eldora, Carlton and Crown Derby. Kreema milk chocolate was advertised as being 'Creamy! Velvety! Delicious!'

Sales were boosted when green sweet jars were replaced by clear glass. Air conditioning was installed in 1927 permitting all-weather packing; wrappers had been introduced in the early 1920s and wrapping was automated in 1928. Up to 1918, goods were shipped either by horse-drawn vans or crated and sent by rail. A fleet of vans was built up and by 1927 there were forty delivery vans, all smartly liveried in chocolate brown. The speed limit was 20mph rising to 30mph in 1930. Rail distribution was terminated in 1950 when British Rail introduced hump-shunting which resulted in unacceptable levels of jar breakages. The firm's vans were requisitioned in 1939 for the war and never seen again.

Needler's innovative chemists perfected clear fruit drops – Glace Fruit Drops – in 1938, resulting in another lift in sales. They had the market more or less to themselves until 1965 before they were commercially challenged. In 1938, production moved away from chocolate although post-war demand for Glace Fruit Drops still exceeded supply until 1957.

Raymond Needler succeeded Percival Needler as managing director in 1970; he promptly bought London confectioners Batger, famous for its Jersey Toffees and Sainsbury own brand products; Dickson Orde of Farnham was acquired next. Chocolate production was finally ended in 1976 under pressure from the likes of Cadbury, Rowntree and Mars. The firm focused on sugar confectionery and toffees, laid off half of the 800 staff and returned a profit in 1977, the first for a number of years.

Like George Cadbury and Joseph Rowntree, Frederick Needler was a Nonconformist and a philanthropist. He was a Methodist Sunday school teacher for many years; he married another Sunday school teacher in 1898 after breaking off a previous engagement and going through a lawsuit for breach of promise. The company had a strong reputation for good industrial welfare: a profit-sharing scheme was introduced as early as 1911, the pension scheme for men started in 1922 and there were excellent dining, social and sports facilities. Needler's renowned Musical Society was set up in 1925, performing occasionally on the BBC. Frederick was a close friend of Tom Ferens of Reckitt's (also a Methodist) who was involved in the founding of University College, now the University of Hull. Frederick Needler personally bought and then gifted Needler Hall in Cottingham to the college as a men's hall of residence.

Hillsdown Holdings bought Needler's in 1986 along with Bluebird Toffee of Birmingham. Nora AS, Norway's biggest food group, purchased the company in 1988, although sweets continued to be produced in Hull under the Needler brand. Amazingly, all Needler's catalogues were photographed in black and white and then skilfully coloured in by hand using watercolours; these colour pictures were then converted into three colour separations and printed up in house.

Nuttall's, Doncaster

Harry Nuttall established this confectionery business in Doncaster. His son William succeeded him and opened a new factory in 1909 in Holmes Market employing 130 people. In 1912, Nuttall's Mintoes were launched; so successful and popular were they that production of other sweets like the Liquorice Lump was suspended to satisfy demand. Later the company was taken over by Callard & Bowser who continued to sell the sweets under the Nuttall's name. Like others in the confectionery business, William Nuttall was a noted philanthropist, donating large sums of money to help the people of Doncaster; on his death in 1934 he left £221,000.

Parkinson's, Doncaster

Doncaster Butterscotch is first recorded in 1848 and was sold by three rival Doncaster firms: S. Parkinson & Sons (possibly the inventors), Henry Hall, and Booth's.

Parkinson Ltd was established by Samuel Parkinson, confectioner, grocer and tea dealer, in High Street Doncaster in the early nineteenth century. Its butterscotch was promoted as Royal Doncaster Butterscotch or The Queen's Sweetmeat, and reputedly 'the best emollient for the chest in the winter season'. It was to become one of Doncaster's most famous exports and a highlight of the St Leger race week. In 1956, the company employed 600 or so people, mostly women. In 1961, Parkinson's was acquired by the Holland's Confectionery Group. The business ceased production in 1977. Today, the firm Amy Smiths, based in Bawtry has brought back Doncaster Butterscotch using the same recipe that was used by Parkinsons. 'It's the recipe that was invented in Doncaster and favoured by Queen Victoria when she came to the races.'

Peppersmith, London

Peppersmith, founded in 2009, specialises in xylitol-based chewing gum, mints and sweet products. Its chewing gum is made with 100 per cent xylitol and contains no artificial flavours, colours or preservatives and no aspartame. Peppersmith gum is accredited by the British Dental Health Foundation for being good for teeth.

Quiggin's, Kendal

One of three companies that make Kendal Mint Cake, the confection famously popular with climbers and walkers. Quiggin's Mint Cake is the oldest surviving mint cake company; the Quiggin family had been making confectionery since 1840 on the Isle of Man when one of the four sons, Daniel Quiggin, moved to Kendal in 1880 and set up the mint cake company. Quiggin's products also include Rum & Brandy Butters, Truffles & Marzipan, Fudges, Chocolate Creams, Herbal Punches, Peanut Brittle, Nougat and Coconut Ice bars.

The cake allegedly came about as the result of a mistake when a batch of glacier mint sweets went wrong. In 1869, Joseph Wiper, who married into the Thompson family of confectioners based in Kendal, apparently left the boiled solution for glacier mints overnight; it turned cloudy and went solid turning into what Wiper called mint cake. His great-nephew, Robert Wiper took over the family business marketing Kendal mint cake as an energy snack used on prestigious expeditions, including the Imperial Trans-Antarctic Expedition led by Sir Ernest Shackleton. Sir Edmund Hillary and his team carried Romney's Kendal Mint Cake with them on the first successful ascent of Mount Everest in 1953. The packaging currently includes the following: 'We sat on the snow and looked at the country far below us ... we nibbled Kendal Mint Cake'. A member of the successful Everest expedition wrote – 'It was easily the most popular item on our high altitude ration – our only criticism was that we did not have enough of it.' This led in no small part to its rise in global popularity amongst the mountaineering and hiking fraternity.

The other two Kendal Mint Cake manufacturers are:

Romney's

Essentially Kendal mint cake with a chocolate coating. Romney's was founded in 1918, its mint cake was sold in Kendal and sent by train to other areas of the north-west for sale.

Wilson's

Wilson's Mint Cake was founded in 1913, when James Wilson purchased a factory in the Stricklandgate area of Kendal. He had previously made and distributed types of toffee. In 1966, Wilson's was licensed to sell a Beatrix Potter range of sweets. By 2007, mint cake production declined as chocolate confectionery took up 90 per cent of orders. The company is now run by W. McClures Ltd, a family business established in Windermere in 1945, and still offering Kendal Mint Cake online.

Radiance, Doncaster

Lines included Devon Cream Toffee, Hazelnut Toffee, Extra Devon Cream, Creme-De-Menthe, Radiance Assortment, Riviera Assortment, Chocolate-Coated Toffees, Brazil Toffee. The company had closed by 1943.

Riley's, Halifax

Fred and J. H. Riley set up their confectionery business in Halifax in 1907. Their premier line was Toffee Rolls, available in seven flavours including fig, rum and butter, date and liquorice. Initially, the factory was in the family home, but saw a move to Hopwood Lane and the Kingston Toffee Mills in 1911, famous for the Riley name on the 120-foot-high chimney picked out in 7ft tall white glazed letters.

On J. H. Riley's death in 1953, Nuttall's bought the company; later, Callard & Bowser, Smith Kendon, Terry's of York and finally Kraft all bought Riley's. Ella Riley wrote down the recipe 'just in case' and it lay dormant in her cookery book for many years until 2008 when it was found by Freya Sykes, her granddaughter.

J. Roggall & Sons, Leeds

Manufacturers of toffees, liquorice and nougat. The original factory was in Rockingham Street, where the Merrion Centre is now. By 1930 it was in Spark Street. It was here that they were granted permission to employ on two day-shifts, 'women of 18 years of age and over in attending automatic wrapping machines and weighing up and packing in the Toffee Department'. By the 1950s the company was in Seacroft.

Sharp's, Maidstone & York

The Sharp's brand was launched in 1911 from the Kreemy Works factory in Maidstone; the company was headed by Edward Sharp, a Congregationalist. Sharp's best-selling line was Super-Kreem Toffee, from 'The Largest Manufacturers of Toffee in the World'. Royal Nougat was another important brand. Over the years the company was taken over by Taverner's, Trebor Bassett and Monkhill and is now part of Tangerine Confectionery of York. The brand was relaunched in 2004 as Sharp's of York in a campaign which resurrected the same monocled, bowler-hatted toff, Sir Kreemy Knut who characterised Sharp's toffee from 1911. The character is much sought after today as a Royal Doulton figure. A 'knut' is a dandy.

A. L. Simpkin & Co Ltd, Sheffield

The company was founded in 1921 by Albert Leslie Simpkin. It was the first manufacturer of travel sweets. The strategy was to make high quality glucose confections using natural flavours and colours and to sell them through chemists' shops, then a niche market which swerved around competition with the large confectionery manufacturers. By 1924, Simpkin had 80 per cent coverage of the UK with 12,000 accounts, employing 180 workers. The range was extended from bulk barley sugar drops in jars to include powdered sweets in 8oz reasonably airtight travel tins. They were called travel tins because they contained barley sugar drops which can alleviate the symptoms of travel sickness. Today, domestic sales are still mainly through chemist and health food outlets.

Slade & Bullock, Dewsbury

Ben Bullock was a Burnley miner who moved to Dewsbury in 1868 and set up a stall selling boiled sweets in Dewsbury and Heckmondwike markets. In 1876, he established his own company and introduced what was reputedly the first example of lettered rock. *The Dewsbury Reporter* takes up the story in 1976:

> Ben turned out his first batch of lettered rock with the words 'Whoa Emma' inside them as a tribute to a popular song of the day. The Whoa Emma rock sold like magic at West Riding markets but bigger things were yet to come. The discovery of a paper which could cover the sticks of rock and yet be removed easily coincided with Ben's decision to take a fortnight's holiday … [in] Blackpool. Shortly afterwards a few hundredweight of Blackpool lettered rock was sent to the resort and the novelty so caught the public fancy that the Dewsbury firm was inundated with orders from seaside resorts all over Britain. [Ben Bullock's] fame spread abroad and demands for lettered rock arrived from all over the world, with exports going to such places as Malta, the Sudan, India and Australia.

Swizzels Matlow, New Mills, Derbyshire

Kraft's takeover of Cadbury in 2010 means that Swizzels Matlow is now the largest independent family-owned confectionery company in Britain, producing 250 lines of sweets, employing 600 people and with a turnover of more than £40 million a year. It all started, says the family, in the early

1920s on a market stall in Hackney, London, with Maurice and Alfred Matlow selling their jellied sweets.

Matlow Brothers was set up in 1928, producing jellies and chews in an East London factory; five years later they merged with rival David Dee, whose forté was fizzy compressed tablet sweets. During the Blitz in 1940 they moved to a disused Victorian wick factory in New Mills, where together they created sweets that are still being eaten today, including Parma Violets, which sold for a halfpenny when they were launched in 1946, and the first chew lolly, the Drumstick, which, as noted previously, Trevor Matlow, Alfred's son, created by accident in 1957 when he was experimenting with a wrapping machine and discovered that it was possible to pour two flavours into the machine – milk and raspberry – and insert a stick.

Today the firm produces more than 14 tons of chew sweets, 40,000 bags of Rainbow Drops and nearly 300,000 Double Dip lollies.

Perhaps the most delightful place to be in the Swizzels Matlow factory is the powder room: not exactly the sort of powder room we hear about in posh hotels of previous generations, but a room where the company's premier brand, Love Hearts, are made. Here a sweet mist pervades the atmosphere as white sherbet is ground to a fine powder, before it is coloured and flavoured and poured through a silver hopper over a hole in the floor. Down below, in a cloud of sugar, the tablet machine applies 8 tons of pressure to flatten the sugar into tablets and stamp those all important messages on them.

More than 7 million Love Hearts are made every day, stamped with 134 different messages ranging from 'My Girl' to 'It's Love' to 'I'm Shy', most of which have been coined by the family . Since the creation of Love Hearts in 1954, an ongoing editing process has been necessary on the inaugural thirty to ensure that the sweets always reflect modern trends and language: passé messages have been ditched, for example – the 1950s 'Hey Daddio', and 'Far Out, Man' from the 1960s – and contemporary ones have been introduced – such as 'Email Me', which was added in 1998.

When meanings change radical action is necessary; for example, 'Go Gay', which a woman from Philadelphia complained about in the 1970s; others were consigned to sweet history when no sense was being made, as with 'Drop Dead Gorgeous' which had all romantic meaning eradicated when it was truncated to 'Drop Dead'. A man tried to mollify his wife after a row by giving her a tube of Love Hearts, but the first message she saw was 'Grow Up'. Her husband was invited to leave. 'Grow Up' is still produced.

More happily, 1-year-old Elijah Swan, who was born on Valentine's Day 2007 with the main arteries connected to his heart the wrong way round, had the words 'Heart Baby' stamped on a Love Heart in 2008 to celebrate his survival.

The company has moved with the times with mechanisation, as evidenced by the fact that in the 1950s the factory could boast 20 lines of sweets; now it has more than 250. Sixty years ago the company produced 5 tons of chew sweets per week; now it is more than 100 tons of pink chew every week.

Swizzels Matlow exports 20 per cent of its sweets to more than twenty countries, mostly in Europe – the Norwegians, for example, love Love Hearts.

Tangerine Confectionery, Pontefract and York

Tangerine Confectionery is headquartered in Pontefract, West Yorkshire, having grown since 2006, through acquisitions into one of the largest independent confectionery companies in Europe and the fourth biggest sweet maker in the United Kingdom. In January 2006, the name of the company changed from Tom's Confectionery to Tangerine Confectionery with new branding following the purchase of the company by a management team from Toms International of Denmark. The UK arm of Tom's existed through the acquisition of three confectionery companies, Taveners, Daintee and Parrs between 1992 and 2001. In 2006, the company acquired the confectionery arm of Blackpool-based Burton's Foods and so increased turnover to £60m, making it the largest independent confectionery company in the UK.

In January 2008, the company bought Monkhill Confectionery from Cadbury plc in a £58 million deal, with factories in Cleckheaton, Pontefract and York as well as a distribution centre in Holmewood, Derbyshire. The purchase included the Barratts, Sharps of York, Jameson's, Trebor Basset Mints, Butterkist and Pascall lines.

Henry Thorne & Co, Leeds

Like others in the confectionery industry, Henry Thorne was a Quaker. His first shop in Briggate around 1837 sold mustard and chicory, but this quickly grew into one of the country's bigger confectionery companies. The firm embraced new technology, notably steam power, and pioneered the use of photography on its tins. By the 1960s, Thorne's (whose slogan was 'The World's Premier Toffee') was producing over 2 million pieces of confectionery a day. In 1971, the business moved into the premises of their sister company C. W. Mattock, confectioners and 'toffery' of Sowerby Bridge, and the factory, in Lady Lane, was closed and demolished. Mabel Lucie Atwell is responsible for some of the Thorne advertising images.

Thornton's, Sheffield

Joseph William Thornton left his job as a sales representative for the Don Confectionery Company in 1911 and opened his first Thornton's Chocolate Kabin shop on the corner of Norfolk Street and Howard Street in Sheffield. Products included Violet Cachous, Sweet-Lips, Phul-Nanas and the curiously named Curiously Strong Mints. Chocolate production began in 1913 in the back room of its second shop on The Moor. Easter eggs and Thornton's Special Toffee were the main lines until the 1950s when the Continental Chocolates range was launched.

In 1948, the company moved to Belper and in 1954, Walter Willen, a Swiss confectioner, joined and created Swiss Assortment – a range of handmade confectionery. The firm was forced to change the name to Continental Assortment after complaints from the Swiss Embassy.

Kendall Mint Cake:
retailer and manufacturer.

Chapter 18

'The Oldest Sweet Shop', Pateley Bridge, the Star Rock Shop, Kirriemuir, and Jubilee Confectioners, Beamish

'The Oldest Sweet Shop', Pateley Bridge

This shop, established in 1827 in Pateley Bridge in beautiful Nidderdale, is recognised as the oldest sweet shop in the UK, an honour ratified by *The Guinness Book of Records*. It deserves a chapter of its own because it symbolises all that is best in sweets, their manufacture and their sale, both retail and online.

The website (www.oldestsweetshop.co.uk/about-us/) tells us how in the very early nineteenth-century days, the Oldest Sweet Shop started off selling sweets and luxury chocolates, including boiled sweets, toffees, herbal and spicy sweets originally prepared, boiled and made within

Inside the Oldest Sweet Shop. (*Photos courtesy of Keith Tordoff, www.oldestsweetshop.co.uk/press-enquiries*)

the sweet shop. In those days, customers were mainly local mill owners, brewery and quarry workers and labourers building the local reservoirs. Children too beat a path to the shop in increasing numbers eager to trade in their pocket money for sweets.

The shop embraced solid chocolate as perfected by J. S. Fry's & Sons, Rowntree's and Cadbury's. The Oldest Sweet Shop soon became exceedingly popular, not just locally but nationally and internationally. In the early twentieth century chocolate saw an upsurge in demand, as disposable income increased, choice expanded, and imported chocolate from France, Switzerland and Germany flooded in. What is more, local chocolatiers like Whitaker's of Skipton, Terry's, Craven, Lazenby, and Rowntree of York, Thorntons of Sheffield and Mackintosh of Halifax fuelled demand so much so that 'the Oldest Sweet Shop was able to sell a selection of the finest British chocolate at that time.' The privations caused by rationing during the First and Second world wars failed to stop the shop, which battled on regardless, selling sweets such as Liquorice Root Sticks and Cinder Toffee to locals, and evacuees from the big cities living at nearby Bewerley Park. The end of rationing in 1953 made sweets more popular than ever with the introduction of such classics as Black Jacks, Fruit Salads, Refreshers, Kola Cubes and Whams – all now referred to as 'retro'. In the 1970s, the supermarkets killed off many a sweet shop with their packets and bags and multipacks, but the Oldest Sweet Shop stuck with tradition, retaining the neat and seductive rows of transparent glass jars.

In the 2020s, the Oldest Sweet Shop continues to thrive and is joined by legions of imitators up and down the country cashing in on the nostalgia evoked by old-fashioned sweets and those neat ranks of glass jars. Sweet shops have come and gone, but the Pateley Bridge shop never went away; it remains pre-eminent in the sector and has become a place of pilgrimage for ardent sweet lovers, 'a national treasure' as one national newspaper called it. Add to this the thriving online business and you have the perfect sweet shop, so indicative of British life and part of the fabric of our nation's social history.

The Star Rock Shop

The Star Rock Shop was established in 1833 by David Ferguson. It still trades today from the same premises in the Roods, Kirriemuir, near Forfar, making it the oldest producing and continuously trading sweet shop in Scotland.

Jubilee Confectioners, Beamish, the Living Museum of the North

In keeping with its authenticity, the marvellous Beamish, the Living Museum of the North, near Stanley in Co Durham features a sweet shop-cum-manufactory. This is what we can expect:

> Jubilee Confectioners represents a typical town sweet shop of the early 1900s, which would sell sweets, toffee and chocolate. Visitors can see sweets being made in the factory at the back of the shop, using traditional techniques and equipment. A wide range of sweets are on sale in the store at the front.
>
> The vast majority of sweet shops in this period were small and family run, with the proprietors often living above the shop. They would specialise in local favourites to be sold at the shop and to other stores in the area. Popular north east sweets included black bullets, cinder toffee, sarsaparilla tablets and Tyne mints. Chocolate from well-known producers such as Rowntree's, Fry's and Terry's was sold, although would be relatively expensive and usually displayed in elaborate hand-painted boxes.

A busy day at Jubilee Confectioners.

Sweetmakers in the region included George W. Horner and Co of Chester-le-Street, Redheads of Blyth, J. Welch of Whitley Bay and J. Vose of Durham. In the sweet factory, visitors will spot a fine collection of sweet rollers, which are used during production to create a variety of shapes, and came from various sweet shops and factories, including in Hartlepool Headland, Houghton-le -Spring and Rowntree's in York.

Courtesy and © Beamish,
The Living Museum of the North

Outside the Star Rock – the oldest sweet shop in Scotland.

Chapter 19

Quotable Sweets

G iven the ubiquity of sweets in life in general it comes as no surprise that sweets feature prominently and frequently in conversation and in quotations; here are just a few words of the wise uttered from the lips of the rich and famous.

I eat a lot of salad, a little meat, and some fruit. That's all. But I like sweets.

Sophia Loren

It was the corner sweet-shop in Australia that first piqued my interest in interior design. I went into this space with a mixture of apprehension and excitement as a child. It was filled, floor to ceiling, with the most incredible rounded glass bowls filled to the brim with bonbons, buttons, and sweets.

Anouska Hempel

I'm really still a child of the Forties. I still think about it a lot, about the repercussions of armed conflict. Until 1953 we had rationing. We couldn't buy meat, we couldn't buy pleasurable goods like cigarettes and sweets. I didn't starve – my family were lucky – but I knew what it was like standing in line waiting for foodstuffs.

Eric Burdon of The Animals

I wish I didn't like sweets as much as I do. I wish I didn't get carried away sometimes.

James Corden

In the 1950s, as food rationing ended, I remember a plentiful supply of sweets for the first time.

Robert Powell

The end of rationing in 1953 resulted in spending on sweets growing by £1,000m in the first year. (*Courtesy of Mark Simmonds, Curator, Hartlepool Borough Council*)

My daughter is a real migraine sufferer; the minute she has a handful of Haribo sweets, she gets a headache. There's a connection between what the liver can't break down with what goes on to trigger a headache. You just have to be aware.

Sheherazade Goldsmith

It's a pragmatist's business, comedy. Start off with good intentions and references to the Pompidou Centre and you end up with boiled sweets and a pantomime cow.

Mel Smith

All you need is love. But a little chocolate now and then doesn't hurt.

Charles M. Schulz

I'm grateful for every day I'm still alive. Everything is still working. I attribute it to eating a lot of processed foods. I think it's the preservatives that keep me going. That, and I eat as much chocolate as I can get my hands on.

Joan Rivers

To me, it's not the end of the world if I end up not being with someone. I love romance. I love sex. I love men's company, but I don't feel I have to be married. Men are a wonderful part of life, like chocolate. But my life goes on whether they're there or not.

Jerry Hall

My wife said, 'Take me in your arms and whisper something soft and sweet.' I said, 'chocolate fudge'.

Tommy Cooper

My beauty secret is… nothing! I don't drink too much water. I don't eat very well. Sometimes I cheat and grab some chocolate. The best thing is to eat what you want, but not very much.

Yoko Ono

I was probably a little bit overweight as a child, being passionate about baked beans on toast and Cadbury's milk chocolate when I could get it.

Roger Moore

My weakness is dark chocolate. I carry little tins of it in my purse.

Sharon Stone

After about twenty years of marriage, I'm finally starting to scratch the surface of what women want. And I think the answer lies somewhere between conversation and chocolate.

Mel Gibson

I need to have dark chocolate in the cupboard – Green & Black's is good, but any will do.

Darcey Bussell

I never do any television without chocolate. That's my motto and I live by it. Quite often I write the scripts and I make sure there are chocolate scenes. Actually I'm a bit of a chocolate tart and will eat anything. It's amazing I'm so slim.

Dawn French

You can't be a grown-up woman and not like chocolate.
Julie Dawn Cole

My father was in the civil service. I can remember standing in a bus shelter in the pouring rain, and that we were allowed candy floss at the end of the holiday if we had behaved.
Honor Blackman

We don't like Jelly Babies, or fruit gums for that matter, so think how we feel standing on stage trying to dodge the stuff, before you throw some more at us.... Besides it is dangerous. I was hit in the eye once with a boiled sweet, and it's not funny.
George Harrison in a 1963 letter to 15-year-old Lynn Smith

Everybody wants a box of chocolates and a long-stem rose. Everybody knows.

And there are no letters in the mailbox
Oh no, there are no grapes upon your vine. And there are, there are no chocolates in your boxes anymore
And there are no diamonds in your mine.
Leonard Cohen

My boy lollipop, you make my heart go giddy up. You are as sweet as candy.
Millie Small, My Boy Lollipop

Anything is good if it's made of chocolate.
Jo Brand

Chapter 20

Sweets in Music & Literature:
'taking candy from a baby' ...

Sweets are a powerful force for nostalgia; they feature frequently in books, plays and poetry, and in music. Here is a small selection of sweets in culture.

Music

A number of bands have taken recourse to sweets and sugar for their names; they include:

Sweet
Hot Chocolate
Vanilla Fudge
Rapper, Vanilla Ice
Sugar Cubes
The Mighty Lemon Drops
The Juicy Fruits
1910 Fruitgum Company
Lemonheads
1980s' hip-hop group the Sugarhill Gang
1990s' punks the Candy Snatchers

– to name but a few.

Reference to sweets, sugar and candy in songs, though, are numerous. Here are just some of them:

- Spangles are mentioned in the (rather disturbing) Kinks' song *Art Lover, (Come to daddy, and I'll give you some spangles)* from their 1981 album Give the People What They Want.
- In 1977 Lieutenant Pigeon released an instrumental single titled *Spangles*.
- The Spangles are a garage punk rock 'n roll band.
- The Fall song *It's A Curse* on the album *The Infotainment Scan* also includes a reference to Spangles: *It's a curse Balti and Vimto and Spangles Were always crap Regardless of the look back bores.*
- Phil Harris wrote a song *Jelly Bean (He's a Curb-Side Cutie)* in 1940. In other words, this guy was useless.

May 2013 saw Australian singer Alison Hams release *Jelly Baby Song* – its lyrics references type 1 diabetics who eat Jelly Babies to overcome hypoglycaemic episodes. This was to raise awareness for type 1 diabetes by the Australia Juvenile Diabetes Research Foundation who sell specially packaged Jelly Babies as the focus of their annual 'Jelly Baby Month' campaign.

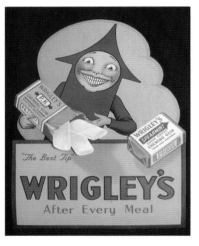

Wrigley's seem to be scaring you into buying their gum in this 1930 showcard.

Chewing gum got a priceless mention from Frank Sinatra when he referred to the Chicago Wrigley Building in his *(Chicago), My Kind of Town*

My kind of town, Chicago is
My kind of razzmatazz
And it has all that jazz
And each time I leave, Chicago is
Tuggin' my sleeve, Chicago is
The Wrigley Building, Chicago is
The Union Stockyard, Chicago is
One town that won't let you down
It's my kind of town!

The quintessential Mars bar song, *Mars Bars* by The Undertones:

> I need a Mars Bar
> Hey raid the Spa
> To help me through the day
> I need a Mars Bar
> I've had total fun
> It helps me, makes me, work rest and play
> It helps me, makes me, work rest and play
> I never eat my dinner
> I push away the plate
> You can see I'm getting thinner
> Because I just can't wait
> To get my Mars Bar
> Hey raid the Spa
> To Patrick Moore and David Bowie
> And all the other stars
> There's evidence here to show
> That there's life on Mars
> I need a
> There's glucose for energy
> Caramel for strength

George Formby helped write and perform the song *With My Little Stick of Blackpool Rock.*

Floating, a Moody Blues song from their album *To Our Children's Children's Children* (1969), has the lines 'The candy stores will be brand new, and you'll buy rock with the Moon right through!', referring to rock being sold at a resort on the Moon.

Brian May of Queen, wrote *Brighton Rock,* which appeared on Queen's album *Sheer Heart Attack* (1974). It concerns a young Jenny and Jimmy's naughty weekend away without their parents' knowledge in a seaside town and showcased May's legendary 'Brighton Rock' guitar solo, which became a standard feature of the group's live shows.

Sweet songs include: *Sweets for my Sweet* by the Searchers: 'Sweets for my sweet, sugar for my honey, Your first sweet kiss thrilled me so...'

THE SEARCHERS Sweets For My Sweet   ●●●● stereo ●●●●   FILE UNDER POP

THE SEARCHERS

Sweets For My Sweet

ORIGINAL ARTISTS • ORIGINAL RECORDINGS

Sweets are an everyday part of life in all countries. For example, they have been ever present in popular music down the years; the aptly saccharine *Sweets for my Sweet* was originally released by the Drifters in 1961 and was later a UK hit for the Searchers in 1963.

Sweets for my sweet, sugar for my honey
Your first sweet kiss thrilled me so
Sweets for my sweet, sugar for my honey
I'll never ever let you go

Then there is *Sweet Talkin' Candy Man* by Nancy Sinatra (1998) and her *Sugar Me* on *How Does it Feel?*: 'Save me, save me Baby, baby sugar me Gotta get my candy free Sugar me by day, sugar me my baby Baby, baby sugar me Gotta get my candy free Sugar me by day, sugar me by night Sugar, sugar, sugar, sugar… Just me and you Honey sweet and caramel-y, Will melt away the bittersweet memory.'

Buddy Rich's *Sonny and Sweets*; *Cyanide Sweet Tooth Suicide* by Shinedown on *The Sound of Madness*: 'Taste like sugar, but it's Novocaine, She's grinding teeth So she can sharpen the pain.'

Songs with *candy* in the title are legion:

Len Barry's 1965 hit, *1-2-3* with the immortal lines:

> Oh, that's how elementary it's gonna be
> C'mon, let's fall in love, it's easy
> (It's so easy)
> Like takin' candy from a baby
> (Like takin' candy)

And these:

The Candy Man, Sammy Davis, Jr
I Want Candy, The Strangeloves
Lollipop (Candyman), Aqua
Candy Girl, The Four Seasons
Candy, Iggy Pop (nostalgic 1990 song about lost love – duet with B-52s singer Kate Pierson)
Candy Man, The Hollies
Candy, Ray Charles
Candy Perfume Girl, Madonna
Candy Says, The Velvet Underground: named after Candy Darling, an actress in some of Andy Warhol's films; Darling identified as a woman and swapped her birth name James for Candy, partly because she loved sweets and partly because, as the song said, she'd come to hate her body, and her new identity's elegant femininity suited her better.

Candy Kisses, Tony Bennett
So Like Candy, Elvis Costello
Candy by the Pound, Elton John
Sweeter Than Candy, Carl Perkins
Candy Man, Suzi Quatro
Candy Lips, Doris Day

Candy, Lisa Stansfield
Candy Shop, Madonna
Candy Man, Donovan on his 1965 album, *Fairytale*
Got Candy, Cyndi Lauper
Candy Man Blues, Mississippi John Hurt: 'All heard what sister Johnson said / She always takes a candy stick to bed / Don't stand close to the candy man / He'll leave a big candy stick in your hand'.

Donovan's *Candy Man* was not just a nice street corner sweet seller but a regular commuter to Morocco:

> Peppermint stick got a little brass band
> I got a peppermint stick I got a little brass band…
> My Candy man he's Morocco bound
> Now I'd give everything in this Godalmighty world
> To bring my Candy man home…
> Candy man, I love the man
> Yeah the Candy man, he gets me high.

This 1965 composition was, of course, of its time, a time when 'sweeties' were drugs and you could, for example, score Preludin – a stimulant drug that was previously used as an appetite suppressant – at 24 for £1.

Cotton Candy Land sung by Elvis Presley in the 1963 film *It Happened at the World's Fair* gives us a children's fantasy world where 'every star is a candy bar, and the moon is a marshmallow dream', offering a psychedelic precursor to Roald Dahl's Willy Wonka's candy factory, which was published the following year.

Then there is *Lollipop Guild* from the *Wizard of Oz*, when Dorothy reaches Munchkinland, and a group of little people who represent a guild named after lollipops comes out to sing her this 23-second song:

> We represent the Lollipop Guild,
> The Lollipop Guild, the Lollipop Guild.
> And in the name of the Lollipop Guild
> We wish to welcome you to Munchkin Land

Here's some liquorice and jelly beans: *There's a Train out for Dreamland*, Nat King Cole:

You'll see a big white snowman
Who melts when he hears you laugh
A singin' mouse
A liquorice house
And a funny-looking jelly bean giraffe

Some try to persuade that *My Boy Lollipop* by Millie Small is replete with sexual innuendo, but it is far more likely that the writers wanted nothing more than to describe a boy who's 'sweet as candy' and a 'sugar dandy'. In any event, lollipop maker Tyler's presented the singer with a 42lb lollipop and 216 regular ones.

Songs featuring sugar are just as many and various although in some of these songs sugar may not mean sugar as we know it:

Sugar Sugar, The Archies; the story is that when the Monkees rejected *Sugar Sugar*, the songwriters 'gave' it to the Archies, a fictional band from The Archie Show; unfortunately, the bit about the Monkees is not true.

Brown Sugar, The Rolling Stones
Pour Some Sugar on Me, Def Leppard
Lips Like Sugar, Echo & the Bunnymen
Real Sugar, Roxette
Sugar Never Tasted So Good, The White Stripes
Sugar, The Pointer Sisters
Sugar Walls, Sheena Easton
White Sugar, Peter Frampton
Sugar Sweet, Muddy Waters
Sugar Daddy, Thompson Twins
Sugar Tongue, Indigo Girls
Blood Sugar Sex Magik, Red Hot Chili Peppers
Sugar Moon, k.d. lang
Sugar Mama, John Lee Hooker
Sugar Me, Lyndsey de Paul

Chocolate

Chocolate figures large in the songwriter's note book; take this from George Harrison on The Beatles' *White Album*: *Savoy Truffle* in tribute to an allegedly chocoholic Eric Clapton in which Harrison took some of the lyrics directly from a box of Mackintosh's Good News:

> Creme tangerine and montelimar
> A ginger sling with a pineapple heart
> A coffee dessert, yes you know it's good news
> But you'll have to have them all pulled out
> After the Savoy truffle
> Cool cherry cream, a nice apple tart
> I feel your taste all the time we're apart
> Coconut fudge, really blows down those blues
> But you'll have to have them all pulled out
> After the Savoy truffle

Dentists must have loved him. Here is the perfect selection box:

Chocolate, Kylie Minogue
Chocolate Chip, Miles Davis
Chocolate Jesus, Tom Waits
Chocolate Symphony, Bee Gees
Cigarettes and Chocolate Milk, Rufus Wainwright
Chocolate Chip, Isaac Hayes, Dionne Warwick
Chocolate Ice, Lulu.

Finally, Leonard Cohen's *Diamonds in the Mine* has this bad news:

> And the trees are burning in your promised land
> And there are no letters in the mailbox
> And there are no grapes upon the vine
> And there are no chocolates in the boxes anymore
> And there are no diamonds in the mine
>
> And, from *Everybody Knows...*
> Everybody got this broken feeling
> Like their father or their dog just died
> Everybody talking to their pockets
> Everybody wants a box of chocolates
> And a long-stem rose
> Everybody knows

Classically speaking there is *Dance of the Sugar Plum Fairy* in Act II of Tchaikovsky's 1892 two-act fairy ballet *The Nutcracker*, where Clara is ushered to the Land of the Sweets by the Prince. This is the realm of the Sugar Plum Fairy, a magical creature inspired by a sweet made up of sugary layers. To honour Clara, a celebration dance of sweets from around the world is performed: chocolate from Spain, coffee from Arabia, tea from China, and candy canes from Russia. Mother Ginger has her children; to end the night, the Sugar Plum Fairy and her Prince dance.

A final waltz is performed by all the sweets, after which the Sugar Plum Fairy beckons Clara and the Prince down from their throne. He bows to her, she kisses Clara goodbye, and leads them to a reindeer-drawn sleigh which takes off as they wave goodbye to all the subjects who wave back.

Chocolate makes an appearance in Mozart's *Cosi fan Tutti*, premiered in 1790 when the maid, Despina, bewails her lot and, overcome by temptation and the smell of chocolate, declares:

'I've been beating the chocolate for half an hour, now it is ready...o gracious mistresses, why should you get the real thing and I only the smell of it? By Bacchus I'm going to taste it; oh, it's so good!'

Literature

Literature too is replete with references to sweets. For example, as we have seen, there are a number of literary references to the burning of medicinal pastilles; they include the short story *The Birth-Mark* by Nathaniel Hawthorne, the poem *The Laboratory* by Robert Browning, and *Jane Eyre* by Charlotte Brontë. They also turn up in Dashiell Hammett's *The Maltese Falcon*. 'A half-filled package of violet pastilles' are among the items found in Joel Cairo's pockets. Vichy Pastilles are mentioned by French author Guy de Maupassant in his short story, *The Magic Couch*.

In 1648, Robert Herrick in his poem *To His Most Fair and Lovely Mistress*, Anne Soame (his cousin), had closely associated his love for her with the sweet smell of 'wealthy spiceries...blooming clove...thus sweet she smells'. Humbugs are referred to in Elizabeth Gaskell's 1863 *Sylvia's Lovers* as being a food from the North.

F. Scott Fitzgerald composed *The Jelly Bean* in 1922, in which he wrote: 'Jelly-bean is the name throughout the undissolved Confederacy for one who spends his life conjugating the verb to idle in the first person singular – I am idling, I have idled, I will idle.'

Charles Dickens' *The Mystery of Edwin Drood* (1870) has Rosa Bud announce: 'I want to go to the Lumps-of-Delight shop' where she explains what a Lump of Delight is, 'occasionally putting her little pink fingers to her rosy lips, to cleanse them from the Dust of Delight that comes off the lumps'. Turkish delight appeared in C.S. Lewis' *The Lion, the Witch, and the Wardrobe,* where it was Edmund Pevensie's greatest passion. In Graham Greene's *Brighton Rock* (1938), Ida says, 'It's like those sticks of rock: bite it all the way down, you'll still read Brighton.'

More recently we see R. K. Narayan's *The Vendor of Sweets* (1969) in which Jagan strives for purity.

Literature too is full of references to sweets, for example: R.K. Narayan's bestselling *The Vendor of Sweets.*

The Goon Show's Bluebottle was often rewarded or bribed, with a quantity of dolly mixtures or jelly babies.

Humbugs have nothing to do with the phrase 'Bah, humbug' from Dickens' *A Christmas Carol* which denotes an aversion to Christmas, although the actual sweets are now often used ironically, for example in an episode of *Blackadder* and in 'The Adventure of the Six Napoleons'; in an episode in *The Return of Sherlock Holmes* series, where Holmes rebukes Dr Watson for offering Inspector Lestrade one of the sweets saying, 'Watson, this is no time for humbugs!' Generally, humbug is a pejorative term first recorded in 1750 meaning something like bullshit, or a practical joke; its use says something about its user – more often than not a posh boy out of touch with the real world with language to match. The B side to Greg Lake's *I Believe in Father Christmas* is titled *Humbug* – no coincidence that.

Unsurprisingly, children's literature and children's authors provide a plethora of sweets:

In *Milly Molly Mandy Keeps Shop* (Joyce Lankester Brisley) Milly yearns for a shop 'like Miss Muggins, where she could sell sweets'. The story concludes with Milly Molly Mandy accidentally giving Billy Blunt one too many aniseed balls. Luckily, Billy spots the error and disaster is averted.

In *Pippi Longstocking Goes Aboard* – Astrid Lindgren – Pippi is let loose in small town Sweden with an abundance of looted gold; in the 'Pippi Goes Shopping' chapter she asks:

'Please may I have thirty-six pounds of sweets?'
'You mean you want thirty-six sweets,' the shop assistant replies.
'I mean that I want thirty-six pounds of sweets,' said Pippi.
She put the gold coin on the counter. The assistant hurriedly began pouring sweets into large bags.

Pippi ends up also buying a small cart to transport the lollipops, green acid drops, jelly babies and chocolate cigarettes out of the shop and into the street where she hands them out to local children and starts a kind of candy-fuelled riot.

Roald Dahl described pear drops: 'Pear drops were exciting because they had a dangerous taste,' in his first autobiography, *Boy*. 'They smelled of nail varnish and they froze the back of your throat.' Indeed, Dahl also tells us how 'the sweet-shop in Llandaff in the year 1923 was the very centre of our lives.'

Sweet shops figure prominently in Peter and Jane's world. In *We Have Fun* ((We Have Fun – Ladybird Key Words Reading Scheme (Peter and Jane book 2a)) Jane is particularly insistent:

Can we have some sweets? Says Jane.
Can we go to the shop for some sweets?
Yes, says Peter.
This is the shop, Jane.
Yes, this is it.
They have sweets and toys.
We want sweets, says Jane.

Strangely when she finally gets her sweets, Jane chooses to place a Liquorice Allsort on Pat the dog's nose, but everyone seems happy; we do indeed have fun.

Chocolate too (liquid and solid) was making its mark in the chocolate houses of Britain. Hester Thrale Piozzi tells us how Samuel Johnson used chocolate as a replacement for alcohol: 'he took his chocolate liberally, pouring in large quantities of cream, or even melted butter.'

Voltaire's Candide learns that the spread of syphilis to Europe by Columbus' explorers was a fair price to pay for the simultaneous introduction of chocolate and cochineal. The works of the Marquis de Sade, one of the more notorious lovers of chocolate, have frequent references to chocolate, consumed ante- and post- coitus and it is a regular prop in his sexual orgies. His petulant letters from prison to Mme de Sade (Renee de Montreuil) betray a genuine personal craving, but also indicate how concerned he was at the same time to establish his aristocratic credentials; this from 16 May 1779:

The sponge cake is not at all what I asked for. 1st, I wanted it iced all over…2nd I wanted it to have chocolate inside as black as the devil's arse is black from smoke, and there isn't even the least trace of chocolate. I beg you to have it sent to me at the first opportunity… the cakes must smell of it, as if you're biting into a bar of chocolate.

De Sade's greatest chocolate moment, possibly fabricated, is told by Louis Petit de Bachaumont in his *Secret Memoirs for the History of the Republic of Letters*: at a ball given by de Sade, the host had laced the chocolate pastilles with Spanish fly, a well known aphrodisiac:

> It proved to be so potent that those who ate the pastilles began to burn with unchaste ardour and to carry on as if in the grip of the most amorous frenzy...even the most respectable of women were unable to resist the uterine rage that stirred within them. And so it was that M.de Sade enjoyed the favours of his sister-in-law...several persons died of their frightful priapic excesses, and others are still quite sick.

The heiress Cecilia in Frances Burney's eponymous novel is given chocolate as one of the accoutrements of prosperity. Jane Austen makes the affluent General Tilney a chocolate drinker in *Northanger Abbey* and Caroline Austen, Jane's niece, tells us how chocolate competed for glory with the wedding cake at her stepsister Anna Austen's wedding in 1814. Later, in his 1859 *A Tale of Two Cities*, Dickens describes how Monseigneur's copious morning chocolate consumption took four men and the cook to administer.

In his 1964 *Charlie and the Chocolate Factory*, Roald Dahl conjured up 'Everlasting Gobstoppers', a fictitious gobstopper that could never get smaller or be finished. In the book, Charlie Bucket walks past Wonka's mysterious chocolate factory every day, with its smells wafting out. When the eccentric chocolatier Mr Willy Wonka, in a brilliant piece of marketing, announces that there are five Golden Tickets to be won, and the prize is a visit to his wonderful factory itself, children everywhere rush to buy his products – but Charlie's family are very poor and can only afford to buy him one bar of Wonka's chocolate each year on his birthday. He never dreams he'll have the chance to see the inside of the factory for himself – but then his dream surprisingly comes true.

Soon Charlie, his Grandpa Jo and his fellow winners are setting out on a magical tour of the factory, where a whole host of extraordinary inventions and a river of melted chocolate await them.

Sir John Betjeman celebrates liquorice and the liquorice fields of Pontefract in his *The Licorice Fields at Pontefract* which starts:

In the licorice fields at Pontefract
My love and I did meet
And many a burdened licorice bush
Was blooming round our feet

And goes on to tell us:

The light and dangling licorice flowers
Gave off the sweetest smells…and little shuttered corner shops.

A plate of liquorice wheels.

In the 2018 film *Johnny English Strikes Again*, the hero (played by Rowan Atkinson) carries a box of Jelly Babies with him – they are actually disguised explosives, 'jelly' being short for gelignite, and they blow up whoever eats them – with fatal results.

TV was also in on the act. In 1962, Jelly Babies were referred to as 'those kids' candies' in a *Supercar* episode, 'Operation Superstork'. Doctor Who was a fan with many a reference: first seen with the second Doctor, they became most associated with Tom Baker's fourth Doctor, who offered them to alien enemies to defuse tense situations, and in one episode actually bluffed an alien into thinking them a weapon.

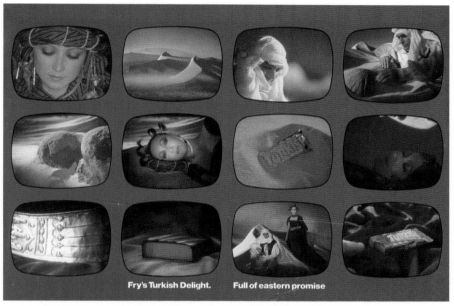

Stills from a Fry's Turkish Delight television advertisement in the 1980s.

The year 2010 saw Cadbury's Flake ditch its famous strapline 'Only the crumbliest, flakiest chocolate'. In the 1970s one of the iconic adverts was taken off air as it was deemed 'too racy ...'.

Chapter 21

The Future: Fairtrade, Health and the Internet

The twenty-first century has already seen significant changes in the chocolate industry in Britain, not least Kraft's £11.5bn takeover of Cadbury in 2010 to add to its earlier acquisitions of Terry and Toblerone. Fairtrade, the agonisingly slow move towards more healthy sweets, and the internet have undoubtedly underpinned the biggest industry-wide developments.

Fairtrade

To help address this crisis, Fairtrade has emerged as a powerful force providing manufacturers to pay growers a fairer price for their raw materials. The Fairtrade website tells us:

> Most cocoa farmers in Ghana and Côte d'Ivoire live on less than a $1 a day. Poverty, and its many related issues, such as child labour, is the key challenge faced by cocoa growing communities. With Fairtrade sales, farmer cooperatives receive the Fairtrade Premium which they spend on improving quality and productivity of their farms, to increase incomes. …The average age of a cocoa farmer is now over 50 because the younger generation cannot be attracted to the profession as the benefits are so poor.
> (www.fairtrade.org.uk/Media-Centre/Blog/2016/October/10-facts-about-Fairtrade-chocolate-to-remember-this-Chocolate-Week)

Fairtrade chocolate accounts for 12 per cent of total sales in the UK – and the trend for Fairtrade-certified cocoa is growing. The Fairtrade Foundation was originally founded by Oxfam and others and the concept was extended into the world of chocolate in 1994 by Josephine Fairley and Craig Sams who insisted that the chocolate she used at their new Green & Blacks organic chocolate company was made from pesticide-free cacao beans. The result was Maya Gold which was not only pesticide free, but also was produced with fair price paid to the Kekchi Maya farmers and received the UK's first Fairtrade certification. The company is now part of Mondelēz International, formerly Kraft Foods.

In 2009, Cadbury's Dairy Milk was Fairtrade certified, thereby tripling the amount of Fairtrade cocoa sourced from Ghana to about 15,000 tonnes a year. The total annual cocoa production of Ghana is more than 600,000 tonnes. Under Fairtrade, Cadbury pays a guaranteed minimum price, even if the open market price falls below it, for Ghanaian cocoa. The move is part of the Cadbury Cocoa Partnership, a £45m initiative over ten years which will help cocoa farmers throughout the developing world.

January 2010 saw the first Fairtrade certified KitKat four-finger bars arrive on shop shelves to the benefit of thousands of farmers in Côte d'Ivoire. As well as the Fairtrade price (or market price if higher) for the cocoa, farmers' organisations receive additional Fairtrade premium payments (currently US$150 per tonne) which is used for business or social development projects. Other facts from the website:

The country produces 40 per cent of the world's cocoa and one in four people directly or indirectly depend on cocoa farming. Most cocoa farmers have never tasted chocolate; cocoa trees begin to yield pods at peak production levels by the fifth year, and they can continue at this level for 10 years. But for all this industry, cocoa farmers earn very little from a hugely profitable global cocoa trade; most cocoa farmers in Ghana and Côte d'Ivoire live on less than a .77p a day; the average age of a cocoa farmer is now over 50 because the younger generation cannot be attracted to the profession as the benefits and prospects are so dismal; 25 per cent of all Fairtrade cocoa growers are women; Fairtrade Africa currently trains cocoa farmers in financial management, governance, good agricultural practices, gender and child labour. This forms part of the Fairtrade West Africa Cocoa Program.

Health

On the continuing issue of alleged health benefits of chocolate, the European Commission Food Safety Authority has ruled that there was still insufficient consistent scientific evidence to support studies which suggest that consumption of certain types of chocolate can lower blood pressure, reduce the risk of heart attack, prevent wrinkles or increase cognitive skills. However, a 2010 study of 19,357 patients (EPIC Study 1994–2006) led by Brian Buijsse of the German Institute of Human Nutrition in Nuthetal, and reported in the *British Heart Journal,* provided some reliable evidence that chocolate does appear to offer some protection against hypertension and stroke: work in progress.

In marketing, the biggest development has undoubtedly been the rise in importance of the corporate and brand websites where companies across the whole range of manufacturers – from Cadbury and Craven to Trebor and Tunnocks – imaginatively and dynamically display all aspects of their lines, manufacturing processes, heritage, recipes and ethical credentials. Individual products have their own sites giving nutritional information and a wealth of other detail; online stores tempt us with attractively presented brands easily and conveniently obtainable without leaving the house.

Josephine Fairley and Maya Gold neatly bring us full circle, back to the Maya Indians and the origins of the cocoa and chocolate industries. Her fairness and the wider work of the Fairtrade Foundation remind us also of the philanthropy we associate with chocolate manufacture through the famous English Quaker companies and others in the US and in continental Europe.

Green & Black ethically sourced organic chocolate bars.

Appendix I

Some Forgettable Brand Names

Oh Henry
Radio Toffee
Voice Gums
Ogo Pogo Eyes
Ainsdale Smilers
Cats' Tails
Bung Carraways
Horehound Tablets
Ching Changs
Bandstrings
Diaboalones

For liquorice there was:

Greyhound Juice
Little Folks' Sticks
Cutty Pipes
Monster London Twists
Peashooters
Spanish Twists
Seville Coils
Japanese Screws
Pomfret Nail Rods
Yum-Yum Twists
Long Virginia
Farthing Starlets and
Jumbo's Chains.

Appendix II

Sweet Places to Visit

Cadbury World
Linden Road, Bournville, Birmingham B30 2LU 0121 451 4180
www.cadburyworld.co.uk

Caleys Cocoa Café
The Guildhall, Gaol Hill, Norwich, Norfolk, NR2 1JP
www.caleys.com/about-cocoacafe

Museum of Brands, Packaging and Advertising
2 Colville Mews, Lonsdale Road, Notting Hill, London W11 2AR
info@museumofbrands.com
www.museumofbrands.com

Thomas Tunnock Ltd
34 Old Mill Road, Uddingston, Glasgow G71 7HH 01698 813551
www.tunnock.co.uk

York Castle Museum
York YO1 9RY 01904 68768
www.yorkcastlemuseum.org

The Sugar Slavery Museum, Museum of London Docklands
www.museumoflondon.org.uk/museum-london-docklands/permanent-galleries/london-sugar-slavery

International Slavery Museum, Merseyside Maritime Museum, Liverpool
www.liverpoolmuseums.org.uk/international-slavery-museum

Wilberforce House Museum, Hull
www.hcandl.co.uk/museums-and-galleries/wilberforce-house

York's chocolate history in action
https://www.yorkchocolatestory.com/the-story/

York Cocoa House
www.yorkcocoahouse.co.uk

Further Reading

Abbot, E., *Sugar: A Bittersweet History*, London, 2010

Angell, S.W (Ed) *Quakers, Business and Industry Volume 4: Quakers and the Disciplines,* Longmeadow MA, 2017

Beckert, S., How Sweet It Is. And How Malignant; review of James Walvin's Sugar: The World Corrupted: From Slavery to Obesity published in *The New York Times*, 23 July 2018

Blum. A., Candy cigarettes. *N Engl J Med*.302 (17), 972, 1980

Books LLC, Confectionery *Companies of the United Kingdom*, Memphis 2010

Bradley, J., Cadbury's *Purple Reign*, Chichester 2008

Brannan, J. and F., A *Postcard from Bournville*, Studley, 1992

Brenner, J., *The Chocolate Wars: Inside the Secret Worlds of Mars and Hershey*, London 1999

Broomfield, M., A *Bournville Assortment*, York, 1998

Buijsse, B. et al.: Chocolate consumption in relation to blood pressure and risk of cardiovascular disease in German adults. *European Heart Journal* 2010, Jul.31 (13): 1616–23

Burg, J: A Guide to the Rowntree and Mackintosh Company Archives 1862–1969, York 1979

Burnett, J., *Plenty and Want: A Social History of Food in England from 1815 to the Present Day*, 3rd edition, London, 1989

Cadbury, D., Chocolate *Wars: From Cadbury to Kraft*, London, 2010

Cadbury Bros Ltd, *The Bournville Story*, Bournville
   Sweet-Shop Success – A Handbook for the Sweet Retailer, Bournville

Chinn, C., *The Cadbury Story*, Studley, 1998

Chrystal, P., Villages *around York through Time*, Stroud 2010
   York Then & Now, Gloucester 2010
   The Rowntrees of York, Pickering 2012
   The Confectionery Industry in York, Barnsley 2011
   Confectionery in Yorkshire, Stroud 2012
   The Rowntrees: Tales from a Chocolate Family in Angell, S.W. (2017), 169–189
   Lazenby & Son (York) Ltd – York's other confectionery company; *York Historian* 36, 2019
   Rowntree's: The Early History, Barnsley 2021

Clarence-Smith, W.G., *Cocoa and Chocolate 1765–1914*, London, 2000

Coady, C., *The Chocolate Companion*, New York 1995

Coe, S.D., *The True History of Chocolate*, London 1996

Coley, N., 'The fight against food adulteration'. *Education in Chemistry* 42 46–49, 2005

Edwards, W.P., *The Science of Sugar Confectionery*. Cambridge, 2008

Feuz, P., *Toblerone: 100 Years – The Story of a Swiss World Success*, Berne

Fitzgerald, R., Rowntree and Market Strategy, 1897–1939, *Business and Economic History* 18, 1989

Fitzgerald, R., *Rowntree and the Marketing Revolution 1862–1969*, Cambridge 1995

Freke, A., *J.S. Fry & Sons: A Rough Guide to the Family & The Firm*, Bristol, 2010

Fuller, L.K., *Chocolate Fads, Folklore and Fantasies*, Binghamton 1994

Goldstein, D., *Oxford Companion to Sugar and Sweets*. Oxford, 2015

Goodall, F., Marketing Consumer Products before 1914: Rowntree's and Elect Cocoa in R.P.T. Davenport-Hines (ed.), *Markets and Bagmen: Studies in the History of Marketing and British Industrial Performance 1830– 1939*, London 1986

Gumbley, E., *Bournville*, Market Drayton, 1991

Hamish F. W., *The Coming of the Mass Market 1850–1914*, London 1981

Harrison, M., *Bournville: Model Village to Garden Suburb*, Chichester, 1999

Head, B., *The Food of the Gods*, London, 1903

Heer, J., *Nestlé 125 Years*, Vevey 1991

Hindley, D., *Advertising in Victorian England 1837–1901*, London 1972

Hitches, M., *Bournville, Steam and Chocolate*, Pinner, 1992

Jackson, E., Joseph Rowntree (1801–1859), *York Historian* 23, 2006; pp 40–63

Jackson, P., *How* did Quakers Conquer the British Sweet Shop? *BBC News Magazine* January 20th 2010.

Jones, I. F., 'Arsenic and the Bradford poisonings of 1858'. *The Pharmaceutical Journal* 265, 938–993, 2000

Keyser, C., The Sweet Tooth of Slavery. *Transition*, 115, 2014, 143–153

Klein, J. D., 'Do candy cigarettes encourage young people to smoke?'. *British Medical Journal* 321 (7257): 362–365, 2000

Klein, J. D., 'Candy cigarettes: do they encourage children's smoking?' *Pediatrics* 89, 27–31, 1992

Knapp, A. W., 'Cocoa and Chocolate'. London. 1920

Knight, C.B., *M.A. Craven & Son Ltd: A History of the Company*, York, 1948

Kotey, R. A., (ed.) 'Economics of Cocoa Production and Marketing'. University of Ghana, Legon, 1974

London J., Tragedy, transformation, and triumph: comparing the factors and forces that led to the adoption of the 1860 Adulteration Act in England and the 1906 Pure Food and Drug Act in the United States, *Food Drug Law J.* 2014; 69(2) :315–42

Mason, L., *Sugar-plums and Sherbet: the Prehistory of Sweets*, Totnes, 1998
Sweets and Candy: A Global History, London, 2018

Mayhew, H., *London Labour and the London Poor*, London, 1851

McCabe, B.J., *Handbook of Food-drug Interactions*. Boca Raton, 2003

Medlin, J., 'Lead: Sweet Candy, Bitter Poison'. *Environmental Health Perspectives* 112 (14), 2017

Miller, M., *English Garden Cities: An Introduction*, Swindon 2010

Minifie, B., *Chocolate, Cocoa and Confectionery: Science and Technology* 3rd Edition, Stuttgart, 2012

Morton, M. and F., *Chocolate: An Illustrated History*, New York, 1986

Moss, S., *Chocolate: A Global History*, London 2009

Needler, R., *Needlers of Hull*, Beverley, 1993

Oddy, D. (Ed), *The Making of the Modern British Diet*, London 1976

Opie, R., *Sweet Memories*, London 2008

Othick, J., The Cocoa and Chocolate Industry in the Nineteenth Century in Oddy pp. 77–90

Richardson, P., *Indulgence*, London 2003

Richardson, T., *Sweets: A History of Temptation*, London 2002

Rogers, T., *A Century of Progress 1831–1931*, Bournville 1931

Roufs, T. G., *Sweet Treats around the World: An Encyclopedia of Food and Culture*, 2014

Royal Botanic Gardens, Kew, Liquorice. (Glycyrrhiza glabra, L.). *Bulletin of Miscellaneous Information* 1894

Rubinstein, H., *The Chocolate Book*, Harmondsworth, 1982

Ryan, O., *Chocolate Nations – Living and Dying for Cocoa in West Africa*, London 2011

Seidel J.S., 'Lychee-flavored gel candies: a potentially lethal snack for infants and children'. *Arch Pediatr Adolesc Med.* 156 (11): 1120–2, 2002

Sheeran, G., *The Bradford Poisoning of 1858*, Halifax, 1992
    'Wholesale poisoning by arsenic at Bradford'. *The Pharmaceutical Journal* 18: 340–43. 1858.

Stroud, J., *The Sucker's Guide: A Journey into the Soft Centre of the Sweet Shop*, Summersdale, 2008

Sumar, S., 'Adulteration of Foods – Past and Present', *Nutrition & Food Science*, 1995, 4, pp 11–15

Taylor, W.B., *The Emergence of a Confectionery Industry in York* in White (2000) pp 213–30

Terry, J., *Terry's of York 1767–1967*, York 1967

Vansittart, J., *Katherine Fry's Book*, London 1966

Vernon, A., *A Quaker Businessman: The Life of Joseph Rowntree 1836–1925*, York 1987

Wagner, G., *The Chocolate Conscience*, London 1987

Walvin, J., *How Sugar Corrupted the World*, London 2017

White, E., *Feeding a City – York: The Provision of Food from Roman Times to the Beginning of the Twentieth Century*, Totnes, 2000

Wild, A., *The East India Company Book of Chocolate*, London 1995

Wilson, B., *Swindled: From Poison Sweets to Counterfeit Coffee – The Dark History of the Food Cheats*, London, 2008

Wilson, V., *The Story of Terry's*, York 2009

Windsor, D., *The Quaker Enterprise: Friends in Business*, London 1980

Wohl, A.S., *Endangered Lives: Public Health in Victorian Britain*, Harvard UP, 1983

Websites

www.dw.com/en/from-status-symbol-to-sweet-poison-a-cultural-history-of-sugar/a-49789645

www.ncbi.nlm.nih.gov/pubmed?linkname=pubmed_pubmed&from_uid=12574033 – Pub med sites

www.york.ac.uk/library/borthwick

www.cocoareworks.co.uk – a website dedicated to the experiences of women who worked at the Rowntree factory.

www.jrf.org.uk – Joseph Rowntree Foundation

www.rowntreesociety.org.uk

www.yorkquakers.org.uk

www. paulchrystal.com

www.yorkcocoahouse.co.uk

It's only fitting that, with York's rich chocolate heritage, chocolate production should resume in the city. York Cocoa House is doing just that with a groundbreaking programme of chocolate making, chocolate workshops, chocolate making tours and chocolate days for school classes. The café and shop allow visitors to taste the chocolate made here and to drink their hot chocolate while deciding what to buy and take home.

Index